(In-)Security and the Production of International Relations

This book provides a framework for analysing the interplay between securitisation and foreign affairs, reconnecting critical security studies with traditional IR concerns about interstate relations.

What happens to foreign policymaking when actors, things or processes are presented as threats? This book explains state behaviour on the basis of a reflexive framework of insecurity politics, and argues that governments act on the knowledge of international danger available in their societies, but that such knowledge is organised by markedly varying ideas of who threatens whom and how. The book develops this argument and illustrates it by means of various European case studies. Moving across European history and space, these case studies show how securitisation has projected evolving and often contested local ideas of the organisation of international insecurity, and how such knowledges of world politics have then conditioned foreign policymaking on their own terms.

With its focus on insecurity politics, the book provides new perspectives for the study of international security. Moving the discipline from systemic theorising to a theory of international systematisation, it shows how world politics is, in practice, often conceived in different ways than that assumed by IR theory. By the same token, by depicting national insecurity as a matter of political construction, the book also raises the challenging question of whether certain projections of insecurity may be considered more warranted than others.

This book will be of much interest to students of critical security studies, European politics, foreign policy and IR, in general.

Jonas Hagmann is Senior Researcher at the Center for Security Studies, ETH Zürich, Switzerland, and has a PhD in International Relations from the Graduate Institute of International and Development Studies, Geneva.

Routledge Critical Security Studies series

(In-)Security and the Production of International Relations

The politics of securitisation in Europe

Jonas Hagmann

Routledge
Taylor & Francis Group

LONDON AND NEW YORK

First published 2015
by Routledge
2 Park Square, Milton Park, Abingdon, Oxfordshire OX14 4RN

and by Routledge
711 Third Avenue, New York, NY 10017

First issued in paperback 2016

Routledge is an imprint of the Taylor & Francis Group, an informa business

British Library Cataloguing-in-Publication Data
A catalogue record for this book is available from the British Library

Library of Congress Cataloging-in-Publication Data
Hagmann, Jonas.
(In)security and the production of international relations : the politics of
securitisation in Europe / Jonas Hagmann.
    pages cm. – (Routledge critical security studies)
    Includes bibliographical references and index.
    1. Security, International–Philosophy. 2. International relations–
    Philosophy. 3. International relations–Risk assessment. 4. International
    security–Europe–Case studies. 5. Europe–Foreign relations–Case
    studies. 6. International relations–Risk assessment–Europe–Case
    studies. I. Title.
    JZ5588.H34 2015
    327.1'7–dc23   2014019757

ISBN 13: 978-1-138-23661-5 (pbk)
ISBN 13: 978-0-415-70834-0 (hbk)

Typeset in Times New Roman
by Wearset Ltd, Boldon, Tyne and Wear

Contents

Illustrations

1 Introduction

Terrorism puts lives at risk; it imposes large costs; it seeks to undermine the openness and tolerance of our societies, and it poses a growing strategic threat to the whole of Europe. Increasingly, terrorist movements are well-resourced, connected by electronic networks, and are willing to use unlimited violence to cause massive casualties [...]. Europe is both a target and a base for such terrorism: European countries are targets and have been attacked. Logistical bases for Al Qaeda cells have been uncovered in the UK, Italy, Germany, Spain and Belgium. Concerted European action is indispensable.

(European Security Strategy 2003: 3)

The strategic consequences of this [previously described] evolution [of the international security context] have deep impact on the security of France and its partners from the European Union. Whereas the danger of a major upheaval in Europe is distant today, the Europeans cannot ignore the instability of the regions surrounding them, regions with which they are intimately connected. Taking part in and profiting from globalisation, they are confronting an increasing number of major risks. In the same time, given the permeability of European territory, they are also vulnerable to the impact of threats from abroad. A major crisis in Asia, for instance, would have serious economic, commercial and financial consequences for Europe.

(Gouvernement Français 2013: 30)

(In-)security as knowledge politics

It has become popular practice in recent years for Western capitals to sketch a wide range of policy themes in terms of security. Whether the object of concern is terrorism, migration, climate change or financial stability – notions of public, national or international insecurity abound in European and North American politics, and rarely are they withdrawn from political agendas again. Yet, not only are security challenges seen to proliferate in these regions. Many of these relatively novel security narratives are also used to describe a world composed of transnational dangers. More often than not, contemporary threats such as migration, climate change or financial instability are argued to represent collective global, North Atlantic or at least regional European policy challenges. According to this view, the Western security environment not only knows a lot of dangers – distinct foreign policy strategies are argued to flow from this security context as well, as collective security problems are claimed to demand collaborative security responses.

In fact, nothing about the contemporary security rationales cited and reproduced above is unproblematic, no matter their popularity with policymakers and policy analysts. Not only does the question arise of how and why diverse topics – from the economy, ecology, society and the military – are transformed into security challenges in the first place. Also, the processes by which threats are turned – or not turned – into dangers posed to entire collectives of states, and how such presentations are, and can be, seized upon to justify distinct types of foreign policy strategies in turn, show themselves as deeply political. Seen from a critical perspective, the politics of defining insecurity – the process of securitisation broadly understood – does, indeed, come across as a fascinating object of scholarly enquiry. How public, national or international understandings of danger are articulated by societies, how they are collectivised to provide larger, often geospatial, assessments of world politics, and how they are appropriated in the foreign policy realm is not only interesting in terms of understanding international politics in itself, it is also fundamental to explaining international politics.

This is the case because, ultimately, every society needs to make sense of its international context *first*, before it can develop policies inside that 'context'. Security policy and foreign affairs do not differ from this basic knowledge requirement. For international relations to actually become possible, world politics must first be rendered intelligible by those who enact it (Weldes *et al.* 1999). Without an understanding of who threatens whom and how, for instance, politicians simply lack the necessary epistemological basis to devise and justify security strategies. Seen in this light, international affairs relies on a heavy dose of knowledge politics: how a country navigates through world politics depends on the ways in which its people recognises that world politics to be in the first place. That description does not rely on some objective interpretation of reality or unanimous national sense-making – it depends essentially on which political faction within a given country succeeds in advancing and popularising its own reading of world politics. As a power-laden process, the knowledge politics involved in producing international relations hence not only refers to the forms that local readings of the international adopt, but also to the articulation and embattling of such authoritative definitions of international reality inside a given political community.

As fundamental as this knowledge (power-) politics is to international affairs, traditional International Relations (IR) theory has given scant attention to the production of national security notions. Even if such theory agrees on the fundamental relevance of security concerns for explaining international relations, it neglects to enquire into how such concerns come about in the first place, and how different ways of articulating these might actually and ultimately be connected to the foreign policy behaviour of states. Traditional IR theorising operates a remarkably theoretical and paternalistic take on the role of knowledge when explaining politics. Champions of such theory consider it more 'realistic' to ground explanations of international affairs on abstract conceptions of anarchy or 'the international system', rather than on empirical engagements with actual policymaker practices, perspectives or statements, yet at the same time they hesitate little to project their explanations of international affairs onto such politicians, providing them with authoritative manuals on appropriate or responsible international conduct (Gusterson 1999). Although national insecurity plays a central role in these frameworks, then, traditional IR postulates insecurity, but does little to enquire into its political foundations and local articulations. Instead of being interested in how national leaders systematise their nation's security context themselves, this context is essentially being systematised on their behalf and the purported mechanics of international politics handed to them (Fierke 2002: 336).

If security and foreign policymaking are to be taken seriously as actual political practices, then explanations of international affairs should become more empirical and less legislative, enquiring more closely into the epistemological politics that come into play when defining national security concerns; concerns that scholars agree are fundamental drivers of international politics as such. In recent years, international political sociology scholarship has contributed a great deal to such a shift in analytical perspective and scholarly practice. Critical approaches to security in particular play a vanguard role in analysing the association of policy themes with security logics, as well as the attendant effects of such conceptual linking. Surprisingly for a body of work evolving in the IR discipline, however, these same critical approaches have not addressed the interplay between the societal formulation of security notions and the national definition of foreign policies in greater detail. While Western policymakers advance an agenda of collective insecurity, linking this agenda in different ways to collaborative security policy strategies across borders, critical approaches to security tend to focus ever more closely on political practices that have relatively little bearing on statist foreign policymaking and thus interstate relations in the classic sense.

This is not to deny the scholarly, intellectual and political relevance of contemporary critical security studies – to the contrary. Apart from some selected works on the topic, however, reflexive IR has become surprisingly quiet on the knowledge politics involved in connecting local (in-)security agendas with national foreign policy strategies, as the scholarly literature seems to have moved away from the more traditional disciplinary concerns with interstate relations and interstate cooperation. As a result, not just traditional IR theory but also the latter, broader, contemporary international political sociology agenda are challenged by an analytical gap when it comes to explaining the effects of securitisation, broadly understood, on statist foreign policymaking and thus international relations. How local conceptions of national and/or international insecurity are connected to larger understandings of world politics is an analytical question that still remains unanswered by that latter reflexive agenda, no matter its merits. The politics of using (in-)security narratives as a means of describing the international in specific ways, and with it also the complicity of such narratives in the production of world order concepts and the conditioning of national foreign policy strategies, still needs to be more systematically unravelled and explained.

Ambition of the book

What happens to international politics when a topic – climate change, terrorism or migration, for instance – becomes framed and recognised as a national security concern in a given society? This book focuses on the process of (in-)securitisation broadly understood – i.e. the production and appropriation of notions of national and international danger (Buzan *et al.* 1998; Bigo 2005). Its ambition is to address the linkage between national security politics and national foreign affairs strategising and, with it, to reconnect central critical security studies arguments with traditional IR concerns about statist foreign policies and interstate relations. In doing so, the book seeks to make analytical, theoretical, disciplinary and political contributions. On the analytical level, the book seeks to denaturalise further aspects of security analysis, moving it towards a relational/positional perspective on security affairs. As will shortly be argued in more detail, the book claims security narratives to speak about distinct configurations of entities causing danger – i.e. originators – but also about victims and antagonisms in world politics, and thus to define distinct actor positions and relationships between select political entities in the international realm. By the same token, security narratives are also shown to work as truth claims – i.e. superior frameworks of reality – and thus to be creative of international relations and foreign policies as such. Rather than debating the broadening and deepening of security or being too intimately interested in the stipulated anti-democratic effects of securitisation and its working conditions, for instance, the book redirects security analysis to enquiring into how security notions are locally crafted, and how security ideas produce the world that they are so often purported to merely describe.

On the theoretical level, the book endeavours to advance an analytical framework – or even mid-range theory – of international relations that cuts across clinical levels of analysis. Since by looking at how political communities create and compete over their own readings of the threatening international, and by looking at how such readings condition national foreign policies in return, that framework eventually makes statements about cooperation and conflict in the international arena. Contrary to popular IR-theoretical explanations of international cooperation based on regime type homology or trust, for instance, the framework posits international cooperation to be stimulated by the political endangerment of the international, and to be brought into distinct forms and alliances by convergent constructions of unsafe spaces. Seen from this perspective, international cooperation is understood to be essentially driven by projections of insecurity and thus insecurity politics: interstate cooperation rests on political communities that consider themselves threatened by a given phenomenon, but also their epistemic construction of transnational insecurity communities and the interlocking projection of such mutually implicating conceptions by different societies. It is the convergent recognition of forming a larger insecurity community that makes cooperation between states possible and explains it, hence the argument of the book.

On the disciplinary level, the book endeavours to contribute a perspective on international relations that abstains from formulating excessively universalising claims, and a perspective that is more closely interested in policymaker practices. Although the basic dimensions of the analytical framework developed in this book are held to be useful for understanding and explaining international relations of the modern period in general, the substantive embodiments of these very dimensions are recognised to differ across history, between nations, but also internally in countries: which dangers a political community recognises, how it mobilises these to systematise its international context and how it appropriates these imageries for foreign policy strategising are posited as empirical questions. There is, indeed, little reason to *a priori* assume that these processes converge across time or space – i.e. to naturalise threats and to assume that a given danger (e.g. terrorism, North Korea) means the same thing to any politician in any country at any period of time. In democratic societies at least, readings of international dangers are continuously negotiated and competed over by evolving alliances of truth-tellers ranging from ministers to bureaucrats, parliamentarians, journalist and scholars, and so contending interpretations of a seemingly singular insecurity topic oftentimes prevail. The general analytical framework provided by this book, then, seeks to empower a historicisation and contextualisation of the politics that it seeks to explain, as it moves International Relations (IR) away from systemic theory and towards a theory of systematisation. Instead of looking at how anarchy imposes itself as a system onto people, it looks at how people systematise the international by and for themselves. Instead of assuming that national security concerns are a given and that they call forth singular paths of action, it looks at how such concerns are formulated, invested with a plurality of contending meanings and appropriated for different kinds of foreign policy programmes.

Finally, on a political level, the book's ambition is to help question further mechanics of security politics. By providing analytical tools for addressing the articulation of transnational insecurity communities – i.e. larger political spaces that are thought to be threatened by the same dangers – the book allows for problematising the production, delineation, positioning and seizure of such political spaces. On the most general level, and notwithstanding the plurivalent meanings of the term, the book thus advances a critical approach to international relations. This approach recognises the local, time- and context-specific power politics involved in endangering international affairs and the performative, inclusionary and exclusionary effects inherent in epistemological systematisations of world politics. As will be discussed in greater detail in the concluding chapter, this approach converses with, speaks back to or challenges some of the discipline's central security theories, ranging from securitisation and regional security complex theory to systemic constructivism and security community theory, and it also raises questions of the transformative and/or emancipatory potential of IR analytics (Marcus 1999).

Argument of the book

What does it mean to US foreign policymaking when a theme such as international terrorism becomes accepted as a major danger to the United States? Moreover, can one expect other nations, whether France, Angola or Argentina, to have a similar reaction to the threat of terrorism, in case that French, Angolan and Argentine politicians follow suit their American colleagues, accepting international terrorism as a danger also confronting their nations? What a threat signifies to local politicians often differs across time and space. Not only is the very validity of specific threat ideas – such as international terrorism – oftentimes questioned. What kind of world these ideas explicitly or implicitly describe is often subject to intense debate as well. Even if all politicians from Washington to Paris, Luanda and Buenos Aires were to agree that terrorism poses a major national security challenge, the term might not mean the same thing to all of them: for some, terrorism might be understood as an existential problem for democracies worldwide, whereas for others, terrorism might be seen as a threat to Western nations only and, for others still, terrorism might be an exclusively domestic issue.

These differences in interpretation matter, so this book, since they represent different readings of world order. From the first perspective, terrorism stands for a world in which non-state actors challenge the international community as such. From the second perspective, the threat creates a club problem, with shared security interests for some states, but not others. From the third perspective, the existence of an insecure space stretching across political borders is denied. Such contending readings are directly relevant to the foreign policy realm, since they empower different policy strategies, depending on which readings dominate where and when. In one case, the reading of the international implicit in terrorism empowers a global anti-terrorism agenda, such as, for instance, via a United Nations framework agreement. In another case, the reading of world order superimposed on terrorism empowers deeper regional security cooperation or, for those who do not see themselves as being associated with that region, indifference or even disengagement. In the last case, terrorism is appreciated as standing for a world with no potential allies – a reading of world politics that works against collaborative international frameworks and in favour of solitary action.

The articulation of national insecurity is an important driver of foreign policymaking, as is evident from the introductory citations from contemporary European security doctrines. Insecurity articulations in themselves, however, do not explain how foreign policymaking will be configured – securitisation as such tells us little about what local politicians mean by the dangers they identify, let alone about the foreign policy implications that they associate with it. This book argues that (in-)securitisation is nevertheless connected to foreign affairs strategising by virtue of the world ordering functions inherent in the articulation of national insecurity. This is so because securitisation subjectifies and subject-positions actors in world politics: the recognition of a threat comes with a need for protection, but also with a definition of enemies, friends and other actors in international politics and thus a distinct positioning of the home nation in a recognised web of antagonistic international relations. Constructed and often contested in their configuration, insecurity narratives thus function as consequential representations of international order. They (1) *endanger* the own nation; (2) *order* the international; and – by virtue of their role as truthful descriptions of reality – (3) *condition* the own nation's foreign policy behaviour in the international context thus described.

Endangering international relations

First, securitisation endangers international relations. Endangering is the process of identification and naming of things as threats, such as the soldiers of one country, the nuclear weaponry of another state, items such as commercial airplanes or processes such as globalisation. The naming of such things as threats is an active process, and necessarily so, since objects and things themselves cannot tell how they will be received and treated by a given society. Only through their framing in and by a social collective do they acquire social meaning and political relevance, and only through routine repetition of such framings over time do objects appear to carry an apparently permanent and thus seemingly natural meaning (Wendt 1992: 396–397). Threats do not evade this basic construction requirement. Unless something is actively named as a danger – i.e. the practice of endangering or securitisation broadly conceived – this something is *not* known and considered as a security issue by a country's inhabitants.

Yet, the endangering of things is not only a mere naming practice. It is also politically effective and a political process in itself. The securitisation of terrorism, for instance, is itself a power-laden process: to define what is considered a threat and what is not – what acts represent terror and what do not – implies selection and thus competition with alternative possible interpretations. By the same token, to name terrorism or any other theme a national danger means to recognise and postulate an essential provocation; to consider the nation endangered is to stipulate a non-reducible necessity for a national policy response. At a basic level, then, the first element in the linking of security politics to foreign affairs and the first function inherent in securitisation is its active endangering of relations between the own nation and other actors in world politics. By naming a threat, securitisation insecuritises and sets out a need to do something against that identified danger. The European doctrines cited above do exactly that. By naming current threats in their respective first chapters, they set out the need for governmental policy responses; policy answers that are then elaborated on in the doctrines' subsequent chapters.

Ordering international relations

Second, (in-)securitisation produces world order imageries. This function is inherent in securitisation, because to articulate a national security concern also means to formulate an idea of *who threatens whom and how*. In doing so, securitisation effectively systematises the international. First, securitisation identifies originators of insecurity in world politics (*who threatens?*). In defining the entities that are held responsible for creating insecurity, it positions the nation against some other thing – a state or non-state actor, a process or a value. Second, securitisation recognises (co-)victims of threats (*who is threatened?*). Securitisation articulates a conception of who exactly is threatened by a given danger. In doing so, securitisation often projects shared security concerns across borders, defining who beyond the own nation is challenged by the same threat. Third, securitisation defines degrees of antagonism between originators and victims (*how is something/someone threatened?*). In assessing the intensity of opposition between originators and victims, securitisation provides a graded ranking of security relations ranging from existential enmity to antagonism, challenge or mere competition. Hence, taken together, securitisation not merely endangers the international by naming a threat and making that threat known to a society. It also populates the international with distinct relations and actor formations and defines the relationships both amongst them and vis-à-vis the own country, thus locating the nation in an actively recognised and graded web of international relations. Securitisation defines world orders, and in doing so it produces international relations.

The need for local policymakers to systematise the international is necessary, in order to anchor threat narratives to concrete subjects, objects and relations. This is to say that the proactive arranging of the international is a powerful ontological security-seeking strategy. By competing over the definition of the nation's context, politicians render that context intelligible – by populating the world with actors and relations, systematisation renders the international known and temporarily stable. This epistemological structuring of the social world responds to societies' need to define its position in a contingent world, thus setting out a basis for action. With its focus on antagonistic relations, securitisation offers a distinct approach to the production of such knowledge about a polity's own position. Its focus on antagonisms coexists and competes with other epistemological systematisation processes outside the security realm, but forms a particularly dominant such practice in modern international affairs. In international affairs, securitisation becomes an influential means – if not *the most* influential means – of making the world known, not least also because its endangering provides a pressing need to act upon the world that has become known.

Conditioning international relations

Third, securitisation conditions international relations. The foreign policy behaviour of states is structured by (in-)security articulations, the book argues, because of the distinct world orders that their societies articulate and accept. Since when providing local systematisations of the international, securitisation describes nothing less than the international reality in which a country finds itself. As authoritative descriptions of the world's basic structures, insecurity narratives create subjects and objects of foreign policy, interpellating both others and the own polity into the so-recognised imagery of world order. Policymakers must refer to those world orders to devise, communicate and justify national foreign policy strategies. Seen in this manner, the world orderings provided by securitisation do not merely 'constitute' foreign affairs. Representations of international order enable foreign policy action, and, as such, a constitutive analysis of their genesis and configuration helps understand foreign politics as a social construct. Representations of international order, however, also interact independently and diachronically with foreign policymaking. Representations of international order causally affect the latter, providing further reasons as to why it is important to address such representations.

The causation at play in this relation is more differentiated than the way in which that mechanism is commonly used in the IR discipline. Representations of world order are not causal in the sense that they predetermine foreign policy responses – the recognition of a global security challenge such as climate change, for instance, hardly translates automatically into a global environmental protection plan. Representations such as the danger of global climate change act, however, as quasi-structural conditions for foreign affairs strategising. They prescribe an imaginary of international relations with which the latter has to deal, furnishing some courses of action to policymakers, but also foreclosing others. By authoritatively defining who threatens whom and how in world politics, securitisation hands a conditioning understanding of the world to foreign affairs officials, agents that act upon those representations in turn, effectively appropriating and instantiating them. Unlike the claims made by reductive standard conceptions of causation, the causal powers at play in securitisation are hence both multiple and recursively related – they take different forms and they rest with knowledges and actors alike.

Structure of the book

The purpose of this book is to dismantle some of the central political ordering effects of naming (and claiming) insecurity and to draw analytical and empirical attention to what it means for foreign affairs and international politics to posit something as a national security problem. Securitisation, as conceptualised by this book, is a power-laden politics of naming and embodying threats with broader conceptions of who threatens whom and how; a politics that is embattled not least because of its conditioning effects in the foreign policy arena. Such an understanding of securitisation as endangering, ordering and conditioning international relations contributes an immanent perspective on the subjectification of world politics. It stands for a perspective on international security politics that expands, challenges and inverts established IR theories of international politics: it expands on the Copenhagen School's basic idea of securitisation to address its world ordering functions, and it reformulates regional security complex theory into a thoroughly reflexive and non-statist account of the politics of creating and enacting regional insecurity. It develops post-structuralist works into a more variable systematisation framework linking national security articulations with foreign policymaking, contributes a reflexive input to democratic peace theory and challenges security community theory for not providing a convincing cause for international security cooperation. Rejecting rationalist and constructivist grand theories of international politics, finally, the book calls into question whether interstate anarchy provides a secure starting point for international theorising.

As a critical and political sociology approach to international threat politics, the book looks at how societies define their world for themselves and others and how they act upon the(ir) world so defined. This focus on national discursive arenas is not to suggest that transnational insecurity narratives are unimportant – transborder social interaction and political communication, and transborder attempts at authoritatively interpreting dangers on behalf of others, is standard practice in many places. Yet, the focus on statist societies depicts an ideal-typical heuristic for analysing the matter in question. That heuristic rests on the insight that reflexive analyses of politics must first and foremost address how *local* actors interact with each other in the naming and defining of policy contexts. In a Westphalian world centred on organised national state apparatuses, international politics essentially derives from national foreign policies operated by government agencies (i.e. statist foreign policies), and these essentially rely on the knowledges available within their own society. The production and negotiation of such local knowledges evolves over time, and it is particularly strongly exposed to local political dynamics – even if fragments of knowledge are imported or translated from abroad (Stritzel 2011) – and this is why an empirical, historicised and contextualised enquiry into statist societies proves useful. It is from this genealogical perspective, then, that this book addresses international relations as a local politics of systematisation of the international and that it revisits and connects the traditional IR concepts of security, international system, regional order and cooperation.

The book consists of three parts, which develop, illustrate and situate the argument that securitisation endangers, orders and conditions international relations. In the first part, two conceptual chapters theorise the security politics/ foreign policy interplay asserted by the two European security doctrine quotes reproduced and problematised above. Reconceptualising security as a relation, these chapters argue that the articulation of national insecurities not only endangers the international, thus provoking foreign policy reactions, but also that such notions systematise the international in specific ways and, in doing so, that they advance authoritative and politically efficacious images of world order(s). The first conceptual chapter of the book discusses how epistemological fear drives such systematisations of the international, and it draws on the work of Michel Foucault and Louis Althusser to conceptualise securitisation as a mechanism of international subjectification and subject-positioning. The second conceptual chapter discusses how representations are produced, instantiated, rejected and reformulated politically. Drawing on the work of Roy Bhaskar and Margaret Archer, it elaborates on how these representations condition, but do not predetermine or merely constitute the foreign policy behaviour of nation-states.

The second part of the book empirically substantiates the argument. Focusing on the security/foreign policy debates of France, (West) Germany and Switzerland between 1945 and 2010, this part of the book presents eight empirical case studies (see Table 1.1 for an overview). Each of these eight chapters draws on local government declarations, parliamentary debates, scholarly assessments and media positions from their respective periods to provide immanent understandings of the various insecurity communities that were articulated, adopted, adapted and rejected by different political factions inside this tri-national space. In doing so, the empirical part of the book serves three larger purposes. First, the chapters empirically substantiate the analytical framework set out in the first part of the book, providing comprehensive genealogies of the interplay between national security and foreign policy debates. Second, by circulating through European space and history, the empirical chapters enable a direct comparative analysis of the interplay between security policy and foreign policy. Through shifting examples within a narrow tri-national space, the second part of the book shows how distinct political communities frequently advance substantially different readings of world politics in the same given period of time, notwithstanding factors such as value convergence, regime homology, geographical proximity or geopolitical location. Third, the genealogies set out in this part of the book unpack European Cold War politics in general. By showing how, on both the continental level and within individual countries, European perspectives on security and world order evolved, sometimes converged and oftentimes conflicted with each other, the empirical chapters provide a differentiated larger genealogy of European Cold War foreign politics, thus challenging popular systemic and fixed regionalist perspectives on that particular space and period.

The third and final part of the book is again more conceptual. Conceived as a single concluding chapter, it puts into perspective the historical evolution of European threat politics, reconnects to the book's central discussion on insecure/insecurity communities and reflects on the perspective on international affairs that it advances. On the empirical level, the conclusion summarises how European societies popularised often surprisingly contending readings of world politics during most of the Cold War period, but also how their systematisations of the international evolved along fairly distinct lines leading up to the 1990s and 2000s. On the analytical level, it addresses the ways in which a focus on insecurity politics inverts established accounts of international politics, given that it questions traditional markers of international history. On the theoretical level, the final chapter shows how the focus on insecurity politics moves IR away from systemic theory and towards a theory of systematisation and how this perspective contrasts with popular international security theories that ground foreign policy behaviour and international security cooperation in elements such as national identity, regionally shared values, trust or routine interaction. On the political level, finally, the conclusion engages a normative discussion on the political production of spaces of inclusion and exclusion.

Table 1.1 Overview of empirical chapters – genealogies of European (in-)security politics

	1940s	1950s	1960s	1970s	1980s	1990s	2000s
Chapter 4	France: Post-war views						
Chapter 5		West Germany: *Westbindung?*					
Chapter 6			Switzerland: Neutrality and non-implication				
Chapter 7				France: Gaullism as world order view			
Chapter 8					West Germany: *Ostpolitik et al.*		
Chapter 9							Switzerland: Collective insecurity or not?
Chapter 10						France: Regional insecurities	
Chapter 11							Germany: Global threats?

Part I

The construction of international insecurity

2 Endangering and ordering international relations

Security and the analysis of international relations

Security analysis has come a long way since the emergence of security studies in International Relations. Initially popularised in the discipline as a narrow concept exclusively concerned with uses of military force by and against states (Morgenthau 1962; Walt 1991), it was expanded by the late 1970s into a notion which also addressed the economic foundations of such military might (Snyder and Diesing 1977; Ellsworth 1978). It was not until the early 1990s, however, that security was turned into a broader and deeper framework which addressed all kinds of policy sectors, ranging from the military to economics, politics, the environment and society (Westing 1989; Buzan 1991; Buzan *et al.* 1998), and which concerned all kinds of referent objects – not only states, but also individuals, groups of states or the entire international system as such (Rummel 1983; Haftendorn 1991; Lipschutz 1992; United Nations Development Programme 1994; Krause and Williams 1996). In turn, discussions on security's appropriate breadth and depth gave way to constructivist and critical understandings of the concept's definition and analytical fixation (Krause 1998; Huysmans 1998a). In the view of the former, security has been defined sociologically as that which nations are concerned with (Mutimer 1998; McDonald 2008). From the perspective of the latter, security is also a political ordering tool that is fought over not only for its thematic content, but even more so for its structuring effects on politics broadly conceived (Booth 1991; Waever 1995; Krause 1998; Buzan 1997).

There is little doubt that over the course of this analytical evolution, and thanks to the reflexive approaches to security in particular, a much greater understanding of the politics of security has emerged in recent years (Williams 2003; Smith 2005; Buzan and Hansen 2009). However, despite the vast and productive range of new security scholarship to which this evolution has led, security analysis has not only become more comprehensive in that process. Since not only does a substantial number of IR security analysts still uphold traditional conceptions of security today (cf. Waever and Buzan 2007). Inevitably, perhaps, for an emergent and institutionalising body of thought, the new perspectives on security have also steered security analysis in fairly distinct directions themselves.

Empirically, for instance, critical security analysis tends to focus on a restrained set of Western topics, such as migration (Doty 2003; Huysmans 2006) or terrorism (Buzan 2006; Aradau and van Münster 2007), or on democratic concerns with the framing and control powers of security talk (Aradau 2004) and apparatuses (Bigo and Tsoukala 2008). Even if the literature continues to expand, and additional issues such as non-Western security (Wilkinson 2007; Hagmann and Korf 2012), alternative authorities for speaking security (Villumsen 2011; Hagmann and Dunn 2012) and the securitisation of new policy fields such as transportation (Salter 2008), public health (Elbe 2009) or environmental protection (Floyd 2010) are addressed, the literature's empirical contributions rather clearly focus on domestic European and North American security issues.

Conceptually, too, IR security analysis evolves along distinct avenues. The two-dimensional understanding of security as a broad and deep concept, for instance, represents an almost inescapable analytical systematisation device for many security scholars and practitioners (see, for example, Barnett 1997; Huysmans 1998a: 491, 1998b: 227; Smith 1999; Buzan *et al.* 1998: 32; C.A.S.E. Collective 2006: 452–453). Similarly, the post-structuralist argument that Othering is complicit in the construction of a society's identity, thus providing an epistemological foundation for national foreign policymaking, is firmly anchored in security studies (Doty 1993; Hansen 2006). The Copenhagen School's understanding that securitisation enables unwarranted norm-breaking effects is widely reproduced (cf. McDonald 2008; Roe 2012), and also a Foucaultian/Deleuzian perspective, according to which security equals or helps establish comprehensive systems of societal control, regulating and locking aspects of life or even life itself into distinct and problematic political mechanisms and finalities, presents a dominant syllogism (cf. Lund Petersen 2012). Regardless of whether or not the proponents of these select frameworks actually sought to affect critical security analysis in such a decisive manner, and also irrespective of critical security studies' explicit concern with diverse lines of inquiry (Baldwin 1997; Krause and Williams 1996; C.A.S.E. Collective 2006; Walker 2007), some critical interventions have found a particularly strong echo, and they have directed security analysis to a distinct set of empirical questions and analytical frameworks (Mutimer 2007).

In terms of knowledge generation, for scholarly, political and methodological reasons, the tendency to inquire into domestic security practices, challenge popular anti-terror agendas and problematise security talk's democratic implications are, of course, all well taken. Also, it is important to note that despite the preponderance of some empirical questions and analytical frameworks, reflexive security studies remains a fairly pluralistic and dynamically evolving project overall, covering a range of themes from gender issues (Hoogensen and Stuvoy 2006; Sylvester 2010) to emancipation (Peoples 2011; Nunes 2012), risk analytics (Hagmann and Dunn 2012; Lobo-Guerrero 2012) and resilience (Lundborg and Vaughan-Williams 2011; Chandler 2012). However, for the purpose of addressing the distinct question of how security frames interact with foreign policymaking and international relations, the directions recently taken by reflexive security studies have not proven all that helpful. Since the 1990s, a considerable part of the literature has turned to the more domestic dimensions of security politics broadly defined, such as the production of exclusionary Western identities (e.g. Weldes and Saco 1996; Weldes *et al.* 1999), the political sociology of local policing (e.g. Salter 2008) or security as a politics of exception (e.g. Williams 2003; Huysmans 2008). As instructive as these debates are – with their focus on select topics, critical approaches to security have come to position themselves surprisingly distant from classic disciplinary concerns with interstate relations and statist foreign affairs strategising. As a result, reflexive security studies has not developed a broader analytical framework that addresses how securitisation becomes a means for creating more complex orderings of international politics.

Indeed, contemporary security studies must be challenged today for not providing sufficient analytical leverage over the question of how the articulation of national insecurity connects with foreign affairs strategising. The above description of security as a broad and/or deep concept is one case in point. This classification scheme clearly allows dangers other than military threats to states to be highlighted, and in doing so helps overcome traditional analytical fixations of the object (Deudney 1990: 462). But the description of security as a danger emanating from one sector and affecting another referent object merely establishes a managerial protection agenda, such as when it states that governments or human beings are challenged by political or economic dangers (e.g. Moran 1996; Rowe 1999). It does not allow for the capturing of those dimensions by which security narratives serve to make sense of world politics, by which they advance differentiated imageries of international security relations and, based on which, they propose distinct rationales for foreign policymaking. The analytical focus on the 'what and the who of security' (Barnett 1997: 408) literally falls flat conceptually – it fails to capture how notions of threat stand for a three-dimensional organisation of international insecurity and thus also of international politics as such, since it does not provide enough analytical leverage for understanding how, with whom and against what national security policymaking is to be designed and directed in the foreign policy realm.

Similarly, the – often post-structuralist – focus on the production of identity does not strike as entirely useful for the question of how the naming of national insecurity interacts with foreign affairs strategising in practice. Certainly, this literature contributes sophisticated accounts of how Othering projects enemy-images abroad, thus assisting in the production of a society's identity – a Self, which, in turn, lays the basis for foreign policymaking (Campbell 1992; Doty 1993; Weldes *et al.* 1999). Yet, its empirical analyses are often insufficiently diverse and too strongly indebted to radical binary oppositions. Its indebtedness to dichotomies (*the*, singular, Other) precludes that body of work from focusing on how Othering may be plural in practice; that is, how a multiplicity of danger narratives – ranging, for instance, from global weapons proliferation to regional insecurity themes and strictly bilateral relations with a neighbouring country – come together in producing at times compatible and at times conflicting local knowledges of both world politics and the own nation's position therein (i.e.

Others and Selves, both in more complex shapes and in the plural). By the same token, the same literature also finds it difficult to acknowledge less self-centred and less antagonistic systematisations of the international (Weldes and Saco 1996; Hansen 2006). Given its focus on the Self as social identity and meta-theoretical commitment to radical (binary) antagonisms, the understanding that a danger (such as terrorism) may be constructed as a global, regional or other form of collective problem also affecting other nations beyond the immediate Self, its construction as a problem of others *without* effects on the home nation or its presentation as a challenge that is *not* as radically threatening compared to other problems cannot be meaningfully accommodated by much of the identity literature. Indeed, in some instances, the stark focus on singular radical oppositions even stands for a preconceived politico-analytical strategy, such as when it is held to be a desirable political mobilisation device (Torfing 1999: 127). Post-structuralist work, then, cannot – and, in some instances, also does not want to – recognise and address more differentiated ways of producing knowledge about both world politics and the own nation, even if it introduces the central idea that security narratives are key to understanding international relations in general.

Also, securitisation theory – arguably the most innovative (Smith 2005) and widely used (McDonald 2008) contemporary security studies framework – happens to both facilitate and impede an analysis of the way in which security framings interact with the international. On the one hand, securitisation theory enables an analysis of the social construction of security narratives, their political embattlement and their performative force. Securitisation theory allows the disciplinary analysis to move beyond narrow materialist and rationalist conceptions of security politics, and this is also why this book draws on that framework in a broader sense. On the other hand, however, securitisation theory complicates the examination of the security policy/foreign affairs interplay. This is so because in its original theorisation, securitisation puts such a strong emphasis on extraordinary force as an elementary load in security framings. The practice of securitisation, so its theory's main contention, not only names threats, but also posits these as existential, thus giving way to extraordinary – i.e. norm-breaking – powers (Waever 1995; Buzan *et al.* 1998). In doing so, securitisation theory has directed security analysis to an ever more detailed inquiry into a distinct kind of political force. Securitisation studies have produced sophisticated accounts of securitisation's procedural unleashing and effect-creating (Balzacq 2005; Stritzel 2007), but they have not given way to empirical assessments of the world order representations that threat articulations are made to transport. Indeed, securitisation also happens to complicate security analysis ontologically, since in arguing that the framing of security performs a specific thing, the theory effectively packages the construction and the uses of security narratives into one single framework. Even if securitisation theory merely points to an 'empowerment' of norm-breaking outcomes (Buzan *et al.* 1998: 23–24) – its lack of analytical differentiation between the production of insecurity narratives on the one hand and the seizure of such narratives on the other precludes analytical differentiation of these two sites of political contestation, thus making it difficult to examine how actors compete over the eventual political finalities of threat narratives. Analytically, securitisation theory in its original variant provides few tools to address the way in which threat notions are mobilised or appropriated in favour of or against some foreign policy strategies and not others, since it is claimed that security 'itself' organises political behaviour in its own ways, inescapable and narrow.

Lastly, the more recently emerging Foucaultian and Deleuzian approaches to security are also not consequently in favour of a deeper examination of the international ordering effects of insecurity enunciations. On the one hand, the notion of governmentality popularised by some of these works seems to provide strong analytical leverage with which to address this question – the idea of governmentality as a rationale for norming, normalising and disciplining social behaviour (Foucault 1991), for instance, is squarely helpful for an inquiry into the politics of ordering social systems and thus potentially also for international security (e.g. Krause 2011). On the other hand yet, quite some works evolving in this tradition claim that such governmentality is radically undesirable (e.g. Hardt 1998; Hallsworth and Lea 2011). It does not matter whether such evaluations are motivated by democratic principles or concerns over the crude reduction of human life to economist finalities – on a normative level, some Foucaultian and Deleuzian works join securitisation theory in presenting security as something that is to be thoroughly resisted or outright rejected (Nunes 2012; Hynek and Chandler 2013). At the scholarly level, such a 'negative' reading of security is of limited use for a differentiated analysis of the political orders that security helps to produce, since it forecloses more graded perspectives on how security might be worked with – i.e. reformed, reconfigured or emancipated. When security is fully rejected, then disciplinary security analysis has no tools with which to ask whether certain security configurations might be considered more warranted than others relatively speaking, even if security does control social life, create spaces of political inclusion and exclusion or empower norm-breaking policymaking practices.

Towards a relational/positional security analysis

Approached through the prism of interstate relations, critical security analysis' recent contributions to the study of the effect of security frames on foreign policymaking are thus fairly mixed. While various works have contributed sophisticated empirical inquiries and thought-provoking analytical schemes, its empirical attention to foreign policymaking is surprisingly limited, and its analytical frameworks only permit the capturing of parts of the wider politics involved in the international mobilisation of threats: analytically, security can be systematised as a broad and deep concept or seen as a means for producing radical binaries in world politics, but it cannot be apprehended as more complex and variable representations of the social world; ontologically, threat narratives may be considered politically effective, but the forms that this effect is given can hardly be problematised; normatively, the use of securitisation is critically engaged, but a graded evaluation of the value of different security configurations is little encouraged. Unsurprisingly, perhaps, given this situation, analyses that address the effect of securitisation on international relations do not actually manage to convincingly connect the two elements. Indeed, when the naming of threats is argued to justify illiberal international interventions (Abrahamsen 2004), to dramatise international politics, so making compromise and interstate cooperation difficult (Morozov 2004), to legitimise issue-leadership, thus introducing hierarchy into the international system and undermining multilateral cooperation (Kelstrup 2004; Buzan 2006) or when it is claimed to reassert state powers in transnational political dialogue (Malvig 2005), then such linkages between the framing of security and international relations often merely rely on securitisation theory's elements of urgency and norm-breaking. These elements are very generic and say little about the substantive world order imageries that securitisation helps to describe and organise, in these cases and for specific countries. They provide ad hoc theoretical support to the attempted linking of the construction of threats with international politics, but not an elaborate conceptual framework for that linkage.

Although national security concerns provide crucial rationales for foreign policymaking in practice, being explicitly codified and presented as such in national security and national foreign policy strategies, IR scholarship finds it difficult to create a conceptual connection between securitisation and foreign policy strategising and thus state behaviour. There is no reflexive framework addressing the way in which the identification of security notions comes with the *variable* construction of complex world order understandings, as well as contending conceptions of the home nation's position in international relations, and how such representations of the international affect national foreign policymaking in return. In contrast to current analytical tenets, such a framework has to be more consciously focused on the production of contested and variable substantial threat representations, as opposed to the production of binary oppositions and process-related and methodological questions of securitisation's anti-democratic effects and measurability. Its conception of security also has to be relational and not two-dimensional – not just identifying what sector-type danger threatens whom, or how Other and Self confront each other, but acknowledging how local security narratives subjectify and subject-position – i.e. how they actually create, describe and order varieties of relations between international political entities and the home nation. Lastly, security analysis' conception of performativity has to be more dialectic, differentiating between the production of security notions and their political appropriation, providing room for a dissection of the different causal powers involved in securitisation as a process of construction and in securitisation as a basis for action.

The following paragraphs develop an analytical model along these lines. To do so, the book's two conceptual chapters rework securitisation theory – the discipline's most important framework for understanding how knowledge of national and international insecurity is produced – into a theory of political ordering. Shifting that theory's primary focus away from linguistic performativity (Waever 1995; Austin 1962) and Arendtian concerns with democratic politics

(Waever 2004), the chapters move securitisation towards the politics of producing, contesting and appropriating social representations. Instead of seeing representations of international danger as producing local and singular identities of the Self, however, it is argued that representations produce a multiplicity of complex and often contradicting world order imageries. As part of this, also the process of securitisation itself is reconsidered. Instead of this process being seen as empowering norm-breaking action, securitisation is shown to be complicit in the construction of world order imageries, since the recognition of a threat always comes with a broader understanding of who threatens whom and how. Reconceptualised in this way, securitisation effectively populates the international with distinct actors and security relations, providing inter-subjective imageries of the world's basic political relations. Speaking insecurity amounts to speaking world order, so the argument of this book, and speaking world order, means locking foreign policy behaviour into some highly distinct patterns.

To develop this argument, the sections that follow will discuss how securitisation *endangers*, *orders* and *conditions* international relations and how such endangering, ordering and conditioning of international relations is often challenged by alternative conceptions of who threatens what and how, and of what is to be done with such a representation in the foreign policy realm. In order to build up the argument, this conceptual chapter focuses on the way in which securitisation endangers and orders international politics. The subsequent chapter then continues with this elaboration, discussing how such 'world ordering securitisation' can be contested politically and how it conditions or causally affects foreign policymaking, thus making the case for an explanatory framework. Part II of the book applies the framework to a set of empirical cases. Part III reconnects with grand IR theory, discussing how the framework proposed here answers established accounts of international security politics and addressing normative aspects in the political production of insecure international orders.

Securitisation and the endangering of world politics

To name a threat – to securitise in a broad sense – means, first and foremost, to endanger the international context as it is seen by a country. When politicians, bureaucrats, experts, journalists and other influential truth-tellers talk about danger, they are locating that danger into their country's international environment. Securitisation constructs and identifies problem situations in world politics as it is understood locally, and it makes the presence of such situations known to the wider public (Waever 1995; Stritzel 2007). By singling out certain themes as special matters of concern, securitisation creates epistemological points of reference for a society, and in doing so its construction creates a basis for political action (Weldes *et al.* 1999: 1). This constructive process is dictated by the world's epistemological indeterminacy. In world politics, nothing has political currency for societies, unless it is actively named, classified and turned into an inter-subjective reality (Berger and Luckmann 1966; Schutz and Luckmann 1973; Wendt 1992; Guzzini 2000).

Securitisation is, however, more than a simple means for constructing inter-subjective knowledge. By setting out problem situations, endangerment also sets out a stimulus. The recognition of danger – whether the securitisation of weapons proliferation, migration or North Korea – creates situations of urgency. The endangerment of world politics creates a requirement for policy action, because it sets out problem situations (Wolfers 1952; Westing 1989; Jahn *et al.* 1987). Regardless of whether the basic rationale of this stimulus for activism is a quest for survival in the face of existential threats (Buzan *et al.* 1998) or the endeavour to master future uncertainty – i.e. risk (Hagmann and Dunn 2012) – endangerment in a basic sense creates knowledge of unacceptable foreign policy situations. Securitisation recognises that a problem exists in world politics. It brings these problems into political being and positions them as mandatory objects of action. Securitisation both provides points of reference for agency and asks for agency at the same time.

How such agency is channelled, however, depends on how danger is sub-stantially circumscribed, beyond simple naming and identification. National insecurities are, indeed, not only portrayed as simple problem situations in policymaking practice – the naming of international danger is always associ-ated with further elements of meaning and organisation. This is because by naming a threat, political communities are doing more than bringing a topic into security logic, creating a problem situation and a need to act. They are also creating broader understandings of who actually threatens whom and how. Securitisation, then, is nothing less than a process of subjectification (Foucault 1982). It creates sources and targets of threats, and it specifies the nature of relations between them, subject-positioning threatening and threat-ened things into distinct relations with each other and the home nation (Althusser 1971). Rather than merely empowering extraordinary political responses, as the Copenhagen School argues, the acknowledgement of danger hence also comes with the production of actors and relations in world politics. Securitisation names, defines and systematises international political orders, populating the world with actors and relations.

Understood as such a process of subjectification and subject-positioning, securitisation has significant epistemological and political functions. On the epis-temological level, the endangering and systematising of world politics gives structure to the undetermined social world. By naming and setting out a defini-tion of a problem, but also by populating the world with originators and victims, securitisation orders the world and makes it actionable. As a systematisation pro-cedure, securitisation responds to and domesticates 'dread' (Croft 2012: 221–223) or 'epistemological fear' (Huysmans 1998b: 235) – i.e. people's fear of not knowing and their urge to make sense of the contingent context in which they evolve. Naming dangers is an ontological security strategy (Mitzen 2006). By giving a confident sense of place and location to the home nation, securitisa-tion divides the de facto, always-evolving and contingent social world inter-national environment into temporarily stable categories of enemies, friends and fellows (Giddens 1984: 375; Walker 1993; Neumann 1999).

On the political level, the articulation of national insecurity creates complex and politically salient ideas about the presence and structure of international danger, advancing conceptions of who threatens whom and how. This means that securitisation is a local description of reality and an inherently political act. Securitisation brings topics to attention, creates necessities for action and structures the knowledge of world politics in distinct ways within a given society. It provides substantial representations of world order and makes, when advanced and accepted as an authoritative reading of international affairs, national foreign policy behaviour dependent on this systematisation. As discussed in more detail in the next chapter, the naming of insecurity has hence both political effects and is a political act in itself. Securitisation creates boundaries of action for subsequent behaviour, but it also emerges from struggles over dominant representations of the world – i.e. a competitive framing process.

(In-)Security and the production of world order(s)

After endangerment, however, how does securitisation create local ideas of international insecurity? Securitisation, the book argues, creates actors and relations in international security by codifying *who threatens whom and how*. Securitisation creates subjects of international security by defining who is held to cause insecurity and who is affected by such insecurity. Further, securitisation defines relationships between threatening and threatened actors in world politics by putting them into antagonistic couplings. The following subsections present and unpack these three dimensions – the identification of sources of insecurity, the recognition of targets of insecurity and the assessment of antagonistic relationships between the sources and targets of insecurity – one at a time. The next section then ties these three dimensions together, using empirical examples to illustrate how they come together to make securitisation systematise the international, thus advancing structured conceptions of the organisation of international security.

Identifying sources of insecurity

The first dimension by which the international is organised through securitisation is the specification of sources of insecurity – i.e. explicit or implicit understandings of whom or what is held responsible for causing national insecurity (*who threatens?*). These sources of national insecurity, the book maintains, are whatever local communities identify as such at a given point in time. Part II of the book shows that it is, indeed, standard practice for societies to recognise a wide array of originators of their insecurity, actors, values and processes alike. Foreign states and alliances have been held to cause such insecurity, but so have military companies, terrorists, warlords, separatists, monarchists, liberals, Jacobins, fascists, communists, intellectuals, financial speculators, migrants and polluters. By the same token, a variety of cultural values, such as local practices and ways of life, religious belief systems, such as Judaism and Islam, and material and political processes, such as globalisation, individualisation and consumerism, have also been recognised as causes of national insecurity by different countries in the past or present.

The way in which securitisation sets out sources of insecurity is thus highly context-specific. What is known to threaten a nation derives not from IR theory, but from the ways in which nations themselves come to acknowledge sources of insecurity. As a contextual process of subjectification, securitisation may, indeed, differ quite radically from traditional IR theory tenets. Traditional IR theory addresses the question of sources of insecurity at the hands of rigid conceptual ideas of statism, military forms of violence and permanent insecurity. Traditional IR theory argues that states are the only viable sources of national insecurity, that physical violence is the only relevant kind of security challenge in world politics and that international 'anarchy' organises these statist origins of military threats in inescapably generalised ways (Morgenthau 1962; Waltz 1979; Walt 1991). This is a problematic analytics. On the empirical level, traditional IR theory's claim that only states can be held to be viable sources of insecurity, as well as its argument that states always necessarily threaten each other given the anarchy situation, do not chime with actual real-world policymaking practices. In such practices, states are only sometimes recognised as sources of national or international insecurity (Schmidt 2002). States are clearly not identified as sources of insecurity universally. Indeed, several countries have come to recognise a large variety of non-state actors, political processes and cultural values as more important sources of national and international insecurity in recent years.

More problematically, traditional theory fails to inquire into societies' own, local ways of recognising international danger, and this omission has fundamental effects on the ways in which international politics can be explained. With its prescriptive analytical framework for who is a threat in international security, IR theory disqualifies itself from recognising how societies engage in a complex ordering of international security. Traditional IR not only fails to recognise that 'anarchy is what states make of it', as constructivists argue (Wendt 1992). Together with constructivism, it also fails to address how concepts of organised international insecurity, one of which could be classic interstate anarchy, are actually formulated and made local knowledge in the first place. Traditional IR theory, in short, is simply incapable of addressing how societies recognise and act out spaces of international insecurity. With 'anarchy', a concept of the organisation of international danger is simply handed to societies. At the same time, that concept is defined in extremely inflexible – namely, in state-centric and generalised – ways.

The politics of recognising and specifying local views of international insecurity is yet of fundamental relevance to understanding international affairs. Depending on who or what is recognised as an actual source of national insecurity, different organisations of international security are projected onto the international. Generalised interstate anarchy – traditional IR theory's basic premise – is one version of the organisation of international insecurity. But it is not the only such systematisation possible and, indeed, seems to not have been, in many places, a very popular reading of international relations in the first place. The empirical chapters show that interstate anarchy has never been recognised as a general and universal state of affairs in France, Germany or Switzerland since 1945. Instead, the identification of other states as sources of national danger has always been limited to select number of cases in these countries, and since the late twentieth century, danger narratives focusing on non-state actors and various kinds of values and political processes have clearly outranked more classic state-centric systematisations overall.

The nuances of the question of who or what actually endangers the own nation matters to IR as a discipline, because the answer to the question provides the basis for explanatory IR theorising. By analytically legislating rather than empirically investigating the question of who is considered to be a threat in world politics, traditional IR theory sets itself up to explain world politics from a skewed foundation. Its *a priori* assumption of the purported presence of an insecure 'anarchic' international system of mutually threatening states forces that theory to always explain international cooperation between states *despite* anarchy. Whether it is realism, liberalism or systemic constructivism – states are outright 'ruled' to threaten each other, given the premise of international anarchy, and so they cannot possibly be considered other than sources of insecurity. Alternative predications of the role of states in world politics are analytically precluded, and so the statist insecurity system – anarchy in the classic, disciplinary sense – cannot be escaped. It follows that policy solutions must always find ways of overcoming this generalised insecurity system, whereas the actual presence and the interpretation of the latter – i.e. the condition that makes the overcoming of the situation necessary in the first place – cannot be verified or even debated.

This perspective of grand IR theory is disciplining and blindfolding. It is a perspective that is of little help in understanding foreign policymaking. Like any other idea about the organisation of international danger, 'anarchy' is not a fact of life, but a representation of international affairs. International anarchy as popularised by traditional IR is one imagery of the international that has or had empirical validity in certain historical and local contexts, but by no means has it transhistorical currency or any higher intrinsic epistemic value than other local conceptions of the international. And, indeed, even a cursory look into local policy debates shows that the archetypal disciplinary anarchy situation is oftentimes *not* the basic interpretation of world politics. Quite frequently, other states are *not* held responsible for the home nation's insecurity in the first place, and this means that international cooperation can and should be explained *because* and not despite of the presence of states in world politics.

An excerpt from historical Franco-German relations (addressed in more detail in the subsequent empirical chapters) helps to illustrate this finding. Both of these nations recognised each other as their respective existential enemy in the wake of World War II. But by the early 1970s, the security debates of each country hardly focused on each other any longer. Instead, the ideas of national insecurity that were now circulating in France and Germany identified various other sources of French and German insecurity, such as communism, the nuclear arms race and, later, environmental degradation. Eventually, some of these ideas saw both France and Germany as affected by the same security challenges, thus suggesting that the two countries were caught up in a shared, larger insecurity context. These interlocking projections of shared insecurity empowered cooperation between France and Germany. For the vast majority of Franco-German post-war relations, cooperation was *not* founded on anarchy – for years, French and German politicians simply did not recognise each other, let alone the entire international system as such, as a threat. Yet cooperation emerged because of the construction of larger, mutually implicating insecurity spaces. During the Cold War, it was the USSR or the so-called superpower directorate that was recognised as a danger to the wider Europe in French and German security discussions, and it was these conceptions of international danger that served as an important knowledge basis for cooperation between France and Germany. Today, that same cooperation rests on the acknowledgement of a host of 'new shared dangers', such as environmental change, migration or economic instability.

This example illustrates that the politics of defining who exactly is held to cause national or international insecurity matters greatly. Securitisation is directly complicit in advancing representations of who is a source of a problem and who is not, and by doing so it assists in advancing distinct ideas regarding the organisation of international insecurity. This organisation matters politically, because it represents knowledge about the presence and structure of the international security context. Whether all foreign nations are considered sources of danger, whether some foreign states are but not others, whether the danger sources are non-state actors, material processes or political values – differential identifications of sources of danger are directly complicit in the production of different local knowledge of the international security environment. Specifications of such knowledge provide important policymaking rationales to foreign affairs, because they indicate against which entity national policies have to be directed and against which they do not.

Traditional accounts of IR black box the politics of identifying danger sources, and with this they do not and cannot acknowledge the construction of such differential representations of the international. By opening up the politics of identifying danger sources, this book denaturalises important elements of international politics and gives IR analytical leverage for the explanation of state behaviour. By seeing the identification of sources of insecurity as a political process, it becomes possible to understand how securitisation subjectifies the international. Securitisation may, indeed, come with the recognition of a variety of actors, processes and values as sources of national and international danger, and by doing so securitisation recognises and presents enemies and other opponents in the international, positioning these vis-à-vis the home nation. As a process of subjectification, securitisation is an utterly political struggle to organise the international and to provide authoritative interpretations of this organisation (Althusser 1971: 174; Torfing 1999: 25–26; Törrönen 2001: 314). Securitisation is about deciding how the international is organised, whereas different such decisions set out different problem definitions to deal with. Indeed, the question of who (or what) is recognised as a danger to the home nation and who (or what) is not is subject to political struggle precisely because such selections are complicit in advancing differently configured, politically salient images of world order.

Recognising targets of insecurity

Securitisation also organises the international by virtue of its definition of targets, or victims, of the threatening international system (*who is threatened?*). Securitisation comes with an explicit or implicit acknowledgement of the various entities affected by a given danger and thus the positioning of further actors in world politics. Also, this process of subjectification rests on a more complex politics than is usually accepted by traditional IR theory. IR security studies' traditional take on insecure entities in world politics is thoroughly statist, and it also seems perfectly self-centric. Generally, it is only states that can be held to be insecure, and states are usually merely held capable of recognising dangers that apply to them alone. This does not enable a differentiated positional analysis of how societies recognise further international actors as threatened by the same security problem as the home nation. The local construction of imageries of larger transnational insecure spaces is not a political process that traditional IR theory is capable of addressing. And how could it be otherwise, considering that traditional IR theory does not approach understandings of insecurity as constructive processes in the first place.

But grand IR theory is not alone in having difficulties in accounting for how notions of collective danger come about. The concepts of mid-range security studies also have difficulty addressing the politics of recognising insecure entities. The idea of 'referent objects' is a case in point. Referent objects have been defined in the security studies literature as 'those objects which are to be secured' (Buzan 1991: 13). Superficially at least, referent objects would thus seem to be a good starting point for addressing the question of how victims, or targets of insecurity, are defined and recognised. But scholars using the concept have done little or nothing to pursue the question of how referent objects come about, and so the idea of referent objects remains locked in its original, narrow managerial perspective on security affairs. As objects that 'are to be secured', the idea of referent objects comes with a straightforward claim to protection and protective policymaking.

Yet the politics of defining referent objects is not about such a claim in the first place. The politics of defining referent objects, this book argues, is one of epistemological construction. This is because the designation of insecure entities works first and foremost as an act of subjectification – the definition of who is threatened by a given danger is a performative sense-making process. Indeed, securitisation often creates entities in world politics that are considered to be insecure in parallel and in addition to the home nation. In doing this, securitisation populates the world with additional actors next to the identified sources of insecurity and the home nation. Securitisation creates fellows of sorts in a shared insecurity context and, with this, it also creates a complex web of relations between international actors – namely, between the recognised sources of national/international insecurity, the recognised fellows in a shared security context and the home nation.

'Fellows' – i.e. the foreign entities recognised as insecure in parallel to the home nation – are not referent objects in the original sense, since recognised foreign insecure entities are not necessarily 'to be made secure'. Indeed, for constitutional and other reasons, countries are usually bound to merely pursue and provide their own security, materially speaking. But even if 'fellows' are not proactively 'made secure', their recognition as insecure actors is nevertheless directly complicit in organising the international in a sense-making perspective. This is because different conceptions of who is insecure in the international system creates different understandings of the latter's organisation. The book's empirical genealogies show how, in practice, French, German and Swiss politicians have only rarely construed dangers as affecting their respective nation alone – rarely did they conceive of an Other merely confronting the Self. On the contrary, their focus on the Soviet Union as a European challenge, their recognition of weapons proliferation as a global security problem, their framing of migration as a regional danger to high-income European countries and their representation of Islamic religious fundamentalism as a threat to democracies worldwide are all examples of securitisations in which larger collective victim communities have been constructed. These constructions of larger insecurity communities have created different imageries of the international, and these imageries have then been acted upon and acted out in the French, German and Swiss foreign policy arenas.

The politics of selecting and defining targets or 'victims' of danger, then, is a fairly complex and important issue. The European empirical cases in this book provide abundant examples of how security has been systematised differently at different points in time. Sometimes, dangers have been known to target only the home nation. Sometimes, dangers have been held to affect not only the home nation, but also a number of neighbouring countries. Sometimes, dangers have been known to pose regional problems to Europe or outright global problems to everybody. Sometimes, dangers have been argued to evolve between other nations only. But dangers have also recurrently been defined transversally by non-statist indicators, such as in cases when a danger was known to target a certain regime type such as democracies, when it was known to focus on material conditions such as industrial states or when it was held to focus on specific sub-state actors, such as workers and citizens, but not residents, linguistic minorities and so on. In many instances, the construction of collective insecurity thus cut across clearly defined scholarly levels of analysis. In all these instances, however, securitisation created imageries of larger insecure communities – not imageries of uniform identity (Anderson 1991), but imageries of communities bound up in a similar problem situation.

This projection of insecure communities is not necessarily agreed on by others. When German politicians construe Greek financial turmoil as a challenge to all of Europe or American leaders present Cuba as a challenge to the entire Western hemisphere (Weldes and Saco 1996: 381–383), the fellows drawn into such wider insecurity communities – Europe here, the Americas there – are usually not asked for their consent to such epistemological collectivisation. And, indeed, other nations sometimes reject, sometimes endorse and sometimes simply ignore such collectivising narratives in practice. What matters locally, however, is that for and inside a securitising society, such collectivisation does have epistemic currency. What matters for local politics is that certain dangers are known to create larger insecure communities. Seen in this way, securitisation does *not* create larger Selves or we-identities when collectivising danger. The emerging French recognition of Germany as a fellow in a shared security context in the aftermath of World War II, for instance, did not construct a singular identity for these two nations – it did not extend French identity to Germany, with Germany suddenly being subsumed into French cultural self-identification. But that collectivisation did recognise Germany as not being responsible for French insecurity, and it also recognised France and Germany as forming a joint insecurity community overall. By advancing collective notions of the organisation of danger, French politicians merely came to know Germany as a distinct category of actor in world politics – an actor that is known to exist in world politics, known not to be a cause of the own country's insecurity and an actor that is projected to stand in a similar insecurity situation to France.

Securitisation's implicit or explicit identification of targets of insecurity, then, makes the naming of danger directly complicit in constructing imageries of international relations. The potential and empirically recurrent recognition of fellows in world politics creates (subjectifies) actors beyond the Other/enemy and the Self. By the same token, knowledge of the existence of such actors creates larger ideas of the organisation of world politics, locating (subject-positioning) the home nation into a complex web of recognised international relations. Politically, such systematisations set out distinct knowledge bases for foreign policy strategising. The collectivisation of danger creates ideas of international or transnational insecurity communities and thus makes interstate cooperation possible, whereas self-centric framings of danger as exclusively affecting the home nation disempower such foreign policy strategies. The politics of recognising and selecting targets of international insecurity, then, is of consequence for foreign affairs, because it populates the international order with different kinds of actor-categories and formations. Whether representations of danger are collectivised and how is subject to contending local interpretations precisely because such decisions advance differently configured and politically salient images of world order.

Assessing antagonisms in world politics

Lastly, securitisation also organises understandings of international security by providing graded assessments of the relations at play between the threatening and threatened actors (*how is something/someone threatened?*). As a matter of course, these relationships are relations of opposition. The specificity of securiti-sation, the preceding discussion of the endangerment of international relations has argued, is its setting out of problem definitions. This understanding of security as representing some form of confrontation squarely echoes the IR security studies literature, but it also goes beyond the stand taken by that liter-ature. This is because in security studies, security is usually claimed to be about generalised destruction and (thus) national survival (Waever 1995; Buzan *et al.* 1998: 21). This is to say that IR security studies generally only accept security as one distinct form of antagonism – namely, existential danger.

The reason why IR defines security in such extreme terms varies with the scholarship in focus. In some cases, the coupling resonates intimately with the destructive potential of modern weaponry – i.e. the nuclear bomb (Morgenthau 1962). In other cases, the equation of security with survival is less materialistic and more cosmological. It has been argued by some that the Copenhagen School's equation of security with survival, for instance, echoes a tacit commit-ment to the conservative and conflict-laden political philosophy of Carl Schmitt (Smith 1999; Williams 2003). Such conservative foundational assumptions are, however, difficult to ascribe to the Copenhagen School wholesale, given that one of its main contributors, Ole Waever, relies strongly on Arendtian and decon-structivist/post-structuralist political theory (Waever 2004, 2011). Then again, post-structuralism, too, is a political theory of radical confrontation. It sees a radical opposition as mandatory for the stabilisation of collective meanings and national identity (Campbell 1992; Walker 1993; Neumann 1999). Indeed, some scholars working within that tradition flatly reject the possibility and viability of non-existential antagonisms in world politics (Laclau 1988: 256; Torfing 1999: 127). Seemingly then, the literature's influential equation of security with sur-vival either derives from material potentials for destruction or from a conflict-oriented political philosophy.

Yet if the exact sources of the equation of security with survival are hard to identify, it still has to be asked what analytical leverage such straight association forgoes. Indeed, when security is strictly equated with survival, then security analysis becomes a fairly binary and limited affair: security situations either exist or do not exist based on the simple yet demanding benchmark of whether a situation is existential or not, and with this all security analysis is forced to pass the test of existentialism. Such an analytical perspective on antagonism has fairly major effects on the ways in which international relations can be thought and known. On the one hand, it only allows the recording of a restrained set of empirical cases of danger politics, as it only permits the registration of a certain type of security relations – namely, existential danger. On the other hand, the analytical equation of security with survival prevents from thinking about the relative overlapping and ranking of coexisting securitisations. The focus on security as survival does not allow putting parallel existing representations of danger into a hierarchy of sorts, since any danger either is, and is existential, or is not, and is thus not a security issue at all.

The parallel framing of overlapping and, at times, unevenly pressing national dangers is, however, everyday practice in reality, and so the disciplinary standpoint appears overdrawn. In practice, the empirical chapters show, security relationships are, indeed, *not* always defined in existentialist terms, yet the recognised dangers are still considered pressing problems, even if they are eclipsed by others. In West Germany, for instance, differentiated assessments of antagonism played a crucial role during the *Ostpolitik* years. Even a cursory look at the manifold official security doctrines of the time make it clear that Eastern Europe was always considered a threat to West Germany in the 1960s and 1970s. But with *Ostpolitik*, Romania, Poland, Hungary and Czechoslovakia were seen as less pressing security problems than the USSR or the German Democratic Republic. This differential assessment of security relations enabled a differentiated West German foreign policy strategy. It allowed for a treaty-based normalisation of relations between West Germany and East Europe, while at the same time upholding full German commitment to NATO, the countering of the Soviet Union and German unification – i.e. the disintegration of the German Democratic Republic (cf. Von Baudissin 1970). The example from the German debates of the 1960s and 1970s – and the same dynamic applies to the French redefinition of its relations with the USSR under de Gaulle, for that matter (cf. Touraine 1993) – shows how a range of different kinds of oppositions were recognised in national security debates in practice, including existential opponents as extreme cases, but also including antagonists and challengers as more graded forms.

Security, empirical evidence suggests, is thus sometimes about survival, but sometimes also not (Ciuta 2010). Given this, it seems useful for both empirical and theoretical reasons to keep security as a more open, graded scheme of relations of opposition and not to let political philosophy commitments curtail the analysis so fundamentally. Empirically, a graded understanding of security as *a* relation of opposition allows more cases of security politics to be covered, as it permits making observations of security politics below the survival threshold. Theoretically, a graded understanding of security relations then permits inquiry into the practical overlapping and relative ranking of parallel existing danger narratives. Securitisation can be understood as a politically contested definition process precisely because of the various politically salient kinds of opposition that it describes, and so it becomes possible to discuss and explain how contending assessments of antagonisms enable different kinds of foreign policy practices.

Security as systematisation

The naming of national insecurity, the previous sections argued, is a complex and context-dependent process of subjectification and subject-positioning. Securitisation is not merely about recognising what kind of sector-type threat challenges what kind of referent object, it is not merely about a radical binarisation of the world into the Other and the Self and it is not merely about empowering extraordinary and decisionist handlings of the themes that have been hauled into security lingo. Securitisation has more fundamental and variable epistemological and political dimensions and effects than this. Securitisation as understood in this book is a complex process of endangering and ordering the international. It makes problem situations known to a public, and it specifies who causes that problem situation, whom it affects and how. The naming of migration, Iran or climate change as matters of national security, for instance, literally *creates* international security contexts according to the view of the securitising actors. It populates their world with subjects and subject-positions – it identifies enemies, antagonists, competitors, but also fellows, and it relates these to the own nation and it assesses the nature of opposition in these relations. In doing so, securitisation creates an entire web of international relations under the larger thematic umbrella of different security themes, and it defines a position for the home nation in the international security context thus recognised.

The concrete ways in which securitisation does create such subjects, positions and relations depends on the kinds of representations of international danger that securitisation creates. Whether climate change or communist expansion represents an existential, state-actor driven or collective threat depends on how securitisation is used to answer the questions of who threatens whom and how – i.e. the previously discussed notions of danger sources, danger targets and antagonisms. By taking differentiated positions on these three dimensions, the securitisation of such topics can (and in practical terms often does) create *contending* knowledge about world order. The danger called 'terrorism' provides one example of how securitisation has created differentiated – at times overlapping and at times contending – understandings of international order(s). In the France of the 1980s, for instance, terrorist acts by radical left-wing and Middle Eastern groups were recognised as existential threats to the national security of France. In September 2001, by contrast, terrorism was known to be a state and non-state actor-sponsored existential threat not only to France, but to all democracies worldwide. Later in the 2000s, terrorism was again systematised differently inside the *hexagone*. For some French politicians, terrorism was still considered as a threat to democracies, but for others it threatened the entire world, while a third group saw it as effectively challenging the United States only. Opinions also diverged as to whether terrorism was, indeed, an existential problem or whether it was not merely more of a nuisance. Table 2.1 provides a schematic overview of these contending systematisations of terrorism. Superscripts indicate

Table 2.1 French constructions of terrorism

		1970s	1980s	September 2001	2000s
Terrorism	Source	N/A	Various groups[D]	Afghanistan[D] Al-Qaeda[D]	Al-Qaeda[D]
	Target	N/A	France[D]	All democracies[D]	All democracies[W] Entire world[W] USA only[W]
	Relation	N/A	Existential[D]	Existential[D]	Existential[D] Problematic[W]

whether a systematisation provided a dominant (D), widespread (W) or more marginal (M) interpretation in the French political system.

The securitisation of terrorism did not only evolve over time, however, nor was its exact definition contested merely in France and by the 2000s. Terrorism was sometimes also systematised differently across borders. In (West) Germany, for instance, as Table 2.2 shows, terrorism had already been securitised in the 1970s. Like the French, West German politicians understood terrorism – in particular, the acts perpetrated by the Red Army Faction – in self-centric terms – i.e. as problems posed to West German citizens, first and foremost. Unlike the later French securitisation of terrorism, however, the dominant West German discourse explicitly framed terror not as an existential threat or act committed by an outright enemy, but as a burdensome challenge posed by criminals. Later in the 2000s, German understandings of terrorism echoed the French interpretations again more intimately. At that time, terrorism was initially seen as a state- and non-state actor-driven existential threat to all democracies across the globe. Eventually, however, the sponsorship of terrorism, the specific communities concerned by terrorism and the intensity of the danger in itself became subject to similar debates in Germany as it did in France, come the late 2000s.

In neighbouring Switzerland, the securitisation of terrorism gave rise, again, to similar and different systematisations of the international. In the late 1970s, it was the Iranian Revolution and the diplomatic turmoil that followed it, but also the unifying front of the oil-producing countries that were considered terrorism by Swiss policymakers. That terrorism was seen as gravely challenging, but not existentially threatening the industrialised world as such – a distinctly material collectivisation of danger and the production of a larger insecurity community encompassing numerous other actors beyond Switzerland itself. In 2001 and later in the 2000s, terrorism was securitised similarly as in France or Germany – i.e. based on important controversies over whom terrorism truly affected. Unlike the French and German discussions, however, the Swiss debates focused more on Al-Qaeda and less on Afghanistan as a terrorism-sponsoring actor. Even more important, there was no sizeable Swiss reading of terrorism as a problem facing the United States only – Swiss analysts consistently framed terrorism as a wider shared challenge, even if they disagreed as to whom it affected exactly (cf. Table 2.3).

Table 2.2 (West) German constructions of terrorism

		1970s	*1980s*	*September 2001*	*2000s*
Terrorism	Source	Red Army Faction[D]	N/A	Afghanistan[D] Al-Qaeda[D]	Al-Qaeda[D]
	Target	German citizens[D]	N/A	All democracies[D]	All democracies[W] Entire world[W] USA only[W]
	Relation	Challenge[D]	N/A	Existential[D]	Existential[D] Problematic[W]

Table 2.3 Swiss constructions of terrorism

		1970s	*1980s*	*September 2001*	*2000s*
Terrorism	Source	Iran[D]	N/A	Al-Qaeda[D]	Al-Qaeda[D]
	Target	Industrialised world[D]	N/A	All democracies[D]	All democracies[W] Entire world[W]
	Relation	Adversary[D]	N/A	Existential[D]	Problematic[D] Existential[W]

The three tables taken together describe what kinds of world order imageries the securitisation of the thing called terrorism has helped to produce in practice. They suggest how systematisations of terrorism evolved over time, how they were sometimes subject to contending readings within a country proper and how they sometimes took quite different forms internationally. This empirical fact lends weight to the argument that a danger theme (such as 'terrorism') does *not* have a fixed meaning in itself and that it does not provide a single inescapable representation of the organisation of international insecurity. Who threatens whom and how by a problem such as 'terrorism' can be, and often is, subject to contending systematisation across time, across political camps inside a country and across international borders. This insight directly asks for a contextualised analysis of security politics. The cases make clear that in order to understand how nations make sense of world politics, it is vital to inquire empirically into the ways in which nations define national insecurity themselves. To understand how nations act out the dangers they recognise, the configuration and relative salience of the locally available threat definitions must be addressed first, since it is that knowledge upon which nations base their foreign policy decisions.

Clearly, this empirical research agenda turns out to be demanding, since not only is it necessary to assess how policymakers fight over the authoritative definition of a single danger as authoritative imagery of the international. In order to understand how countries act out their reading of their international security environment, it is also necessary to address the totality of all danger rationales available in a given country. This is because, in practice, nations rarely recognise only one single national danger. More often than not, nations recognise a host of dangers at the same time, whether they be Iran, climate change, weapons proliferation, poverty and so on. Each of these dangers systematises the international in its own ways, and each narrative is potentially subject to contending interpretations about ordering in themselves. Taken together, this means that national security politics may (and empirical analysis suggests that they quite often do) rest on a complex and potentially contradictory set of representations of international danger. In their multiplicity, securitisations may create contradictory readings of the international, since parallel subjectification mechanisms may give rise to incompatible subject-positions (cf. Althusser 1971: 107; Davies and Harré 1990: 48). National security doctrines such as those cited in this book's introduction illustrate this situation well. More often than not, their enumeration

of different kinds of contemporary danger creates a *pluriverse* of local understandings of the international; a multiplicity of world order descriptions that are
not always fully compatible with each other.

Potentially, local interpretations of international security can thus become
contradictory. French post-war security debates illustrate the way in which tensions
between contending readings of the international can be paramount. In the late
1940s and early 1950s, as Chapter 4 of this book shows and Table 2.4 indicates,
French politicians not only recognised a number of major dangers to the nation, the
challenges of Germany, the USSR and 'American capitalism' in particular. French
politicians were also fundamentally divided as to the exact meaning of each of
these dangers. Whom exactly Germany was seen as threatening – France only,
Western Europe or the world in its entirety – was hotly debated, as was the fundamental question regarding whether Germany still posed a problem to the security
of France. Whether the USSR – a former wartime ally – posed a problem, and if it
really did, then to whom, and whether it paralleled or eclipsed the German danger
(if that danger was held to be still viable) formed another virulent controversy, as
did yet another view of international politics, according to which the United States
and capitalism writ large were held to threaten French independence and well-
being. Only by the late 1950s, the subsequent empirical chapters show, did a distinct new reading of the international security context (namely, 'Gaullism') become
hegemonic in France, stabilising the country's conception of international affairs
and sense of its own location.

Conclusion

The naming of international danger comes with a larger and, indeed, formidable
politics of endangering and ordering international relations. Securitisation is
directly complicit in advancing authoritative frameworks of international danger
reality: whether it focuses on communism, terrorism or climate change, securitisation makes clear who the enemy or opponent is, whom it affects, how and
what the position of the home nation is in a wider recognised web of international relations. As a subjectifying and subject-positioning process, securitisation creates structured representations of international order under the umbrella
of distinct insecurity themes. It advances truth claims about the organisation of
international security as it is understood by a community. These truth claims
matter when explaining foreign policymaking, because they project distinct
kinds of symbolic orders onto the international at a given place and point in time,
making specific foreign policy options available at a given social and historical
moment (cf. Jameson 1971: xiv). What kinds of symbolic order are projected by
danger narratives, however, depends intimately on which interpretation of
danger takes the upper hand in a country at a given point in time. Securitisation
is subject to political struggle, because it advances contending frameworks of
international security reality. These frameworks empower certain kinds of state
behaviour but not others, and this is why their configuration and relative epistemic validity is hotly debated in political practice.

Table 2.4 French constructions of international (in-)security after World War II

		Late 1940s	Early 1950s
Germany	Source	Culture of militarism[D]	Culture of militarism[W] Fascist West Germany only[M]
	Target	France only ('historical prime enemy')[D] Everyone (incl. wartime Ally USSR)[W] Western Europe[W]	Everyone (incl. wartime Ally USSR)[W]
	Relation	Existential[D]	Existential[W] Problematic[W] Manageable[W]
Communism/USSR	Source	French communists[W] USSR[W]	USSR[D] French communists[M]
	Target	French democracy[W] Europe (incl. Germany)[W]	Europe (incl. Germany)[D]
	Relation	Challenge[W] Existential[W] No threat[M]	Existential[D] Challenge[W]
Capitalism/USA	Source	Capitalist economy[W] Foreign power/alliance[W]	Capitalist economy[M] Foreign power/alliance[M]
	Target	Workers[W]	Workers[M]
	Relation	Existential[W] No threat[W]	Existential[M] No threat[W]

3 Contesting and conditioning international relations

Contesting international relations

In order to understand how ideas of danger can be subject to contestation, it is necessary to address the way in which such ideas are produced in the first place, beyond systematisation alone. Ideas of national or international danger are produced by acts of naming (Buzan *et al.* 1998). On the substantive side, securitisation is the process of taking examples, of framing these as problems and of specifying who causes that problem, whom it affects and how. It is the rendering of things, events and processes as politically relevant, a making-signify all sorts of objects in a specific manner. As already argued, such construction is mandatory, given that people act on the meaning that objects have to them and not on objects in themselves prior to their interpretation (Wendt 1992: 396–397; Searle 1995: 34–35; Cox and Sinclair 1996: 51; Fearon and Wendt 2002: 58). The Red Army's occupation of Eastern Europe is an example of an event that did not signify anything prior to its interpretation. The securitisation of this occupation eventually made the Soviet Union signify a danger to the West, but this meaning was not inherent in the action under scrutiny – and indeed, others saw the occupation of Eastern Europe not as a threat, but as the agreed upon result of Yalta or even as an act of self-defence (e.g. Aron 1949: 252–254). Things, events or processes only become known as dangers when rendered as problems, and the question of how things, events and processes are valorised as dangers is as much political as the question of which things, events and processes are recognised as valid empirical observations for collective interpretation in the first place (Feyerabend 1975).

On the procedural side, ideas of danger are interpretations that are made collective truths. The naming of threats is paralleled by a process of making such interpretations politically relevant – i.e. of turning individual identifications of danger into more general public knowledge. This means that securitisation involves a process of convincing larger audiences about the truthfulness of the very imagery of international relations that it advances. Different factors cater to this process of creating inter-subjective knowledge. By speaking from positions of power such as councils, ministries or universities (Mutimer 1998), invoking a public mandate bestowed by democratic election or professional function

(Weldes *et al.* 1999: 17–19), mobilising ideational and material support systems such as IR theories, expert systems and media channels (Ashley 1987; O'Tuathail and Agnew 1992; George 1997; Büger and Villumsen 2007), pursuing distinct visualisation strategies or rhetorical tactics such as the paradiastolic reframing of old knowledge and the likening of new danger ideas to existing folk knowledge about the world (Balzacq 2005; Stritzel 2007), the interpretations of a few people can be advanced as larger truths within distinct social networks and discursive arenas and possibly even within an entire country.

Seen in this way, securitisation refers to an entire politics of speaking danger. In this politics, the very meaning of a threat narrative can be contested exactly because its transformation into public knowledge requires – in democracies even more so than elsewhere – a collaborative interaction between a plurality of people with potentially contending opinions and agendas. Securitisation as understood in this book is both about a knowledge system that names and describes things in specific ways and a process of producing, reproducing and potentially also reformulating that knowledge. This means securitisation is better understood as a social representation than as a speech-act, here. Social representation theory refers to acts of representing (the constructive process) and presentations (the imageries constructed) as such (Moscovici 1973: xiii; Verkuyten 1995: 265), and it acknowledges the role of a plurality of oftentimes unequally powerful groups or milieus in these constructions and the seizure of collective knowledge (Mérand 2007). As social representation, so the position adopted in this book, securitisation can thus be turned into a fuller sociological framework of security politics, given that it addresses both construction and that which is constructed. Conceptualised this way, securitisation resonates more intimately with the sociology of knowledge of Berger and Luckmann, the collective representation of Durkheim, the critical sociology of Bourdieu or the ethnomethodology of Garfinkel (Farr 1987: 346) than with Austin's more limited socio-linguistic speech-act theory, even if acts of naming form part of the articulation of social representations (Parker 1987; Bauer and Gaskell 1999).

As a social representation, securitisation creates knowledge about the world and lays that knowledge out for discussion. This means securitisation empowers political agency by virtue of being in itself a collective sense-making process: securitisation allows recognised members of society to endorse, reformulate or outright reject a representation of danger, and in doing so it makes it possible for there to be political competition over true knowledge. Empirical evidence suggests that securitisation is, indeed, often contested. Not only are some actors more resourceful than others in making their interpretation of world politics heard inside a society. Often, a variety of formal and informal tactics are also used to passively or actively prevent the articulation of contending readings of the nation's security environment. In the media, publishers and broadcasting stations often print or air only those analyses that are in line with their own political agendas, while in the academic arena, seniority and other kinds of access restrictions allow some but not other interpretations of world politics to be disseminated. In the parliamentary arena, so the case studies show, rival perspectives regarding the world are shouted down or labelled as deviant, and regulations are used to limit the time given to smaller parties to articulate contending positions on the floor.

In the broader politics of producing and arranging knowledge, such practices are complicit in making certain sorts of knowledge about the world more important than other sorts. They help to ensure that some types of knowledge, but not others, are hegemonic for an entire society, to the point where the validity of such privileged knowledge becomes self-evident (Gramsci 1971). Seen in this way, securitisation not only carries the possibility for dissent and contestation, it also entails the potential for articulations of few or singular superior truths. The interpretation of reality is a battle of ideas, and in this contest some frameworks can be invested with more epistemic currency than others, to the point where the validity of some knowledge is harder to challenge or not subject to debate at all. Securitisation, then, can be contested politically, reformulated or challenged in its entirety, but it can also be stabilised into more or less dominant systematisations of international relations: as a political construct, securitisation may establish situations in which a number of contradictory danger narratives coexist, such as in the French example of the late 1940s and early 1950s mentioned in the preceding chapter. But as a political construct, securitisation may also result in a situation in which only a few such systematisations coexist and are unevenly powerful at that. This was the case during the West German *Ostpolitik* years, when the dominant political camp divided Eastern Europe into different kinds of challenges, and a more marginal camp maintained an existential rendering of the entire Eastern Bloc as a whole. Finally, as a political construct, securitisation may also only allow a single overarching master narrative regarding international affairs, as the Swiss case shows. Until the 1980s, the Swiss understanding – that East and West confronted each other, but did not threaten neutral Switzerland in so doing – provided for a hegemonic reading of the international, a knowledge that stood unopposed by other systematisations of the international and a knowledge whose epistemic validity was not open to debate.

The understanding that knowledges can be contested but also popularised and stabilised over time within society is analytically relevant and has methodological implications. Analytically, it means that multiple danger narratives may coexist inside a society, working with or against each other in making sense of the country's international context and its own position therein. Methodologically, it means that securitisation can usually be studied as the (re-)production of relatively stable knowledge formations. Securitisation as systematisation can produce temporary imageries of the international. These imageries provide for objectified or frozen local pictures of reality, even if they are subject to constant reproduction over time (Fierke 2002: 337). Ideas of international danger can become structural conditions to a political system, 'real-existing truths of world order that appear fixed, canonic and binding' and thus cannot be wished away (Nietzsche 1887: 180; Berger and Luckmann 1966). Subjectification and subject-positioning, then, may undergo 'sedimentation' over time – for instance, by virtue of epistemic institutionalisation: world order understandings can be (and often are) engrained or written into strategy papers, doctrines, IR theories, material investments and mandates of international organisations, to the point where readings of world order reproduce themselves almost autopoietically (Jameson 1971: xii). Systematisations of the international can become de facto social facts to a country, even if they are always produced and instantiated by society (Törrönen 2001: 315; Hall 1992; Žižek 1994). This means that systematisations of the international can be studied, and given their potential for becoming de facto social facts to society, they also *should be* studied.

Conditioning international relations

Given the inter-subjective nature of national knowledge about international affairs, the contestation of danger narratives' subjectification mechanisms is always possible, but it may be practically more prevalent at certain times than others. Once, however, security concerns are articulated and disseminated, systematising the organisation of international insecurity in different ways, policymakers must act upon the representations of international danger that are available to them when crafting foreign affairs strategies. Politicians must justify their actions in relation to the knowledge circulating in their society, given that they have no other means of knowing the international. Securitisation therefore directly influences the way in which states can design foreign policies. Securitisation as understood here sets out problem situations and advances authoritative readings of the international, and this is why the construction of danger is ultimately important for explaining state behaviour.

The effect of such knowledge on foreign policymaking is, however, not causal in the classic sense. Representations of the international organisation of danger do not impose themselves on to foreign affairs directly as ideologies would. They do not predetermine behaviour, given that they are always instantiated by actors who can choose to do otherwise, and hence they are no independent variables. Nevertheless, representations of world order do condition foreign policymaking by providing the epistemic material with which policymakers must work. This means that representations of international danger empower some types of foreign policy action and foreclose others, and as will be argued shortly, this means that they causally condition foreign policymaking in an Aristotelian sense of the term.

As already briefly noted in the preceding chapter, securitisation theory as formulated by the Copenhagen School provides limited help for such a dialectical understanding of the political effects of securitisation, according to which knowledge sets out ranges of possibilities, but does not lead to one single unavoidable outcome. Not only has securitisation theory in its original variant been more directly interested in the democratic implications of security as naming, shying away from inquiring into the substantive world order imageries that danger narratives produce. By arguing that the naming of danger directly empowers extraordinary policymaking practices, securitisation theory has also packaged the effects of securitisation into its naming in an ontological manner, forgoing a differentiation of the construction of danger and its appropriation as two separate but interlinked spheres of political debate. Securitisation in its original conceptualisation popularises a 'coupled' understanding of social action, in which those who frame security also define what is to be done with it – namely, the deployment of extraordinary measures. Once security is enunciated, a narrowly circumscribed politics of security is then claimed to be at work, to the point where its outcomes are no longer to be debated (Huysmans 1998b: 234). This means that even if securitisation is inspired by a democratic/Arendtian concern with the closure of political discussion through security, the theory itself makes the appropriation and redirection of security to anything other than extraordinary ends impossible to discuss. The politics of instantiating and appropriating security narratives for some projects but not others is cut short in securitisation theory and by securitisation theory itself.

The decomposition of construction and bringing-into-effect poses a major challenge to securitisation theory (Roe 2008; Guzzini 2011). The difficulty that securitisation theory has with differentiating this question stems seemingly from its intimate reliance on a linguistic model of politics and its ambition to make a strong case for the performative and unwarranted effects of rhetorical moves in security affairs. These commitments – so it is widely understood in security studies – produce an argument according to which ideas of danger give way to clearly defined outcomes, once these ideas are invoked and enlarged so as to enter the sphere of public knowledge. Ontologically speaking, this means that the Copenhagen School ends up advancing a structural and causal theory of politics, since if securitisation necessarily leads to extraordinary policies, then policymakers become mere rule followers, at least as regards these latter dimensions of security politics. Policymakers may be considered to actively partake in the naming of national danger, but once this danger is identified, the distinct effects of danger narratives are simply held to impose themselves on the political arena without further ado. The conceptual and political implications of such an analytics should not be underestimated. If this is the argument that the Copenhagen School sets out, then that School effectively reifies policymakers as cultural dopes (Giddens 1979: 52, 1995: 17–18) when it comes to the effects of security. This means that the powers and responsibilities of policymakers for enacting ideas of danger in some ways but not others are glossed over or at least gravely underestimated.

However, the answer to the question of whether the Copenhagen School is effectively making this kind of structural argument about security is not as straightforward as it might seem. Although the view that extraordinary actions necessarily follow the naming of danger has been widely understood as a key component of securitisation theory in security studies, the Copenhagen School, in fact, employs a number of guarding statements that relativise such a deterministic reading of the theory. In some places, it is merely argued that securitisation 'opens the way' for a mobilisation of extraordinary powers (Buzan *et al.* 1998: 21). Elsewhere, securitisation has been said to merely advance 'claims to right' to the use of such existential powers (Waever 1995: 51). The broader agenda of securitisation analysis, too, has been described as an inquiry into 'the results' of securitisation, among other things (Buzan *et al.* 1998: 32). Also, more recent Copenhagen works have begun asking for more contextualised assessments of securitisation (Waever 2011; note the plural in both cases). Seemingly, then, the effect of securitisation on political action is much less direct, and it may also be much more diverse, than how it is generally understood. A dialectical ontology can seemingly be read into the theory, alternative outcomes of securitisation can be envisaged, the roles and responsibilities of policymakers in using security ideas for different ends can be addressed and a pluri-causal model of security politics can possibly be postulated, even if such things are not explicitly addressed by the Copenhagen School.

It quickly becomes clear that whether securitisation proposes a structural or a dialectical theory of security depends a lot on the exact meaning of 'audience acceptance' in the Copenhagen framework. If audience acceptance of a securitising move merely turns 'claims to right' into collective knowledge, then 'claims to right' are merely bolstered inter-subjectively and outcomes of securitisation remain contingent. The claim might be accepted throughout society in such a case, but whether and how it is invoked remains a completely different issue. By contrast, if audience acceptance sanctions 'claims to right' in the authoritative sense of granting permission for something that is then certainly going to be performed, then these 'claims to right' are directly transformed into actual extraordinary policy practices, and securitisation is a structural theory of security politics. Problematically yet, the under-theorisation of the audience – not just who it entails, but also *what* it is held to accept or reject – in securitisation theory makes it impossible to discern what the audience's role is held to be according to the Copenhagen School and thus to determine on what ontological side its theory ultimately falls. It is important to point out this ontological ambivalence, because it is a source of fundamental ambiguity in securitisation theory. It has an analytical role to play in figuring out the exact role that danger narratives play in international politics, and it has a political role to play in opening or blocking an emancipatory agenda of security. Depending on the ontology with which securitisation is invested, causal claims can or cannot be identified, and the interplay between security and foreign policy is either a matter of explaining or a matter of understanding. Depending on the ontology on which securitisation is made to rest, alternative outcomes to security politics can or cannot be thought of and catered to.

Beyond constitutive analysis

Yet, there is no need for security studies to await clarification of this issue from the Copenhagen School authors. Even if the Copenhagen texts and/or their reception are ambiguous with regard to ontology and causal powers, this situation does not alter the fact that securitisation theory must ultimately be made to rest on a dialectic theory of politics. This is so since, in the last resort, no sophisticated theory of politics can operate a structural ontology that does not grant a place to contingency, especially not if it is going to be made to explain political process in democratic societies. Social groups do rely on human agency: even if they are at times steeped in structural contexts, there is always some human ability to reformulate political practices and thus do and use things differently, and human agency is also involved throughout in the mere reproduction of social reality (Emirbayer and Mische 1998; Fuchs 2001). This basic fact of social life *requires* securitisation theory to operate a dialectical model of politics, in which representations of danger and their seizure are recursively related. A sociological model of securitisation such as social representations theory is directly useful for advancing such an ontology. Unlike the linguistic model of Austin drawn on by the Copenhagen School, social representation theory overtly differentiates between constructing actors, objects of representation and the association of uses with such representations (Farr 1987; Foster 2003: 236; Laffey and Weldes 1997: 211). In doing so, social representation theory acknowledges the ability of agents to appropriate insecurity narratives for different finalities. Seen in this way, securitisation is not precluded analytically from giving rise to a variety of contending uses, and it is not precluded from relying on distinct policymaker actions for their instantiation and enactment.

The necessity of theorising politics in such a dialectical manner is, of course, not a new insight for reflexive IR. Systemic constructivism has prominently argued that meanings of anarchy (as structures) make different kinds of state behaviour (agency) possible (Wendt 1992, 1999), and post-structuralists, too, have shown how the framing of Others determines (as structures) the identity of the Self, thus making specific kinds of interaction (agency) with those Others possible (Doty 1993; Weldes and Saco 1996; Milliken 1999). Importantly, however, the dialectical ontology that these kinds of reflexive scholarship are advancing into IR is generally claimed to be non-explanatory. It rests on an understanding that social science research can either explain or understand social actions (Hollis and Smith 1990), and it rests on a fairly broad disciplinary consensus that reflexive IR is about the latter and not the former (e.g. Dessler 1989; Klotz and Lynch 2007). This view derives from the general understanding that reflexive IR studies reasons and not causes and that it should therefore not advance causal arguments akin to those of traditional theory (Kurki 2006: 194). It derives from a criticism of traditional IR for taking as unproblematic the possibility that a particular decision or course of action could actually happen. This is why, from the 1990s onwards, reflexive IR distanced itself from traditional IR, positioning itself as an agenda that addresses 'how-possible questions' – i.e. conditions that make social action possible in the first place. Such conditions are held to be constituted and not caused. It is held that they are *not* about an independent variable causing changes in a separate and posterior dependent variable, and this is why reflexive IR has so broadly abandoned 'why questions', causal mechanisms and explanation (Wendt 1998).

Back in the 1990s, this intimate linking of reflexive IR scholarship with constitutive theorising was also motivated by reasons internal to academia. At the time, the newly emergent reflexive IR research agendas were being pressured by the discipline's figureheads to sketch an explanatory research agency modelled on classic positivist science (cf. Keohane 1988: 392–393), and yet much reflexive IR was unwilling to provide such causal arguments. Reflexive IR had just criticised mainstream theorising for its structural determinism and its clinical imputation of 'rational' interests to policymakers (Wendt 1987, 1992; Weldes 1996), and so the seemingly logical consequence was to reject what was held to be this scientific model of traditional IR, causal analysis. By embracing constitutive theorising, then, reflexive IR sought to carve out space for its own work inside a discipline which, although formally a social science, was still strongly wedded to material, mechanistic and systemic understandings of social behaviour.

It is likely that the securing of such a distinct and legitimate domain for reflexive IR theorising has been important to its further institutionalisation and development. In hindsight, however, it is important to recognise that the very syllogism on the basis of which reflexive IR was made to abandon explanatory arguments is far from unproblematic. And, indeed, reflexive IR's decision to turn to constitutive theorising *à la* Wendt and others complicates its own scholarly inquiry, making its agenda less powerful than it could be. The shortcomings of constitutive theorising by and large derive from the very special kind of dialectical solution to the structure-agency problem that has been popularised with constitutive theory in IR – namely, the social theory of Anthony Giddens. It is on his so-called 'structuration theory' that Wendt, who has been particularly influential in advancing constitutive theorising in IR, draws intimately in arguing against causal analysis in reflexive IR and in favour of constitutive relations and 'how-possible questions' (cf. Wendt 1987: 362, 1998). Structuration theory was a prominent dialectical social theory at the time, a model of social action that acknowledges that social behaviour results from a combination of both structural and agential powers (Thompson 1989; Bieler and Morton 2001; Stueber 2006). Structuration theory posits structure as 'system of generative rules and resources' (Giddens 1976: 127; 1984: 17), and thus it shifts its meaning conceptually from the classic negative idea of delimitation and predetermination to a new and more ambivalent concept of both possible curtailing and enabling of social action (Giddens 1979: 54). Structuration theory sees structures and agents as 'two sides of the same coin' (Giddens 1984: 374) and thus as jointly complicit in the production of social behaviour. When Wendt calls for constitutive analysis and an inquiry into the making possible of situations, he is mobilising this very ontology as a replacement for the traditional causal model of IR scholarship. It is Giddens' theory of structuration that allows him to differentiate between 'how' and 'why' questions and that empowers him to inquire into the making-possible of situations taken for granted by traditional IR. But it is also the very same theory of structuration that forces him– and, by extension of the popularity of constitutive analysis, also reflexive IR more broadly – to disqualify causal and explanatory analysis.

Structuration theory is, however, only one possible solution to the recursive relationship between structure and agency (Dessler 1989; Lewis 2002), and it is important to note the way in which it affects the way social behaviour can be understood analytically. Indeed, structuration theory not only fuses structure and agency into one model, thus providing analytical leverage for those questions of how things become possible that have been ignored by traditional IR. It also effectively collapses the two elements into a single amalgamated process. By describing structure and agency as 'two sides of the same coin', the two sites of power are conflated analytically to the point where inquiry into the independent properties of each is made impossible (Hay 1995: 197). Structure and agency are 'elided' in structuration theory. They are pushed together conceptually to the point where their distinction becomes meaningless and the independent properties of either are lost (Bhaskar 1979; Taylor 1989; Layder 1997). Applied to IR, this means that structuration theory and constitutive analysis helps understand how, for instance, meanings of anarchy (as structures) make, together with their instantiation and appropriation by policymakers (agency), certain international relations possible. However, by regarding structure and agency as duality rather than dualism, by melding the two into one phenomenon instead of treating them as separate but connected phenomena (Carlsnaes 1992; Sibeon 1999), it precludes a deeper analysis of the exact interplay between such knowledges and actions (McAnulla 2002: 279; Bates 2006: 156). It makes it impossible to determine what kind of power each has in determining social behaviour, and thus, in analytical terms, it invites, if not forces, an uncritical rejection of causal argumentation and explanatory theorising (Hagmann 2013).

But this is not the only problematic aspect of constitutive theory. In a similar way to that just noted, the same elision also directs IR scholarship towards static analyses of social action. Although Giddens himself acknowledged that all social activity was inscribed in a larger, evolving 'world time', his sociology essentially sees social action as consisting of routines. It is the repetitiveness of daily activities that provides the material grounding of the recursive nature of social life in his ontology (Giddens 1984: xxiii), and structuration theory therefore has an inbuilt tendency to direct inquiry to the immediate moment (Layder 1981; Stones 2001). This analytical evacuation of time is squarely shared by constitutive theorising, despite intermittent references to evolution. As Wendt describes constitutive IR theorising:

> Constitutive theories account for the properties of things by reference to the structures in virtue of which they exist. Cummins calls such theories 'property' theories. Unlike transition theories, which explain events through time, property theories are static. Their goal is to show how the properties of a system are constituted. The systems whose properties they explain may be dynamics, and indeed all systems, natural and social, are always in process, continually being reproduced through time even if they do not change. But constitutive theories abstract away from these processes and take 'snapshots' instead, in an effort to explain how systems are constituted.
>
> (Wendt 1998: 105)

Such an analytical perspective affects the way in which international relations can be understood and researched. Although it lends due weight to the way in which situations are made possible and the importance of routines in producing social outcomes, the focus on constitution also makes it difficult to assess evolution, as opposed to mere reproduction (Gouldner 1970). With constitutive theorising, it becomes very hard for reflexive IR to explain how knowledges become challenged or transformed, since by conflating structure and action, the possibility of explaining change in terms of their interaction over time is ruled out from the start (Taylor 1989: 149). Defined as constitutive analysis, then, the focus on understanding invites reflexive IR to focus on snapshots, as opposed to assessing genealogically how situations may evolve or be evolved over time. Applied to the question of how representations of international danger affect national foreign policymaking, constitutive analysis thus provides little analytical assistance for apprehending how the two elements interact with, and impact on, each other in a dynamic fashion, and in doing so it also works against genealogical empirical enquiry (Hagmann 2013).

(In-)Security theory as transformative ontology

It is important to address the ontology of any IR or security theory. Ontologies codify how scholars and research agendas understand social relations to be configured in their most basic sense – i.e. what is held to affect what and how (see Table 3.1 for an overview of ontological choices and their implications for theorising the interplay between security politics and foreign affairs). And even if such basic understandings are at times tacitly compacted into larger arguments (such as in the case of securitisation theory), no security theory can shy away from adopting such ontological stands (Wight 2002: 26; Carlsnaes 2002: 335). This is so because the making of ontological commitments is simply inevitable for any social science theorising. Yet, ontologies are not innocent analytically, as they direct the way in which political processes can be analysed and apprehended. Among the various ontological stands possible, constitutive theorising represents just one distinct set of commitments, and an ontology that comes with both benefits and limitations. As an alternative to structural theorising à la Neo-Realism or World Systems Theory, for instance, it permits inquiry into the way in which situations are made possible and hence the addressing of research questions that traditional IR theory simply takes for granted (Wendt 1987). At the same time, however, the ontology of constitutive theorising also creates difficulties for IR theorising. By melding the interaction between structure and agency into a single instance, it makes inquiry into the distinct properties of each impossible, and it removes evolution/time from the analysis. Applied to the interaction between imageries of international security and national foreign policymaking, constitutive analysis does not allow either to be thought of as distinct sites of causal power, and it does not allow addressing their dynamic recursive interplay.

Table 3.1 Contending ontologies of social action and the interplay between knowledge of international danger and national foreign policymaking

	Reductionist ontologies		Dialectical ontologies	
	Structuralism	*Voluntarism*	*Structuration*	*Morphogenesis*
Role of structure/ systematisations of the international	Structure imposes social action. Knowledge of international danger dictates foreign policy.	N/A. Structure is epiphenomenal. Once-formulated knowledge of international danger is not binding on policymakers.	Structure and agency co-ally to produce situations and make outcomes possible. Knowledge of international danger and policymaker action come together to make international relations in a given snapshot moment.	Structure and agency come together to produce international relations, having different characteristics and interacting over time. Knowledge of international danger conditions foreign policy, but is also instantiated, activated, etc. by policymakers.
Role of agency/ policymakers	N/A. Agency is epiphenomenal. Once-formulated knowledge of international danger imposes itself on foreign policymakers.	Agents decide on social action as they want. Foreign policy is not required to follow knowledge of international danger.		
Conception of ontology	Upward conflation: Reification of agency.	Downward conflation: Reification of structure.	Elision/central conflation: Static *duality* of structure and agency.	Stratified and transformative *dualism* of structure and agency.
Type of relation/argument	Causal (Cartesian/Humean): Causation as observable regularity determinism in systemic environment, strongly generalisable and parsimoniously explainable. Causation also works for voluntarism if rationality is imputed on agents (and voluntarism is thus de facto subverted).		Constitutive: No causal argument, due to recursive relation of factors and non-material constitution of reality.	Causal (Aristotelian): Recursively related and 'real' conditioning and activating causes of social action.

Source: Ontological differentiation draws on Archer 1995, 2000: 4–6.

Surprisingly, these limitations of constitutive analysis have been very little debated in the discipline. Often, constitutive analysis seems to be used simply as a ready-made model for reflexive IR, as a fail-safe justification for not doing explanatory IR. Yet its limitations are too important to let it pass uncritically, and the question arises of whether other ontologies of the social could help avoid or mitigate the limitations of constitutive theorising. And, indeed, more recent theoretical advances in social theory – in particular, Margaret Archer's morphogenetic reworking of Roy Bhaskar's critical realist philosophy of science – suggest that constitutive theory's rejection of dynamic and causal analyses might not be necessary, and that the current placing of reflexive IR as understanding might not be as warranted and well-elaborated as thought. Morphogenesis, indeed, allows for the regaining of analytical leverage over the analytical limitations of constitutive theorising. Morphogenesis represents another dialectical social theory in which social outcomes are recursively related – like structuration theory, morphogenesis also proposes a dialectical ontology, in which, to paraphrase Marx, 'men make history but not under the circumstances of their choosing'. As such an ontology, inherited structures are understood to influence action, but they also rely on agents to be instantiated and thus take effect. Unlike structuration theory, however, morphogenesis is a social theory that does *not* see structure and agency as 'two sides of the same coin' or duality. The Giddean conception of the structure-agency interplay is rejected for 'sinking rather than linking' (Archer 1995: 102) the differences between the two elements. As Archer criticises structuration theory:

> Issues surrounding the relative independence, causal influence and temporal precedence of the components have been eliminated at a stroke [...]. Because 'structure' is inseparable from 'agency', there is no reason in which it can be either emergent or autonomous or pre-existent or causally influential.
>
> (Archer 1995: 93–94, 97, respectively)

Morphogenesis unravels this problem by conceptually separating and temporally sequencing the structural and agential sites of power. In its ontological model, structure and agency come together in endless cycles of both structural causal conditioning and agential causal instantiation (Bhaskar 1989: 77). Morphogenesis (re-)introduces time and difference into the interplay of structural and agential powers, arguing that structural conditions logically predate the action which they transform, and structural elaboration logically postdates those actions (Archer 1995: 15). This temporal differentiation makes it possible to think of evolutionary dynamics in the structure-agency interplay, no matter what recursive relation there is between structure and agency, as past actions turn into present structures, present structures influence future action and future action reformulates further structure. As Archer describes this transformative understanding:

Action is ceaseless and essential both to the continuation and further elaboration of the system, but subsequent interaction will be different from earlier action because conditioned by the structural consequences of that prior action. Hence the morphogenetic perspective is not only dualistic but sequential, dealing in endless cycles of structural conditioning/social interaction/structural elaboration, thus unravelling the dialectical interplay between structure and agency.

(Archer 1990: 76)

With its temporal separation of the elements, then, morphogenesis proclaims an ontological 'dualism' of structure and agency, as opposed to the compacted 'duality' of Giddens. This differentiation directly affects the ways in which knowledge of international insecurity can be understood to interact with national foreign policymaking: morphogenesis helps disentangle the interplay between the making of knowledge about international danger on the one hand and the seizure of such knowledge for foreign policies on the other hand. Rather than postulating a direct mechanism between the production and seizure of insecurity, as the Copenhagen School (seemingly) does, it reconstructs that linkage as a dialectical recursive relation, in which the former conditions the latter, but the latter also instantiates and potentially elaborates on the former. Rather than setting out a mere constitutive relation between knowledge of the international and its enactment, morphogenesis thus allows for the differentiation of the two aspects as two distinct, albeit intimately related, sites of power and politics.

Transposed to securitisation theory, a morphogenetic ontology has analytical and conceptual benefits. Analytically, the temporal separation of the creation and seizure of danger narratives allows for the dissection of the distribution of responsibilities in security politics in more detail. With morphogenesis, it becomes possible to differentiate between actions that aim to describe the international as it is, actions that aim to redescribe such imageries and actions that aim to use such descriptions for distinct foreign policy purposes. These actions can be differentiated in time, as knowledge production and seizure stretch over a temporal horizon (Bhaskar 1979: 46; Wight 2000: 428), and they can be differentiated spatially by social fields: the production of knowledge about international danger, for instance, can be found to evolve in a variety of arenas, including parliament, bureaucracy, academia and the media, whereas actions that aim to seize such knowledge for purposes of foreign policymaking tend, for reasons of institutionalisation and formal-political organisation, to be located in the legislature and the executive only.

Conceptually, the transposition of securitisation theory on to morphogenesis allows for the re-engagement with the question of what kinds of powers are or can be held complicit in the production and the seizure of knowledge. Morphogenesis is a 'stratified' ontology, in which structure and agency have different kinds of powers. Their interplay is recursively linked, yet their effects are not necessarily of the same nature, as each element has a different kind of influence over the other. This means that the interplay between the production and the seizure of knowledge about international danger can be formalised as a *differentiated* pluri-causal model. This model recursively relates the powers involved in security politics in a complex causal nexus. The powers that it acknowledges are multiple, affecting each other as structural and agential causes, and as discussed in the following subsection, they are also different in their nature. This means that morphogenesis allows the setting out of an explanatory/ causal theory of security, even if it does not accept the idea of ideal-typical dependent and independent variables (Carlsnaes 1992: 257; Lewis 2000: 264). In the view of morphogenesis, causal powers are necessary but also insufficient, determining and determined by each other, and their interaction is not as linear as in a classic conception of causation.

Securitisation as a dialectical causal argument

As an explanatory social theory, morphogenesis differs quite substantially from constitution. Crucially, unlike constitutive theory, morphogenesis allows the idea of causation to be re-engaged in reflexive IR theorising. And, indeed, the reintro-duction of causal analysis into reflexive social scientific theorising is the key contribution of that ontology, making morphogenesis an explanatory, albeit dia-lectical, theory (Archer 1985: 61; Piiparinen 2006: 425). The causal powers to which morphogenesis appeals are yet not of the classic type. The classic concept of causation, which is also the idea of causation that reflexive IR scholars have been rejecting, indeed lends itself poorly to dialectical reflexive IR theorising, given its distinctively 'Cartesian and Humean' framing (Kurki 2006): in the classic conception, causation is understood as akin to mechanistic processes, as regular 'push and pull' factors (Cartesian), and it is assessed in utterly empiricist ways (Humean). Causation in the classic sense of the term refers to the constant conjunctions between two observable events or independent and dependent vari-ables (cf. King *et al.* 1994: 81–82). Analytically, this understanding of causation directs scholarly analyses to observables (given the empiricist philosophy), a maximalist search for broad covering laws (given the mechanistic focus on con-stant conjunctions; Winch 1972; Wendt 1987: 353; Gerring 2005) and 'parsimo-nious' explanations (given the quest for strong causal effects; Kurki 2006: 196).

This understanding of causation is excessively restrictive for reflexive IR the-orising (Steinmetz 1998: 172–173; Marsh and Furlong 2002: 19–20). Reflexive IR is interested in the production and forms of inter-subjective knowledge, a rather non-material factor in world politics. It is concerned with the ways in which meanings are attached to materiality and the ways in which given mean-ings and actions are brought to interact. A materialistic and regularity-deterministic understanding of causation lends itself very poorly to this. By the same token, reflexive IR is generally also interested in multifaceted contextual-ised analyses of politics and not in the subjection of scholarship to an abstract dictum for parsimonious argumentation. For reflexive IR, which sees causation as equating Cartesian/Humean causation, these are reasons enough to reject the explanatory scientific model of traditional IR. As Kurki describes the situation:

Robert Cox for instance argues that the concept of cause is applicable strictly to the positivist framework and that his 'historical explanation' cannot be equated with 'causal explanation' since 'causal explanation' cannot capture the complexity of the social world as the historical mode of analysis can. Causal analysis is associated with the 'ahistorical' neorealist frameworks and the 'scientific' claims of objectivity of the mainstream. Causal analysis, then, is understood in accordance with Humean assumptions and, as a result, rejected altogether.

(2006: 198; referring to Cox and Sinclair 1996)

The inner logic of this syllogism is important to recognise. Practically, it means that reflexive IR's move to constitutive analysis is not only motivated by the very conceptual needs that reflexive IR identified for itself; reflexive IR's focus on constitutive theorising is not only driven by the recognition that a sophisticated reflexive epistemology necessitates a dialectical theory of the social. The syllogism suggests that reflexive IR's move to constitutive theorising also rests on a narrow interpretation of what causal analysis is held to be in IR and on a forgoing of a more sustained discussion about what other kinds of causal inquiry there might be aside from Cartesian/Humean analysis. This means that if constitutive analysis is held to make explanatory analysis impossible, given that social relations do not consist of separable independent and dependent variables (Wendt 1998: 105), then it is a distinct dialectical ontology (namely, structuration theory in Wendt) that is made to bar an equally distinct concept of causation (namely, Cartesian/Humean causation), whereas the actual multiplicity of both ontological and causal frameworks is left unaddressed.

As a contending ontology, morphogenesis allows such syllogism to be avoided. Morphogenesis allows thinking of differential powers in the production of social action, even if it advances a dialectical model of structure and agency. By the same token, a contending conception of causation such as Aristotelian causation also allows these powers to be circumscribed differentially in a non-mechanistic way, so subverting the disciplinary fixation of reflexive IR to mere understanding. In a morphogenetic theory of security, an Aristotelian conception of causation lends itself particularly well to being an alternative to Cartesian/Humean causation. Unlike such classic causation, an Aristotelian conception is philosophically 'deeper', and it is also conceptually more pluralistic and differentiated (Bhaskar 1989: 34, 1993: 92). It is 'deeper' because it draws not on empiricism, but on critical realist philosophy for its grounding of what can be held to be valid study objects and transmission mechanisms. Critical realism differentiates philosophically between layers of reality, identifying three such layers: 'the empirical', which refers to experience only, 'the actual', which includes experiences and events, and 'the real', which circumscribes experiences, events and mechanisms (Bhaskar 1978: 13). With such a philosophical grounding, causality is considered that which is 'real'. It happens independently of whether it is or can be observed, and so the question of whether or not something can be of a causal nature does not depend so much on sensorial experience as on the effects it has on social behaviour. Knowledge is an example of the 'real'. It affects social behaviour, even if it is inter-subjective rather than material and thus not as easily observed (Lewis 2002: 21; Kurki 2006: 201).

The Aristotelian conception also lends itself well to a morphogenetic theory of securitisation because it is pluralistic, acknowledging the necessary complicity of multiple factors in producing social outcomes. Morphogenesis, it has been argued, does not consider linear and mono-causal explanation as an appropriate model of social inquiry in the social sciences. In morphogenesis/critical realism, social relations are held to develop in open and evolving social systems, not in closed laboratories. In open social systems, structural and agential causes are held to interact recursively, and social outcomes are seen as determined by variable constellations of causal factors, rather than a single factor or constant set of factors (Bhaskar 1979: 17; Steinmetz 1998: 173). Indeed, it is held to be the defining feature of the social sciences that they are unable to isolate and test singular causal mechanisms, given the nature of the material – humans and social relations – with which they work. This does not mean that the possibility of science is rejected – critical realism does not formulate a postmodern argument at all. But a different – and, indeed, considerably more demanding – vision of science is advanced by critical realism, a model of the social in which multiple sources of causation, material and other, interact across time, conditioning and empowering social action in ways that are not fully predictable (Bhaskar 1978: 12). With morphogenesis, then, social science can be about more than mere understanding, and yet the explanatory accounts that it can formulate cannot be expected to generate systematic predictions, given the dialectical nature of social being. It is a pluralistic and contingent kind of causation that morphogenesis looks at, not regularity determinism in the Cartesian/Humean sense of the term (Collier 1994: 58, 161; Bernstein *et al.* 2000: 48; Steinmetz 1998: 181–182).

Aristotelian causation accommodates this idea of contingent causation. From an Aristotelian perspective, the concept of cause (or *aition*) is very general at the outset, referring to 'anything that contributed in any way to the producing or maintaining of a certain reality' (Cartwright 2004: 805). In practice, according to Aristotle, four distinct types of powers come together, but each in its own way, in order to produce this reality – namely, efficient causes, formal causes, final causes and material causes (Aristotle 1998: 115). *Efficient causes* (that which incites a result) refer to the traditional 'prime mover' of social action, the 'push and pull' factor on which the traditional concept of causality focuses exclusively (Harré and Madden 1975: 5; Harré 1993: 98). However, in contrast to the traditional connotation of 'push and pull' factors, efficient causes are not considered mechanistically, but as embedded in the other three types of causation. *Formal causes* (that which the result is to be) describe and define the structures that give meaning and being to things – i.e. the internal systematisation of reality. *Final causes* (that which the result is for) refer to the intentionality of human behaviour, the motivations or reasons that direct actors and because of which certain actions are being taken, and *material causes* (that which the result is to be made of) point to the passive potentiality of concrete matter as a factor that both enables and limits possible ways of being or changing (see Table 3.2 for an overview of the Aristotelian powers and their application to the interplay between security politics and foreign affairs).

This Aristotelian framework of causation is directly helpful for theorising the interplay between securitisation and foreign policymaking in explanatory terms. This is because, although all four powers come together to produce social life, two powers each can be associated either with structure or agency. Material and formal causes are causes proper to structures – they are *conditioning* causes – whereas efficient and final causes are causes proper to agency, as *activating* causes (Kurki 2006: 207–210). When differentiated according to the Aristotelian doctrine, the acting out of knowledge about the international can be understood as an *efficient* cause (that which incites a foreign policy outcome), and the representation of the international can be seen as a *formal* cause (that which the international is systematised to be in the first place). The purpose for which foreign policymaking is intended is, then, a final cause (what the result is for, reaction to a recognised problem situation), and the knowledge out of which foreign politics is crafted a *material* cause (the truths out of which policies are to be made).

Securitisation and the production of international relations

What is the interplay between securitisation and international relations? What happens to a country's foreign policy behaviour when a theme becomes recognised as a danger? The ontological and causal discussion of the preceding section sets out the social theory of this book's argument, and in doing so it allows that

Table 3.2 Aristotle's doctrine of the four causes and the interplay between knowledge of international danger and national foreign policymaking

		Definition	*Ontological association*	*Securitisation and foreign policymaking*
Conditioning causes	Material	What the outcome is to be made of.	Specific to structure: Conditions and empowers.	The availability of truths about the world in a local context of contending interpretations.
	Formal	What the outcome is to be.		The systematisation of the international through insecurity.
Activating causes	Efficient	What incites an outcome.	Specific to agency: Activates and instantiates.	The seizure of knowledge about the international.
	Final	What the outcome is for.		The reaction to an identified problem situation.

Source: Causal differentiation draws on Lewis 2000.

argument to be brought full circle. Securitisation, this book argues, stands for the creation of a systematising and politically consequential local knowledge of the international (see Figure 3.1 for a schematic overview). Securitisation endangers, orders and conditions the international, and in doing so it effectively produces international relations both epistemologically and practically; securitisation endangers and orders the international by framing distinct things, events or processes as distinctly configured kinds of problem situations. It sets out policy stimuli to which a given society must react, and it makes situations known to that society. By the same token, securitisation structures these stimuli by defining who threatens whom and how. Securitisation names and defines the organisation of international insecurity, and it positions the home country in the web of international relations thus recognised.

This endangerment and ordering is a deeply political process. What is being endangered and how a danger is understood to be organised internationally – the nature and shape of the larger insecurity communities that it produces – denotes a veritable battle of ideas. Depending on tactics, power relations, convictions and intentions, these battles of ideas create different kinds of local world order imageries or frameworks of international reality. These imageries can become more or less stable local truths, and they may or may not allow congruent subject-positions of others and the self. Knowledge of one kind of insecurity (e.g. migration) might well describe a different kind of world order than knowledge of another kind of insecurity (e.g. nuclear arms race), and this is why

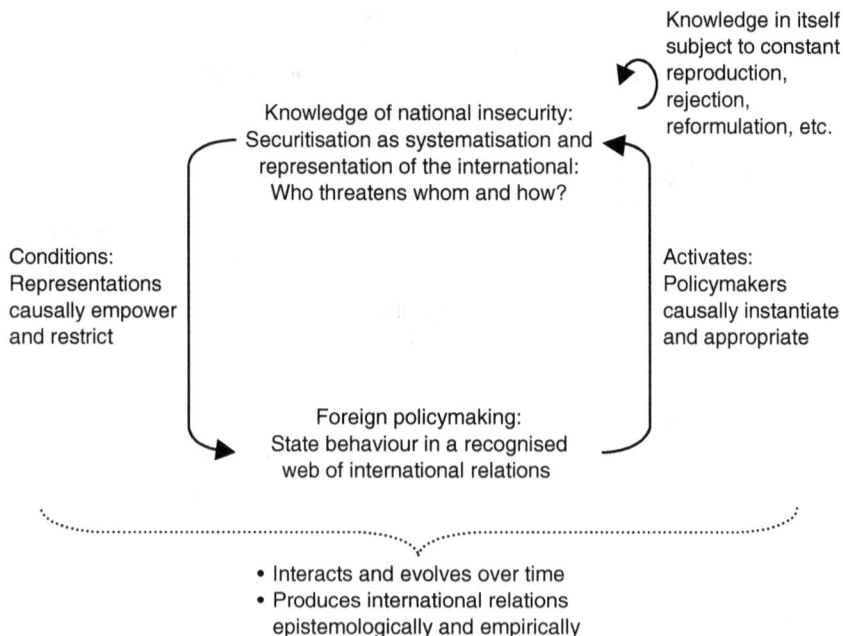

Knowledge in itself
subject to constant
reproduction,
rejection,
reformulation, etc.

Knowledge of national insecurity:
Securitisation as systematisation and
representation of the international:
Who threatens whom and how?

Conditions:
Representations
causally empower
and restrict

Activates:
Policymakers
causally instantiate
and appropriate

Foreign policymaking:
State behaviour in a recognised
web of international relations

• Interacts and evolves over time
• Produces international relations
  epistemologically and empirically

Figure 3.1 (In-)securitisation and the production of international relations.

complex, at times convergent and at times divergent understandings of the home nation's position in the international may be formulated in terms of national insecurity. As the French case of the late 1940s and early 1950s suggests, the originators of one national security challenge may be posited as co-victims of another challenge, and thus the totality of locally available danger narratives might not necessarily provide a clear-cut understanding of world order and the home nation's position therein.

Dominant knowledge(s) of the international do, however, have a causal effect on foreign policymaking. As representations of international order, securitisation advances realities with which policymakers must deal when crafting foreign policy responses to recognised security problems. These realities condition foreign policymaking as material and formal causes; hegemonic knowledge(s) of the international both empower and disqualify certain foreign policy actions. Insecurity narratives organise the international in specific terms, and in doing so they make some policy responses but not others appropriate under their own definition. However, insecurity narratives only condition foreign politics when instantiated and activated by policymakers. The interplay between representations of the international and their seizure is dialectical, but not merely constitutive. Representations of the international do not mechanistically impose themselves on policymakers, thus strictly predetermining foreign policies (as securitisation is understood to argue in its original theorisation), but nor can policymakers wish these representations away, ignoring their epistemic currency as claims to truth (as a voluntarist security theory would claim). Instead, the production of knowledge and its seizure evolves over time, and the creation and enactment of international (in-)security are two separate, albeit intimately related, sites of power and politics. Coming together in a causal nexus, these two sites are complicit in producing international relations. The naming of national danger creates imageries of world order(s) epistemologically, and because they have causal effect on national foreign policymaking practice, they also 'produce' international relations empirically.

Conclusion

As a systematisation of world politics, securitisation produces international relations epistemologically, and via the enactment and activation of such systematisations by policymakers, securitisation also 'produces' international relations empirically. Part III of the book addresses how this relational/positional perspective on security politics makes new analytical, theoretical and political contributions to international relations. Before doing so, however, Part II of the book substantiates the book's analytical framework. The empirical case studies illustrate how in France, (West) Germany and Switzerland different security themes helped systematise the international in distinct ways between 1945 and 2010, setting out different imageries of who threatens whom and how. Travelling through European space and time, the case studies discuss how these frameworks of reality were challenged and reformulated over time and how they empowered some foreign policy strategies but not others. With this, the empirical chapters also show how European Cold War security politics played out in a much more differentiated, complex and oftentimes contradictory manner than what is usually argued.

The case studies address the major local (in-)security themes. As genealogies, they indicate stable and volatile phases of knowledge elaboration and appropriation, pointing to continuities, ruptures and gradual shifts in the French, German and Swiss ways of systematising and enacting the international. The retrieval of local insecurity syllogisms rests on primary sources, given that this allows for the assessment of the historical state of local debates closer to their own vantage point. To triangulate the empirics, Part II of the book draws on the realm of formal politics – i.e. government, parliament and parties – but also on statements made by major media outlets and academia. This methodological strategy rests on the understanding that national security and foreign affairs rationales are (and were) produced primarily in and across these three discursive arenas. Publications of the national parliaments and lead newspapers – i.e. *Assemblée Nationale, Deutscher Bundestag, Schweizerischer Nationalrat, Le Monde, Die Zeit* and *Neue Zürcher Zeitung* – are referenced frequently throughout the subsequent chapters and thus abbreviated correspondingly. All quotes are translations and all tables compiled by the author. Following the categorisation scheme introduced in Chapter 2, tables include superscripts to indicate whether a particular systematisation provided a dominant (D), widespread (W) or more marginal (M) interpretation of international insecurity.

Part II

Genealogies of European insecurity politics

4   France's troubled post-war years

Enacting the 'German threat'

At the end of World War II, France's views on international affairs were clearly structured. Emerging from a protracted and devastating armed conflict with the fascists, French politicians saw their country, together with the United States, the United Kingdom, the Soviet Union and a number of other allies, as having been existentially threatened by the Axis powers. Among these latter relationships, however, the bilateral Franco-German antagonism clearly stood out as the most intense. Even if France suffered less during the war than others, given the rapidity of the French defeat in 1940, World War II represented no less than the third war with neighbouring Germany over a 70-year period. It is hardly surprising, then, given this historical trajectory that the threat of German militarism continued to be an extraordinarily important theme in French security politics for years also after the 1945 defeat of the Third Reich (Rovan 1951: 60; Karst 1959: 55). German militarism and aggression was considered to be nothing less than a cultural, constant and hereditary enemy. There was widespread fear that the emergence of a fourth German Reich was inevitable, and that it could be expected to happen sooner rather than later (cf. Coudenhove-Kalergi 1939: 383f; *Le Monde* [LeM] 1950c). Neighbouring Germany, according to the dominant understanding in France, would never respect any international treaty whatsoever, and it would never, ever be willing to cooperate on European security affairs.

This securitisation of Germany was embodied in the foreign policies of the new, but politically volatile, French Fourth Republic. In 1947 and 1948, France concluded long-term alliance treaties with the United Kingdom, as well as the Benelux countries. The 1947 Dunkirk Treaty between France and the United Kingdom was set out to last for no fewer than 50 years. Directly aimed at Germany, its purpose was to prevent any possible resurgence of German aggression or expansionism. In the view of French politicians, the Dunkirk Treaty ensured that the United Kingdom would be ready on the mark at the time of the next 'Prussian awakening'. Earlier, bitter accusations had been directed at the United Kingdom for having failed to intervene in European security when it mattered – from the perspective of French scholars, politicians and the French media, the UK had failed spectacularly to understand the Nazi menace (Géraud 1937, 1940: 18; Assemblée Nationale [Assemblée] 1954b: 2388; LeM 1948e).

The 1948 Brussels Treaty with Belgium, the Netherlands and Luxemburg also embodied the French reading of Germany as the primordial danger, even if this alliance was designed more broadly than the Dunkirk framework with England. Indeed, the Brussels Treaty not only formalised a military alliance, but it also promoted economic, social and cultural collaboration between the four signatory countries. Moreover, the treaty focused on any kind of armed attack in Europe, even if Germany remained the key concern. The Brussels Treaty also instantiated an understanding of France as being situated in an international insecurity community, since France, Belgium, the Netherlands and Luxemburg were claimed to be equally menaced by German and European danger (Wallace 1947: 276f). Inside the French political system, this reading of world order was hegemonic and not open to debate in the mid- to late 1940s. The Dunkirk and Brussels Treaty were based on security rationales that were fully supported by the legislature and the media (cf. LeM 1948c, 1948d, 1948f; Assemblée 1954f).

This, then, was the rendering of the 'German threat' with which the French political system embarked on the post-war era. In this reading, France's national security was existentially threatened by Germany. The latter was not only endangered, however – i.e. proclaimed to be a problem. It was also proclaimed to affect others besides France: Germany was understood to effectively create a larger insecurity community of sorts, endangering a larger collective of nation-states in similar ways. This collectivising understanding of the 'German threat' directly conditioned French foreign politics, enabling the creation of military alliances against that danger. From a conceptual perspective, the 'German threat' thus not only presented the single most important security topic in post-war France. It also stood for a distinct danger narrative that ordered world politics in certain ways. In the mid- to late 1940s, the idea of Germany posing an existential threat both to the Fourth Republic and Europe at large was hegemonic. Neither the endangering of Germany nor the ordering of this danger narrative was questioned in parliament, the French media or the French scholarly arena.

Eventually, other ideas of national insecurity joined this first and primordial French post-war danger narrative. The Brussels Treaty already spoke more broadly of threats of armed conflict in Europe at large, and remarkably, the foreign policy enactment of the 'German threat' also took an intimately Western shape. Although Germany was recognised as posing a problem to many countries, the way in which that danger was enacted in the foreign policy realm suggested that, in actual fact, some countries were included in the insecurity community created by the German danger, while others were not, the most notable omission being France's wartime ally, the Soviet Union. And, of course, as the subsequent empirical narrative shows, the Soviet Union itself was soon recognised as a pressing kind of danger in France. This emerging securitisation of communism did not simply replace the German danger narrative, however. The German threat was still very well 'known' for years to come, and only at a certain point in time did the former become seen as more important than the latter.

France's reconstruction of communism

The second major French national security theme to emerge in the post-war era focused on the Soviet Union. When and by whom exactly the Soviet Union first became conceived of as an enemy in the French public policy debates in the late 1940s is somewhat difficult to specify precisely. Although government declarations, parliamentary statements and academic articles give a certain indication of the events whereby France's former wartime ally was reconstructed into a menace, the National Assembly archive in Paris contains only sparse public records of national security and foreign policy matters from the tumultuous Fourth Republic. According to the data available, the communist takeover in Hungary in May 1947 was construed as a particularly crucial turning point in French-Soviet relations (cf. LeM 1948a, 1948b, 1949b). Robert Schuman, for example, who held the offices of Finance Minister in 1946, Prime Minister twice in 1947 and 1948 and Foreign Minister in eight different cabinets between 1948 and 1952, repeatedly mobilised 'Hungary' as proof that the Eastern Bloc was aggressive and had 'constituted itself first', although Truman's containment doctrine had been formulated even earlier (De Chambrun 1949: 355). In parliament, others joined Schuman in this understanding of communism. The foundation of Cominform, the perceived Soviet delaying of European economic reconstruction, coups in Romania, Bulgaria, Poland and Czechoslovakia and the (first) Berlin blockade were all understood to confirm the new inimical relationship between the USSR and France (Assemblée 1953: 5221ff). Scholars were relatively fast to adhere to this view (Mayer 1954: 250; De Maupeou 1956: 144f), exceptions notwithstanding (Aron 1949: 260).

Domestic elements, too, became recognised as proof of communist hostility, especially the activism of European communist parties. In France, the Communist Party won a formidable 28 per cent of the vote in the 1946 elections. By the late 1940s, its calls for strikes and militant echoing of Soviet policy positions was seen as an increasingly overt and offensive alignment with the Soviet Union (Strauss 1960: 8). Interpretations of international and domestic observations thus came together in the reconstruction of communism at large as a source of French national insecurity. By the late 1940s, it became increasingly legitimate in the parliamentary arena and the press to see the USSR no longer as an ally, but as a hostile, intransigent and hypocritical power with hegemonic ambition regarding Europe at large (Debré 1953: 374; De Maupeou 1956: 144; Mayer 1954: 250; Assemblée 1954e: 6879/Rousseau 1959b: 379ff./Conte; LeM 1949c). In this re-description process, the Soviet military arsenal in particular became a major cause of concern. Compared to 16 or so Western divisions, the Red Army was estimated to have maintained at least 175, and soon enough these were claimed to be in a state of high readiness (Assemblée 1954a: 4575/Reynaud, 1954c: 2784/Foreign Affairs Committee speaker Billotte). As one analyst dramatically argued in 1950:

> Since the Europeans had woken up from the immediate post-war situation, they recognised with anxiety that an immense army of almost 200 divisions

was camping at their doorstep and that this army could, if it only wanted to, easily get to the Atlantic and the Pyrenees in a couple of days, if not a couple of hours.

(Gascuel 1950: 440)

It was recognised at the time that this securitisation of France's former ally represented a fairly dramatic reconstruction of French security politics (De Chambrun 1949: 357). However, the securitisation of the Soviet Union solidified quickly in increasingly wider spheres of French public life, and it was soon acted upon by French foreign policymakers. At the Moscow conference of April 1947, Foreign Minister Bidault went on record as wanting Germany to benefit from the Marshall Plan, and in 1949 members of government openly declared that without American support, the defence of France and Europe against the Red Army was no longer possible (cf. Assemblée 1959d: 3669/Foreign Minister Couve de Murville). Also in 1949, the same endangering of the Soviet Union enabled the signing of the Washington Treaty and France's accession to the North Atlantic Alliance. As with the Dunkirk and Brussels treaties, French membership of the North Atlantic Alliance did not rest merely on the recognition of a given pressing danger. It also derived from the getting-to-know those dangers as collective threats that also affected other actors in world politics – i.e. one very distinct process of securitisation.

This construction of the USSR as driver of a larger, collective insecurity context is important in itself, given the explanatory power that this construction entails. But it is particularly remarkable in that it was so little influenced by geographical considerations. While the Dunkirk and the Brussels Treaty had presented Germany as a danger to its immediate neighbours, the Soviet Union was construed as a collective security challenge to countries of Europe and North America more by virtue of the political regime type, social organisation and economic structures that it was held to challenge (Centre d'Etudes de Politique Etrangère 1953: 402). These are very immaterial categories upon which to craft a danger narrative, and as such the very distinct ways in which the Soviet Union was securitised underscores the relevance of knowledge and imageries of international relations. The securitisation of the USSR epistemologically imputed similar positions to a variety of nations, and it is this 'real' knowledge of the organisation of international danger that enabled French accession to the North Atlantic Alliance. This creation of a larger insecurity community evolved irrespective of the fact that, materially, these nations could not actually be threatened in similar ways by the Red Army, not least because the Red Army had no intercontinental strike capabilities before the late 1950s.

In the Fourth Republic, this positing of the Soviet Union as a source of French and others' national insecurity became known as the 'Atlanticist' perspective. As distinct knowledge of the organisation of international (in-)security, Atlanticism had gained impressive epistemic currency in French power circles by the turn of the decade, and later it even motivated a powerful rewriting of history. By the mid-1950s, Atlanticists in the French National Assembly were starting to retrospectively present the Dunkirk and Brussels treaties as anti-communist projects (Assemblée 1953: 5223/Gouin, 1954a: 4570/Mendès-France, 1954c: 2783/Billotte), which, as previously demonstrated, had not actually been the case originally. In the early twenty-first century, the North Atlantic Treaty Organization's (NATO) website also proclaimed the Atlantic Alliance to be a direct result of those treaties, although the alliance's original focus rested on Germany and not the Soviet Union.

In the 1940s and 1950s, and irrespective of its heightened epistemic standing in the French political system of the time, the Atlanticist systematisation of the international was yet never without alternatives, and it remained a hard-fought position. Even if contending perspectives were dismissed as 'divisive communist manoeuvres' or disqualified as 'failures to recognise the real threat' by the Atlanticists in power (cf. Assemblée 1952: 336/Foreign Minister's declaration and discussion), the French clearly did not buy into the Atlanticist narrative in its entirety. Indeed, the idea that the Eastern Bloc posed a danger to France and Europe had never been accepted by some people in the first place. Scholars such as Raymond Aron, for instance, suggested that the sovietisation of Eastern Europe could not be considered an extraordinary or even hostile act, given that this division of Europe had been agreed on at Yalta. The Soviet toleration of the Berlin Air Bridge was also construed as an argument for the West's non-hostile relations with the USSR (Aron 1949: 252–254). Seen from this perspective, the Soviet Union's suggestion that it join the North Atlantic Alliance in defence against a potentially resurgent Germany was judged to be consistent. After all, the United States in 1947 itself proposed to the USSR such a two-pronged alliance against possible Nazi resurgence, a proposal which the Soviet leaders, however, then rejected (De Maupeou 1956: 145). From the perspective of some, then, even the very basic endangering of the Soviet Union had not been supported.

Reasserting and re-differentiating the 'German threat'

Others loosely accepted the idea of Soviet danger, but did not securitise it as an existential challenge to France. According to this perspective, the Soviet Union was, at most, of secondary importance compared to the danger of Germany (Assemblée 1952, 1954g: 7009/Loustaunau-Lacau). This camp in French politics considered that Germany's quest for *Lebensraum* was still inevitable, and that its resurgence had to be prevented by any means possible (Debré 1953). Going into the 1950s, this unbroken existential securitisation of Germany enabled a series of initiatives towards/against France's neighbour, first and foremost among them an international neutralisation strategy. Right after the war, this idea of a neutralised Germany had enjoyed broad popular support not only in France, but also amongst its allies. As early as 1946, US Secretary of State Brynes had tentatively proposed to unify the Allied occupation zones, hold democratic elections in unified Germany and keep Germany militarily neutralised for 25 or even 40 years. Later in the 1950s, the USSR also supported such an initiative, although for reasons deriving more squarely from the new political situation of that time – i.e. the German division into East and West (Strauss 1960: 5; Aron 1949: 256; De Maupeou 1956: 143).

As already noted, this neutralisation strategy featured a preventive component in the form of westward alliances with the UK and the Benelux countries. At the same time, the neutralisation of Germany was also pursued through attempts to remove Germany's access to its iron ore and coal deposits. In France, the ore- and coal-rich Ruhr region, in particular, had been seen as the fief of the grand magnates of German industry and finance – indeed, as representing 'the German arsenal' par excellence – and thus it had to be withdrawn from Germany's reach (Grappin 1950: 78; Mayer 1954: 252; Assemblée 1953: 5228/Gouin). As one scholar stated regarding the French agenda towards Germany:

> It is by removing, whether by control or by cooperation, the exclusive usage of the Ruhr's coal and steel resources from Germany that we hope to prevent it from dominating the entire continent.
>
> (Gerbet 1956: 535)

In practice, this identification of German industry and militarism as a danger to Europe at large eventually enabled the French initiation of an international control organism –i.e. the European Coal and Steel Community (ECSC) – as well as the European integration agenda that later followed. This agenda joined other French attempts at handling the known German threat – the defensive pacts in particular, but also the amputation of German territory. Indeed, in 1947, France outright removed the Saarland and its population from Germany. It turned this small yet coal-rich and industry-heavy territory from an occupation zone into a fully-fledged independent state called the *Saarstaat*. Only in 1957 did this newly created country reintegrate with Germany again – i.e. the Federal Republic of Germany – after a local plebiscite.

Concerns about Germany were widespread and deep-seated after World War II, yet the securitisation of Germany also became quickly riddled with altern- ative threat frames inside France. By the early 1950s, for instance, French com- munists were suggesting that it was capitalism and not communism which posed a danger to French independence and well-being, thus introducing another security theme into the debates. French communists also argued that West Germany was a fascist regime, whose transformation into the next, Fourth, Reich was imminent (LeM 1950d; Assemblée 1954a: 4582–4583/Casanova, 1954e: 6872/Vallon). In doing so, the French Communist Party brought some differenti- ation into the question of who exactly caused French insecurity, suggesting that Germany's Western, but not its Eastern, part presented an existential danger. Like the focus on capitalism, this re-securitisation of Germany stood in opposi- tion to the one of other French politicians, who felt that Germany *as a whole* caused French national insecurity. Similarly, it was also rejected by those who saw communism as threatening European peace and French independence (Karst 1959: 55–56).

Still, the upcoming Atlanticist perspective did call the neutralisation of Germany into question, and a certain reconstitution of Germany gradually became seen as necessary in France. But this reconstruction of Germany was not tied in all quarters to a securitisation of the Soviet Union. In some quarters, the view emerged that for simple reasons of maintaining law and order, a disarmed and occupied Germany would require a gendarmerie and police force, and that given the size of the country, the production of such forces would require a fairly serious paramilitary rearmament (Aron 1949: 256). Another rationale saw German neutralisation as perpetuating a power vacuum in the heart of Europe and thus as problematic in itself. Germany was seen as a 'pivotal power' for central Europe, and a vacuum in central Europe was not considered helpful for continental stability, irrespective of whether communism was an enemy or not (Assemblée 1953: 5221/Gouin, 1959a: 322/Foreign Minister Couve de Murville). Finally, the argument was also advanced that even in a neutralised country, leaders would be of a specific political colour, and that, as such, Germany would inevitably lean either west- or eastwards, depending on the political party in office (Assemblée 1954d: 2788/Defence Committee speaker Badie). The reconsideration of the French-led international neutralisation of Germany, then, in part also evolved outside the new anti-Soviet danger narrative.

Eventually, however, it was the securitisation of the Soviet Union that played the greatest role in the gradual rejection of the international neutralisation agenda. As Atlanticism became an increasingly dominant worldview in many parts of the French polity, Germany became cast as an ally in a shared international security context by some, against the wish of others, and German rearmament was advanced as a viable foreign policy option. Inside France, however, the push for German rearmament was greeted with ardent opposition, and many denounced Atlanticism as a foreign policy agenda imposed onto France. Seen in this way, German rearmament was claimed to be an American and British agenda that caught France 'by complete surprise' (Debré 1953: 367; LeM 1950a; Gerbet 1956: 533), although this agenda had been introduced into the debate by the French press back in 1949 – i.e. one year ahead of US General Clay's call for such a policy (cf. LeM 1949a, 1950e). In the Fourth Republic, the attempt to reformulate Germany from enemy to ally was hence anything but consensual. As Grappin and Rovan – two analysts of the time – set out their discontent with the Atlanticists' and allies' repositioning of France's neighbour:

> The same people who came, from America in particular, to extirpate German militarism are now offering weapons to the Germans, who don't want them.
> (Grappin 1950: 73)

> The allies fought German militarism. If they are now calling upon the military potential of this same Germany, they completely repudiate their own position.
> (Rovan 1951: 62)

In the early 1950s, however, this discontent at German rearmament became increasingly difficult to sustain. During this time, Atlanticists successfully mobilised the Korean War as a means of validating the superior truthfulness of their focus on the communist danger. According to these political camps, the Korean War underlined the imminence and utter deadliness of communism (LeM 1950b; Furniss 1954; De Clermont-Tonnerre 1954), and even scholars previously sceptical of its securitisation came to adhere to this position (cf. Aron 1986: 230). The Korean conflict was held to lend authoritative weight to the argument that communism was both an existential and global danger (Assemblée 1953: 5223/Gouin). By the early 1950s, this reading of world politics had become even more powerful than the ongoing securitisation of Germany. And although the balance was tight, with one of the rationales winning over the other depending on the political circles in question and the political alliances of the day, overall the perception of communist danger started to prevail more often than not. As one witness of the time soberly assessed this evolution towards a new dominant world order perspective in the French political system at the end of the Korean War:

> I would accept as a hypothesis that the greater part of the public and parliamentary opinion now acknowledges that a certain amount of German rearmament is inevitable, and that its containment cannot continue indefinitely.
>
> (De Clermont-Tonnerre 1954: 170)

France and the knowledge of incompatible world orders

In the late 1940s and early 1950s, as the above overview of epistemic positions suggests, a sizable multiplicity of evolving and, at times, competing understandings of French insecurity had been produced and circulated in France. Depending on the political camp in question, French national security was thought to be challenged by Germany alone, by Germany and the USSR jointly, by capitalism or by communism alone. At the same time, the identification of these enemies was accompanied by differential systematisations of the international, and the truthfulness of these systematisations was subject to fierce discussions. Whether Germany as such or only parts of Germany were causing insecurity, whether that danger was existential or merely secondary compared to the problem of communism, whether capitalism threatened the French population and workers worldwide or not, whether communism affected Europe alone, the transatlantic region or the entire world all presented highly contested epistemic positions. And, seemingly, the reason why these positions were so fiercely debated was exactly because of the differential world orders that they, as securitisations of different themes, described. The reason was that by accepting some of these positions but not others, the security narratives defined different positions for others and the home nation in the international context. Just as importantly as the question of whether Germany, capitalism or communism posed a danger or not, they advanced different concepts of the very shape and structure of the international security context in which France was held to be located.

Seen in this way, a central element in explaining French foreign policymaking in the post-war period is not so much the question of what threatened France, but how France saw itself as being threatened. If France was truly caught up in an insecurity community against Germany, who was affected by German aggression and who was not? If the superior challenge to France was international capitalism, how did this reposition France's interlocutors in world politics? And if France was better understood as challenged by communism, how existential was that challenge in practice, and did it imply that Germany was an ally of France? In France, the securitisation of Germany and communism in particular set out influential yet overlapping and partially contradictory conceptions of the world, each of which conditioned French foreign politics in its own distinct way. The anti-German representation of the international enabled a variety of cooperative, military and economic containment initiatives. But it also disenabled, as did the securitisation of capitalism, German accession to an anti-communist alliance, as witnessed in the 1950 French veto against German accession to the Washington Treaty (De Clermont-Tonnerre 1954: 169). As the fear from communism became an ever more powerful frame of systematisation, however, the government of France had to ponder the contradictions between the insecurity communities that the respective danger narratives described. Indeed, a number of French politicians realised by the early 1950s that France was caught up in a Western insecurity community anyway, and that an ardent rejection of German rearmament against the USSR might eventually be to the detriment of those westward alliances that France had already concluded in the late 1940s, based on the anti-German frame (Assemblée 1954c: 2784/Billotte; also De Clermont-Tonnerre 1954: 185f.).

With the *Plan Pleven* of 1950–1954, this contradiction of contending world order perspectives reached its climax. Named after the then-Prime Minister of France, the *Plan Pleven* sought to establish a European Defence Community (EDC) together with Germany, Italy and the Benelux countries, thus rearming Germany, but also avoiding its independent reconstitution. According to this French initiative, all the member states armies would be integrated into a single European army, except for the French colonial army, which was permitted to remain under independent French control, and German troops would be integrated into this European army in small and dispersed numbers. The *Plan Pleven* further stated that a commissariat of nine would direct the EDC, with two commissaries each for France, Germany and Italy and one commissary each for the Benelux countries, and that the production of arms would be internationalised as well (De Clermont-Tonnerre 1954: 171).

With its discriminatory clause regarding the colonial army, the plan strongly favoured France over its EDC partners. Nevertheless, French diplomacy managed to enlist all the parties' agreement to this treaty, and so the foreign ministers of all six countries signed the plan in 1952. Within the French political system, however, support for the EDC project was not nearly as clear. Certainly, members of government had advocated for the project as a 'regrettable though necessary' means of addressing Europe's new security context. They warned against Germany becoming increasingly nationalistic and uncooperative, and that only a subordinated integration of German power into a European organisation led by France could ensure that nationalism was kept in check. Government ministers also stressed that by vetoing West Germany's accession to the Washington Treaty in 1950, France had successfully delayed German rearmament by a couple of years, but that it had also done everything it could short of destroying France's Western alliances (LeM 1950f).

In the National Assembly's debates on the EDC project, however, these arguments were not accepted by a heterogeneous majority, including communists, nationalists and others. From the perspective of the political majority of the moment, ratification of the *Plan Pleven* was seen as empowering the 'revanchist German business elite and warlords', allowing them to 'train new Prussian men with military souls' (Assemblée 1952: 4575/Reynaud). Many speakers also argued that the EDC would institute not French but German supremacy. Picturing the idea of German EDC troops 'protecting' *La Manche* (the English Channel) or France's Mediterranean coast in the name of European defence, they feared that Germany would easily be capable of swaying the votes of the Benelux countries within the commissariat and would thus effectively be able to control the EDC (Grappin 1950: 77–78). Other parliamentarians also claimed that the EDC was not specific enough about banning a possible German nuclear bomb (LeM 1954b), and strategists feared that the French colonial army could no longer be reinforced with metropolitan units, given that such transfers would have to be accepted by the EDC commissariat (De Clermont-Tonnerre 1954: 172–174, 182–183; LeM 1954a). In a well-known pamphlet, Michel Debré – later an influential Gaullist – expressed at its fullest this discontent at German rearmament:

> The EDC gives Germany soldiers, generals and military equipment – and one can also say that as a result of the kind of spirit that is dominates it, the EDC also brings pardon and forgetting. The EDC reconstructs Germany's sovereignty inside a community in which France is losing hers, and where the rupture between France and the French Union [i.e. the colonial territories] is taking place definitively.
>
> (Debré 1953: 382)

In August 1954, this unbroken adherence to the anti-German narrative of world politics enabled a surprising and quite dramatic rejection of the *Plan Pleven*. Rather than supporting its own government's initiative for the creation of an anti-Soviet military European alliance, an alliance that institutionalised French privilege on the continent and was agreed on internationally, the National Assembly refused ratification of the EDC Treaty. This means that different and, indeed, incompatible world order imageries dominated in different circles of the Fourth Republic. For the government and a parliamentary minority, the EDC built on the conception of Germany as ally in a shared European security context. For the parliamentary majority of the day, however, this guiding rationale was not held to be truthful, or it was held to be secondary to the existential danger that either Germany or capitalism at large were seen as posing to the world. These were incompatible conceptions of the shape and nature of the insecurity community in which France was known to be situated, and it is their uneven co-presence in the French political system that explains why the *Plan Pleven* was both advanced and rejected by France at the same time.

After the failure of the EDC project, this pluralistic, insecurity theme-based conflict of worldviews continued in France. However, with the dramatic collapse of France's efforts to handle the German question, France effectively lost international leadership on the issue. Only one day after the rejection of the EDC by the French National Assembly, the United Kingdom demanded the integration of West Germany into the Brussels pact. At the London conference one month later, Italy's and Germany's accession to the Washington Treaty was decided by the allies, and in late October, the legal documents for their accession were signed in Paris. When the French parliament decided on the ratification of these accords in December 1954, the same epistemic dividing lines as seen in the EDC debate reappeared, and critics still argued forcefully against any German rearmament:

> The French people does not want these accords, because they mean the rearmament of the West German militarists, and because they create a terrible danger of war for Europe and the world, given the territorial ambitions of the German leaders in Bonn.
>
> (Assemblée 1954e: 6881/Pierrard)

> War, and war on our soil, in our skies, this is what we accept when we agree to rearm Germany. Only she, in Europe, has a motive for wishing war!
>
> (Assemblée 1954a: 4580/Auerman)

But in the Fourth Republic with its fragmented political blocks and rapidly shifting alliances, and in the France of late 1954 with its violent immersion in a rapidly deepening Algerian crisis, a majority in parliament had now come to reluctantly accept the London and Paris Accords. By December 1954, there was a widespread sense that if France would not accept those accords, it would be bringing its Western alliances to a definitive end (Assemblée 1954b, 1954d: 2787/Badie, 1954e: 6874–6875/De Moro-Giafferri). Mendès-France, who was both Prime Minister and Foreign Minister at the same time between June 1954 and February 1955, set out the government position:

> I know well that, in the minds of a certain number of you, any solution that includes or permits the rearmament of Germany, even if limited, even if controlled, is in itself bad. I do not hesitate to accept this; the reasons that they invoke are respectable, the feelings by which they are animated are not foreign to any French citizen. But the realities themselves cannot be ignored either. Long gone are the times when one could affirm here and in all

honesty that a priori, all German rearmament was purely and simply inadmissible [...]. Today this rearmament is ineluctable and imminent.

(Assemblée 1954a: 4573/Mendès-France)

Other parliamentarians supported this perspective, stating explicitly how ratification of the two accords was required by the new international security context that was now held to be true:

We must not forget the reason that forces the free people of this world to permit Germany's rearmament – it was the attitude of Russia, yes, Russia which in lieu of disarming after the war, as the United Kingdom did, as France did, as America and all the other allies did, not only maintained its army but also equipped it with the most fantastic destructive capabilities, her only aim being to submerge the world with the fears which she is proud to inspire.

(Assemblée 1954e: 6879/Rousseau)

For years to come, then, the competition between these two major danger narratives was reproduced in the French political system, as was the comparably more marginal anti-capitalist perspective advanced by France's extreme left. By 1955, however, the securitisation of Germany, while not entirely unravelled, has been authoritatively reassessed as being of secondary importance compared to the existential threat of communism (Robin 1995: 171; Strauss 1960: 6; Assemblée 1959a: 319–323/De Murville, 1959b: 380ff./Billoux). With this, Germany was not so much de-securitised as re-securitised at lower levels of antagonism. And, indeed, Chapter 7 of this book shows that it would not be until the 1970s that the German threat would be no longer merely eclipsed by another danger narrative, but removed from the national repertoire of national security narratives altogether.

Conclusion

The security and foreign policy debates of post-war France were dominated by danger narratives centred on Germany and the USSR. These narratives were not the sole security topics to be discussed in the Fourth Republic. Capitalism, too, had been identified as a danger by certain quarters, and a debate also emerged focusing on the organisation of insecurity in the Mediterranean space. During the accession process of Turkey and Greece to the Washington Treaty, parliamentarians questioned the trustworthiness of these potential allies, given that Turkey had not declared war on Italy in 1940, despite treaty obligations. Politicians also wondered why Morocco, Algeria and Tunisia were not accepted into the same alliance (Assemblée 1952: 327/Mutter). As Chapter 7 shows, this latter point would eventually be expanded into a questioning of the true 'shape' of the insecurity community embodied by NATO. In the immediate post-war years, however, Germany and the USSR provided the most powerful local concepts of international insecurity, and they conditioned French foreign politics accordingly. The anti-German rationale enabled a distinct kind of westward alliances and a variety of other neutralisation efforts, but it also disenabled the accession of Germany to the Washington Treaty in 1950 and ratification of the *Plan Pleven* by parliament. The Atlanticist anti-communist rationale, by contrast, enabled France's own accession to the Washington Treaty and, indeed, the very formulation of the *Plan Pleven* (see Table 4.1 for an overview of the French post-war security narratives and their interplay with French foreign policymaking). As incompatible yet often similarly powerful knowledges of world order, these narratives plunged the Fourth Republic into crisis. Only after the institution of the Fifth Republic in 1958 was there an attenuation of this epistemological contradiction and an articulation of a hegemonic conception of world politics and France's position therein. As the next chapter shows, the substantive and procedural ways of securitisation thus differed strongly between France and West Germany. Other dangers were identified and similar themes were construed differently in post-war West Germany, and patterns of political debate also evolved in other directions than was the case in France.

Table 4.1 French constructions of international (in-)security after World War II

		Late 1940s	Early 1950s
Germany	Source	Culture of militarism[D]	Culture of militarism[W] Fascist West Germany only[M]
	Target	France only ('historical prime enemy')[D] Everyone (incl. wartime Ally USSR)[W] Western Europe[W]	Everyone (incl. wartime Ally USSR)[W]
	Relation	Existential[D]	Existential[W] Problematic[W] Manageable[W]
	World order description	A distinct enemy existentially threatening France only or threatening a global or European collective of states also beyond France	A distinct enemy, competitor or problem state threatening a larger collective of states also beyond France
	Conditioning effects	Go-it-alone neutralisation of Germany, global containment of Germany or Western containment of Germany	Cooperative containment of Germany, not necessarily at all costs
	Policy enactment	Dunkirk Treaty, Brussels Treaty, occupation of Germany, territorial amputation of Germany, vetoing of German accession to Washington Treaty	Continuation of neutralisation strategies, but also cooperation in the international control of rearming Germany through EDC, NATO and European institutions

Communism/USSR	Source	French communists[W] USSR[W]	USSR[D] French communists[M]
	Target	French democracy[W] Europe (incl. Germany)[W]	Europe (incl. Germany)[D]
	Relation	Challenge[W] Existential[W] No threat[M]	Existential[D] Challenge[W]
	World order description	Emergent if not existential danger from without and within, affecting a Western collective of states and France's social order	Existential or problematic international danger, affecting a Western collective of states and France's social order
	Conditioning effects	Collective Western or global responses, including by Germany, to an identified collective danger	
	Policy enactment	Washington Treaty	EDC initiative, European integration, London and Paris Accords
Capitalism/USA	Source	Capitalist economy[W] Foreign power/alliance[W]	Capitalist economy[M] Foreign power/alliance[M]
	Target	Workers[W]	Workers[M]
	Relation	Existential[W] No threat[W]	Existential[M] No threat[W]
	World order description	A collective of states and industrial magnates endangering the freedom of workers worldwide	
	Conditioning effects	Rejection of cooperation with capitalist powers, proposals for closer union with USSR and Eastern European countries	
	Policy enactment	N/A (marginal view not translated into official foreign policy), but support to all factions opposing German rearmament or Western alliance	

5   *Westbindung*, winning paradigm in West Germany

The return of security politics

Different aspects of security politics returned to West Germany at different points in time after World War II. On the formal level, West Germany did not assume control of foreign and security affairs before 1955. Although the *Grundgesetz* of 1949 established the basic structures of a parliamentary democracy in West Germany, institutionalising the division of Germany into two countries, this provisional constitution merely granted limited political rights to West Germany. Also, the 1951 revision of the Allies' occupation statute transferred only limited responsibilities in the areas of foreign affairs and economics to the newly founded West German authorities, keeping the winning powers' occupation forces still in place. Only after West Germany's integration into the West European Union and NATO in 1955 was the military occupation of West Germany lifted and the country's sovereignty fully restored. Given this development at the formal level, it is hardly surprising that scholarly analyses of West German foreign and security affairs do not usually start before the year 1955 (cf. Haftendorn 1983; Hanreider 1989; Roth 1993).

However, societal and partisan debates on national security and foreign affairs re-emerged in occupied Germany much earlier. Although Germany was devastated and Allied commanders held full powers over their occupation zones, public life – and with it, the politics of defining public policy agendas for, and on behalf of, the German population – resurfaced soon after the war (Von Schmoller 1951). By Allied decree, publication of select national newspapers such as *Die Zeit* and scholarly journals such as *Europa-Archiv* had been permitted again as far back as 1946 and 1947, and some regional governments had been (re-)constituted similarly quickly. The (re-)organisation of the partisan landscape was also in full swing only a few months after the war, and different groupings competed with each other in communal and regional elections as early as 1946. A few years later, in 1949, the Allies handed over select public policy powers to the newly created federal authorities. Political parties competed for the leadership of these new national authorities, with the Christian Democratic Union (CDU) candidate, Konrad Adenauer, winning federal elections by a narrow margin over his competitor from the Social Democratic Party (SPD),

Kurt Schumacher. The CDU formed a coalition government together with the liberal Free Democratic Party (FDP) and the national-conservative German Party (DP).

Despite the wartime destruction and post-war hardship, this surprisingly fast resurgence of political life after 1945 was also accompanied by debates surrounding the distinct question of what threatened West Germany. Five contending propositions can be differentiated from these debates. The very first post-war perspective focused on Germany, securitising 'Germanness' itself. In the view of a heterogeneous yet influential group of clerics, politicians and decommissioned army officers, the fascists' success in mobilising the German population for genocide and total war revealed the profound vulnerability of German society to militarism and nationalism. Given the immense suffering and destruction that the Third Reich brought upon both the world and its own populace, any resurgence of these traits had to be prevented. Analytically speaking, this securitisation of 'Germanness' thus provided a first, and highly specific, idea of both who was causing insecurity (the Germans themselves) and who was affected by this danger (world society), and it also came with a fairly existential rendering of that danger. In line with this organisation of the threat, advocates proposed to keep Germany neutralised, and they rejected any national or international attempt to rearm. The *Bruderschaft der Bekennenden Kirche*, for instance – at the time a particularly powerful Evangelical Protestant movement – harshly criticised Chancellor Adenauer for his attempt to develop West German foreign and defence policies, denying him any right or legitimacy to even launch discussions on national defence (Cornides and Volle 1950: 3584ff.). Retired army officers and decommissioned generals joined this position, rejecting German reconstruction and rearmament as warmongering, as did some social democrats (Rovan 1951; *Die Zeit* [DZ] 1952a). Theodor Heuss, West Germany's first President, also supported this first and most immediate post-war type of securitisation practice, seeing Germany itself as the only source of national and international insecurity (Grappin 1950: 72–73).

However, not all Germans identified their own nation as the single or supreme source of national insecurity in post-war West German politics, and a second major post-war insecurity narrative focused on Germany's historical opponent, France. Contrary to what more recent assessments of Franco-German relations suggest, a highly antagonistic framing of the neighbouring country did, indeed, subsist in West Germany for quite a while and in several quarters after the disintegration of the Third Reich. No matter that France had been quickly defeated by the Nazis and that its contribution to the fall of the Third Reich was minor compared to other Allies – in West Germany, France's repeated attempts at occupation and territorial annexation were widely interpreted as proof of its unbroken if not eternal hostility. France did, indeed, continue to intervene actively in German affairs after World War II. In the late 1940s, for instance, it detached the *Saarland* from Germany and turned it into an independent state – the *Saarstaat*, essentially a French protectorate. Only in 1957 did this territory return to Germany following a local plebiscite, and until that year the *Saar* question provided the platform for a series of unfriendly verbal exchanges between politicians from each country (DZ 1952a; Deutscher Bundestag [Bundestag] 1954a, 1954b). The *Schuman Plan* and other attempts at European integration were also construed as signs of French hostility by West German politicians, and considerably more widely so than contemporary textbooks on European integration suggest. Indeed, France was securitised not only by fascists in the early 1950s (cf. Bundestag 1949b: 741–742/Richter NR). Chancellor Adenauer and opposition leader Schumacher, too, had rejected French integration policies as 'appropriation' of the German coal and steel industry, 'nothing new' and 'a simple continuation of the French control regime over the Ruhr' (cf. Cornides and Volle 1952: 5023). In the late 1940s and early 1950s, then, the securitisation of France as a direct threat to Germany was seen as undeniable in fairly significant parts of society. As shown subsequently, this reading of world politics would eventually wane, yet at the turn of the decade, observers commenting on the state of affairs clearly deemed rapprochement between France and Germany illusionary (Barandon 1952).

The above two threat narratives were highly popular in the immediate aftermath of World War II. However, a third insecurity narrative focusing on the Soviet Union and communism at large gradually emerged. As was the case with Atlanticism in France, the securitisation of communism became increasingly salient in West Germany after the 1949 and 1950 incidents in Czechoslovakia and Korea. Contrary to what some accounts of West German politics suggest, however, this framing was not only advanced by the Christian conservatives. Indeed, this camp was not clearly convinced of the validity of the communist threat, nor was it the only group to securitise the USSR as such. The CDU, for instance, was reluctant to accept what it initially considered to be an internationally imposed securitisation of the USSR, and even in 1950 it merely agreed to an unenthusiastic 'general readiness' to participate in the anti-Soviet European Defence Community (or *Plan Pleven*) proposed by France (Cornides and Volle 1950). By the same token, the SPD was not monolithically opposed to the adversarial framing of the USSR either. While the party's first statement on the European Defence Community rejected the EDC as 'undue rearmament against the East', party leaders were split on the issue. Unlike Schumacher, for example, who rejected securitisation of the East, deputy party leader Erich Ollenhauer gradually endorsed a moderately antagonist framing (Cornides and Volle 1950: 3582–3584), while Carlo Schmid, another influential SPD cadre, advanced a straightforwardly existential rendering of it (Bundestag 1949a: 440).

Seen this way, it was the liberal party that advanced the securitisation of communism early on with particular force, with figureheads such as FDP co-founder August-Martin Euler explicitly positioning the 'Russian threat' as 'the mandatory point of departure for all future German foreign policy' by 1949 (Bundestag 1949a: 417–418). It was not until the mid-1950s, following the deepening Berlin crisis and Soviet repression of revolts in East Germany and Hungary, that the securitisation of communism became more salient in West Germany overall. At this point, the ruling Christian conservatives, too, started to fully endorse the rendering of communism as an extreme danger. Referring to developments in Eastern Europe and East Asia, the CDU leadership now rejected the USSR's 'unabated expansionism against Germany and all of Europe', describing it as a 'massive hostile space of 800 million people of fanatic totalitarian ideology' (Bundestag 1954a: 3120–3121, 3146/Kiesinger CDU). Religious groups then gradually joined this narrative, demanding the 'defence of Christian Europe' against the atheist communists (Bundestag 1954b: 3182). As the ruling party began to support the idea of communism as an existential and collective danger ever more strongly, it also began to more actively and forcefully press for what was called *Westbindung* – that is, West Germany's integration into Western alliances.

The securitisation of communism, then, gained significant influence after the founding of the Federal Republic of Germany (FRG), but it nevertheless coexisted with alternative interpretations of international reality. Indeed, not only did the fear of communism compete with the previously discussed perspectives on 'Germanness' and France, ideas of national danger which had been very salient in the immediate post-war years. The securitisation of communism also competed with further conceptions of national danger, such as the one characterising the United States as the enemy. Configured as some sort of mirror image to anti-communism, this fourth local insecurity narrative considered German and other European populations to be collectively and existentially threatened by the US and 'its' capitalism – not merely because of the latter's destructive exploitation of the populace, but also due to its warmongering and purported preparations for war against the East, a practice that was deemed inherent in capitalism's quest for new markets (cf. Bundestag 1949a: 427/Reimann KPD, 1950: 2497/ Nuding KPD). As with the securitisation of other themes, the securitisation of capitalism also advanced an ordering conception of international relations. The securitisation of 'America' codified yet another understanding of who threatened whom and how in world politics, and in doing so it conditioned foreign policy-making on its own terms. Based on its systematisation of international relations, the *Schuman Plan* for a European Coal and Steel Community (ECSC), for example, was rejected as unwanted project, and membership in the NATO 'war pact' was ardently resisted too, since these initiatives all suggested cooperation with actors who were held to cause West German national insecurity in the first place (Bundestag 1949a: 427–429/Reimann KPD). In the period around 1950, the epistemic power of this fourth insecurity narrative was considerable. It was skilfully connected to the strong anti-militarist sentiments of the time, and it also partly colluded with the revanchist securitisation of France described above.

The fifth and final major threat narrative of post-war West Germany focused on Eastern Germany. In the view of many inside the Western Allied zones and, later, the FRG, West Germany was the only legitimate representative of the German people as such, if only for the simple reason that it reunited the greater part of the (former) Allied occupation zone. Seen from this perspective, the Democratic Republic of Germany (GDR) was held to 'amputate' the German people, posing an existential obstacle to its regaining of nationhood. According to West German politicians – with the exception of the local communists, who described East Germany as peace-loving and anti-fascist – East Germany's communist regime held its populace hostage to totalitarian rule and kept the German nation from reconstituting. As a result, the regime (though not the populace, whose material hardship was recognised and thus given humanitarian assistance) had to be actively countered by West German foreign and 'inner-German' policy alike (Bundestag 1949b: 736/Ollenhauer SPD, 1954b: 3196–3197/Baade SPD; Cramer 1970). Between the foundation of the GDR and the late 1960s, this existential securitisation of the GDR government enjoyed extraordinary currency inside West Germany. As shown in the next section, this perspective empowered the pursuit of a specific foreign policy programme, and it also contributed to the subsequent fortification of the inner German border (Gasteyger 1958; Karst 1959).

Westbindung as a winning programme in the FRG

What the West German political system recognised as a current danger after the demise of the Third Reich, between 1945 and 1955, when the FRG finally joined NATO and integrated into the West, was thus anything but given or predetermined. Different factions competed over the question of what could be held to be a valid threat to West Germany and what could not, with different views gaining and losing salience in different political camps in the years following the war. As the preceding overview of major security themes shows, also different conceptions of the international were advanced and projected abroad under the umbrella of distinct ideas of danger. These imageries of the organisation of international insecurity at times complemented and at times contradicted each other. The idea that capitalism endangered Germany, for instance, was partially compatible with the view that France threatened Germany, since in either case, France was positioned in strong opposition to the home nation. The securitisation of communism as an existential threat to both Germany and a Western group of states, however, stood in strong tension with the historical securitisation of France. These two narratives organised world politics differently, and they subject-positioned actors differently in relation to both each other and West Germany. In one case, France was a fellow in a shared security environment together with West Germany; in another, it was the primordial source of German insecurity.

The ways in which the domestic politics of interpreting national danger played out are important for understanding the foreign policy strategies that the West German leaders proposed, adopted and maintained, both before and after the Allies put them in charge of national policies. By the mid-1950s – i.e. by the time West Germany finally obtained full sovereignty – these dynamics had already evolved quite substantially, and the institutionalisation of formal federal structures in 1949 influenced this process fairly strongly. With the *Grundgesetz*, the political arena had been radically restructured. Following the founding of the FRG, new national sites of politics with their own set of rules and regulations were created. Also, following the founding of the FRG, elections arranged political powers in new ways at the national level. Allocating numbers of seats to different parties, elections ranked and temporarily froze the power differentials between different political camps inside the Federal Republic. This formalisation of federal politics, then, structured its dynamics anew, affecting the question of whose epistemic position on national security and foreign policy matters could be articulated. The *Bundestag*, for instance, became West Germany's new primary site of politics, and on this site fascists and communists were soon marginalised by an informal alliance of the three most powerful democratic parties: the CDU, the SPD and the FDP. When fascists demanded revenge against the wartime enemies or re-annexation of the territories that the Allies had turned over to Poland and Czechoslovakia, for instance, or when West German communists demanded the blocking of the capitalist warmongering of the West and support for Soviet proposals for a neutralised variant of German unification, the democratic parties joined forces to ignore, vocally interrupt or overrule the articulation of such positions, not hesitating to leave the plenary empty or to remove such talking points from parliament's order of the day by simple procedural voting (cf. Bundestag 1949b: 741–742ff., 1951: 4263ff.).

Certain ways of securitising, then, had become considerably more difficult with the institution of the new federal system. In the new system, fascists and communists won few popular mandates in the beginning, they were actively marginalised or countered on the floor and they increasingly lost the support of the electorate as time progressed. More importantly, even, in 1952 and 1956 significant parts of these quarters – namely, the fascist *Reichspartei* and the German Communist Party (KPD) – were ruled illegal by the constitutional court, which meant that these parties lost all of their public mandates. Running parallel to this development on the level of formal politics, however, the securitisation of communism as a superior and collective (westward-directed) danger also gained traction among the democratic parties and in West German society as such. On the partisan level, conservatives asserted ever more uniformly that it was the East which posed the supreme challenge, and social democrats also began – much to the joy of the ruling parties – to accept at least the basic configuration of the 'communist danger'. This is to say that the biggest opposition party also began to endorse the idea that communism truly posed a danger, and that it endangered a larger collective of nations, of which the FRG was part (DZ 1952b). Somewhat unlike the conservatives, however, social democrats remained split on whether communism was a problematic or an existential challenge. For Ollenhauer, for example, the USSR necessarily had to be understood as a problematic rather than existential challenge, both for pragmatic reasons and because other sources of insecurity, including German nationalism itself, were more important (cf. Bundestag 1954a: 3137). This differential ascription of antagonism to the East, this book's second chapter on Germany shows, would soon be of fundamental importance to West German foreign affairs.

The communist threat became an accepted truth in larger segments of society as well. To some, the implicit association of West Germany with the Western democratic camp assisted the creation of a new, post-fascist identity, providing democratic credentials to a country that had championed totalitarianism only a few years earlier (Haftendorn 1983: 70ff.). Others started to associate the developing anti-communist stance with their own material well-being, as West Germany's rapid economic reconstruction was seen by many to have followed from a decision against the East (DZ 1957b). The pacifist camps, which had so successfully opposed the designation of any foreign source of insecurity in the past, by contrast started to lose influence on domestic politics at this time. This development was driven in part by the distinct ways in which West German rearmament had come to be enacted. The new *Bundeswehr* emphasised the 'democratic' vetting of officers and the civil rights of conscript soldiers, its command structures were intimately integrated into NATO and it was held materially dependent on allied heavy weaponry and ammunition, and with this the previously widespread fear of uncontrolled militarism was actively addressed (Karst 1959; Strauss 1960). In this context, the threat of communism became increasingly widely accepted by society at large as valid, and by the mid-1950s it was so salient as to guide the national foreign policy agenda in powerful ways. By that time, the apprehension of West Germany as evolving in a larger Euro-Atlantic community of insecure states was directly conducive to certain types of cooperative foreign policy strategies – namely, political and military alliances with these co-threatened nations and against the identified source of danger. The distinct ways in which communism was securitised, then, did not merely set out a provocation and, hence, a need for policy response. Importantly, it also defined the international in ways that allowed the FRG to adhere to NATO and the Western European Union (WEU), and in ways that made the FRG stick to those alliances after 1955.

Yet if the securitisation of communism became widely supported by the mid-1950s, it would still be reductive to suggest that it was the only truth available in West Germany, since other security narratives continued to condition West German foreign policymaking as well. The focus on Eastern Germany, for instance, remained particularly powerful. Concerns with German unification – i.e. the reattachment of Eastern Germany especially, but also of the *Saarland* and the Eastern Territories (those parts of the former Reich that were ceded to Eastern European countries right after the war) – indeed continued to run high for decades (Grewe 1959). Seen from this perspective, any attempt to withhold German unification was considered a hostile act against the FRG and had to be forcefully countered. In foreign and inner-German policy, this stance practically played out in the form of what was called *Politik der Stärke* (policy of strength) – a framework of forceful and persistent diplomatic, political and economic rejection and overpowering of the East German government (Bundestag 1955: 6168/Kiesinger CDU). The *Hallstein Doktrin* also formed part of this broader policy framework. According to this foreign policy doctrine, any international recognition of East Germany as an independent state constituted an unfriendly act against Germany. With the *Hallstein Doktrin*, West Germany pledged to automatically break off diplomatic relations with all countries that recognised the GDR, treating them as de facto opponents.

Finally, it is also important to recognise how the projection of an endangered larger Western space was, indirectly at least, eventually also conducive to Franco-German reconciliation (Cornides 1963; Kaiser 1986). As mentioned earlier, there were few revanchists left in the *Bundestag* by 1960, and so by that time, assisted by the *kleine Wiedervereinigung* (small reunification) with the *Saarland* in 1957 and West Germany's integration into NATO (and not the EDC, which would have privileged French leadership by institutional design), reconciliation was turning into a broad and multi-partisan agenda (cf. Bundestag 1963: 3424). This meant that by the late 1950s, conservatives, too, had broken with the extreme right's demands for *revanche* against France, finally endorsing the description of France as a fellow in a shared insecurity context. Certainly, select conservatives such as Ernst Majonica eventually also criticised the emergent Gaullist foreign policy strategy as 'pro-communist' (Bundestag 1963: 3420), but this argument too meant that France was no longer recognised as the independent source of existential danger that it was earlier held to be. In 1963, this ever clearer subjectification of France as a fellow (and not as an opponent) in world politics enabled the conclusion of a bilateral friendship treaty. Eighteen years after the war, the Elysée Treaty institutionalised regular high-level meetings and consultation on foreign and security policy between the two countries (Abelein 1963). Adenauer's assessment of this treaty exemplifies just how much the West German conception of France's role in world politics and relationship with Germany had changed by the 1960s. Making the case for the Elysée Treaty in parliament, the Chancellor now praised it as 'the logical continuation of the spirit of the *Schuman Plan*' (Bundestag 1963: 3417) – the very same plan that the very same Chancellor had rejected as illegitimate French appropriation of the German coal and steel industry a little over a decade earlier.

Towards the *Politik der kleinen Schritte*

After an initial period of strongly divergent interpretations, then, the major (but not all) political forces of West Germany were converging on communism as a supreme danger by the mid-1950s. By the 1960s, the more distinct ways in which the East was securitised gradually turned into a new point of contestation. An emergent group of actors – journalists and peace researchers especially, but eventually also social democrats and liberals – came to see the prevailing securitisation of the East as a homogeneous bloc and existential danger as increasingly unhelpful (cf. DZ 1957a, 1960, 1965c). Seen their way, the accepted way of securitising the East reproduced and deepened – but definitely did not solve – the partition of Germany. By the 1960s, the GDR had, indeed, become more deeply integrated in the Warsaw Pact (Tudyka 1966). What was more, the communist regime had started to fortify and militarise the Berlin border, preventing citizens from moving to the West and even killing them when they tried. And if that was not enough, the *Hallstein Doktrin* also seemed defunct. Arguably, this foreign policy doctrine had initially prevented neutrals and allies from recognising East Germany, thus sustaining support for reunification. In the 1960s, however, East

Germany succeeded in opening consulates in Tanzania, Egypt and Yugoslavia, and thus it managed to obtain de facto recognition as an independent state, in spite of the *Hallstein Doktrin* (Frei 1965).

By the 1960s, then, the *Politik der Stärke* was being increasingly forcefully challenged for its lack of success. Still more importantly, it also started to be criticised on epistemic grounds. Opposition forces, academics and journalists started to argue that the national foreign policy programme rested on an outdated and thus incorrect understanding of world politics. The 'current map of the world', they claimed, consisted not of one but of a multiplicity of communist actors, each of whom had different kinds of relations with West Germany, with the West, but also with the Soviet Union. Importantly, the East was still considered to pose an important danger to West Germany, according to this alternative perspective. Yet communism was a danger that had to be differentiated epistemologically, since the Eastern Bloc could no longer be held to be perfectly aligned and uniformly hostile (Brandt 1964). The Sino-Soviet confrontation, Romania's opposition to the deepening of the Warsaw Pact and Yugoslavia's opposition to Soviet control were seen as observations that were supportive of this perspective, and it was argued that West German foreign policy necessarily had to recognise this new reality (Cornides 1963; Allen 1964; Bartsch 1965; Brock 1968).

After Adenauer ceded the chancellorship to Ludwig Erhard in the mid-1960s, then, *two* slightly different securitisations of communism started to oppose each other inside the FRG. These two ways of securitising communism were compatible with each other insofar as they recognised communism as a security threat to a Western collective of states, including but also going beyond West Germany. They stood in tension with each other, however, with regard to the exact types of antagonist actors and relations that they identified under the heading of communism. The conservative camp defended an understanding whereby the East was a homogenous block existentially threatening the West (Schuster 1963). In the view of others, however, Eastern European nations in particular were positioned differently 'in reality'. With reference to past uprisings and Soviet repressions in Hungary and Czechoslovakia, Eastern European governments became portrayed as victims of Soviet enmity as well (DZ 1965a). Analytically speaking, Eastern Europe was thus differentiated from the GDR, which was maintained as an existential problem, both for its very existence and its fortification of the inner German border, but also from the USSR, whose rhetoric and military arsenal continued to inspire awe in the entire West German political system (Mackintosh 1968). Eastern European nations were still securitised. As members of the Warsaw Pact, they remained recognised as important sources of danger. Yet their opposition to the West was sketched as somewhat 'unintended', given their subordination to Soviet policy control, and hence these nations were posited both in less tense relations towards Germany and in more antagonistic relations towards Moscow (DZ 1965b).

After the 1966 federal elections, these partially contending systematisations of the Eastern danger became tied together in the executive. In 1966, liberals no longer helped the conservatives to form a parliamentary majority, and thus West Germany's first grand coalition government was formed. With Kurt Kiesinger of the conservative Christian Democratic Union holding the chancellorship and social democrat Willy Brandt directing the Foreign Ministry, however, tensions quickly emerged on issues of foreign relations and defence (DZ 1966b, 1967), and a compromise foreign policy doctrine by the name of *Politik der kleinen Schritte* (policy of small steps) was devised (Mahnke 1971). This new foreign and security policy doctrine kept the FRG firmly anchored in its Western alliances, but it also set out the intention of improving relations with Eastern European governments, in the form of state visits or bilateral trade agreements, for example (Erler 1964). Overall, however, this second foreign policy element remained largely subordinated to the former, and when West Germany's first white book on defence was published in 1969, existential fear of the Red Army and a strong commitment to NATO clearly prevailed overall (Bundesminister der Verteidigung 1969). Also, conservatives and social democrats continued to confront each other with their respective interpretations of world politics in the *Bundestag*, regardless of the grand coalition or the new foreign policy doctrine (Apel 1984; DZ 1969a), and each side drew on arguments formulated by allied politicians in an endeavour to bolster their cause (Kawalkowski 1964; Kissinger 1966).

Conclusion

West German foreign and security politics re-emerged much faster than what scholarship usually argues, and it was considerably more dynamic than what externalist accounts of West German politics so often argue. Instead of having been predefined by Allies, the structural character of the Cold War or the seemingly self-evident nature of communist danger as such, discussions surrounding the question of who threatened whom and how in world politics were fairly diverse in postwar West Germany, at least in the beginning. Irrespective of the fact that Germany was occupied, West German society had hence not been stripped of its own sensemaking capabilities and dynamics. And, indeed, a closer look shows that the West German political system was marked by interpretative dynamics that were fairly particular to it, such as the lingering revanchist focus on France or the influential auto-directed securitisation of 'Germanness', to insecurity narratives that each conditioned foreign policy strategising differently under their own terms (see Table 5.1 for an overview). If local securitisations practices were not predetermined substantively from the outside, however, it holds true that the institutionalisation of the Federal Republic restructured the local political sphere and that this benefited the articulation of some perspectives more than others. As discussed in Part III of this book, this latter impact of formal political rules on epistemological debates is interesting at an analytical level, given that it puts into question the linkage between democratic institutions and political debate. Democratic institutions may be mandatory for pluralistic debates in general, but they might not necessarily give rise to particularly pluralistic security discussions, West Germany shows, and the subsequent Swiss case study demonstrates in an even more impressive manner.

Table 5.1 West German constructions of international (in-)security after World War II

		Late 1940s	Mid-1950s	Early 1960s
'Germanness'	Source	Vulnerability to extreme nationalism and militarism[D]	Vulnerability to extreme nationalism and militarism[M]	N/A
	Target	Germany and world[D]	Germany and world[D]	N/A
	Relation	Existential[D]	Manageable[W] Existential[M]	N/A
	World order description	For cultural reasons, the German nation is self-destructive and existentially threatens others	The German nation is self-destructive and	N/A
	Conditioning effects	Support for neutralisation of Germany, rejection of rearmament and membership in military alliances		N/A
	Policy enactment	N/A (view not translated into formal policies, as government was not sovereign on such matters before 1955)		N/A
France	Source	Historical enemy[W]	Historical enemy[M]	N/A
	Target	Germany[W]	Germany[M]	N/A
	Relation	Existential[W]	No threat[D] Existential[M]	N/A
	World order description	Neighbouring nation does not cease to seek reduction, amputation, subjugation, etc. of Germany		N/A
	Conditioning effects	Opposition to (non-cooperation with) France, including possibly retaliation, reunification with Saarland, rejection of *Schuman Plan* and French attempts at European integration		N/A
	Policy enactment	N/A (view not translated into formal policies, given the limited salience of this frame by the time of FRG sovereignty)		N/A

USSR/communism	Source			
	Target	USSR (incl. Eastern Europe)^M / West (incl. West Germany)^M	USSR (incl. Eastern Europe)^D / West (incl. West Germany)^D	USSR^D / West (incl. West Germany)^D / Also Eastern Europe^D
	Relation	Existential^M / No threat^D	Existential^D / Problematic^D / No threat^M	Existential^D / Problematic^D
	World order description	Eastern bloc existentially challenging Western order, of which FRG is part	USSR existentially challenging Western order, of which FRG is part	USSR existentially challenging West, of which FRG is part, but USSR also subjugating Eastern Europe
	Conditioning effects	Collective 'Western' reaction (incl. France) to identified collective danger	Collective 'Western' reaction (incl. France) to identified collective danger	Collective Western (incl. France) or even European (incl. Eastern Europe) reaction to identified collective danger
	Policy enactment	N/A (view not translated into formal policies and view of little salience yet)	1955 NATO membership (and continuation thereof later), support for European integration plans (Westbindung)	Support to European integration, 1963 Elysée Treaty, promotion of relations with Eastern Europe (Politik der kleinen Schritte)
USA/capitalism	Source	Capitalist economy^W	Capitalist economy^M	N/A
	Target	Workers worldwide^W	Workers worldwide^M	N/A
	Relation	Existential^W / No threat^W	Existential^M / No threat^D	N/A
	World order description	Existential danger promoted by a distinct actor (the US), affecting all nations and the German populace	Existential danger promoted by a distinct actor (the US), affecting all nations and the German populace	N/A
	Conditioning effects	Rejection of westwards alliances (NATO especially) and opposition to capitalist cooperation (European integration), support to alternative social programmes (e.g. communism)	Rejection of westwards alliances (NATO especially) and opposition to capitalist cooperation (European integration), support to alternative social programmes (e.g. communism)	N/A
	Policy enactment	N/A (view not translated into government policies, except for opposition to 'French' European integration agenda)	N/A (view not translated into government policies, except for opposition to 'French' European integration agenda)	N/A

continued

Table 5.1 Continued

		Late 1940s	Mid-1950s	Early 1960s
East Germany (regime only)	Source	Existence and opposition to unification[D]	Existence and opposition to unification[D]	Existence, opposition to unification, deepening integration in Warsaw Pact[D]
	Target	German nationhood[D]	German nationhood[D]	German nationhood[D]
	Relation	Existential[D]	Existential[D]	Existential[D]
	World order description	Existential obstacle to the reconstitution of the German nation		
	Conditioning effects	Forceful rejection and overpowering of GDR government, opposition to anyone accepting division of Germany		
	Policy enactment	N/A (FRG not yet in charge of policies, FRG and GDR formally funded in 1949)	*Politik der Stärke, Hallstein Doktrin*, humanitarian aid	*Hallstein Doktrin*, humanitarian aid

6 Neutral Switzerland and the non-recognition of direct danger

Neutralism as hegemonic interpretation of international politics

French and West German security debates evolved in different ways in the post-war context, yet they also partly developed from epistemic positions that had been elaborated during or even before World War II. The same situation applies to Switzerland, where neutralism was an important 'inherited' factor of this kind in the late 1940s. As an epistemic world ordering perspective, neutralism had, indeed, already enjoyed a strong standing in the Swiss polity at the beginning of the European post-war period. As a distinct reading of international politics, however, neutralism proposed a fairly specific idea of the international. Particular to Swiss neutralism was the understanding that although international danger existed, it did not directly threaten Switzerland as such (Hagmann 2010). This is not to say that Swiss policymakers would not have understood the international security context as heavily confrontational in the 1950s and thereafter – policymakers, scholars and journalists explicitly recognised the antagonist dynamics at play between NATO and the Warsaw Pact throughout the Cold War, and they considered opposition between East and West to be the supreme challenge to international security as such (e.g. Schweizerischer Bundesrat 1966, 1973, 1975). This insight notwithstanding, however, confrontation between these two blocs was *not* considered to represent a direct danger to Switzerland as such. At worst, Swiss policymakers feared that flank elements of this conflict could spill over onto Swiss territory, if, for example, some of the battalions of one side were pushed onto Swiss soil (Schweizerischer Bundesrat 1966: 858–865). It was thought that such an intrusion into Swiss territory would, however, be accidental and fully unintended, as Switzerland was not known to have antagonistic relations with any camp.

Seen in this way, neutralism endangered and ordered the international, but it did so in a peculiar manner. And, indeed, the Swiss perspective on armed conflict between East and West systematised the international in ways that are not seen in the other two case studies in this book. In the Swiss view, two opposing camps existentially threatened each other as collectives, but the link between Switzerland and their opposition to each other was one of radical disconnect.

Analytically speaking, this means that the international was understood in ways that attributed to Switzerland an utterly disengaged position – according to the Swiss reading of world politics, Switzerland was simply not implicated in the Cold War conflict, which, as existential as it may have been for its participants, was a conflict between others and had nothing to do with the Swiss nation itself. Instead of situating Switzerland in parallel to possible fellows in a shared insecurity context, then, the securitisation of the East–West conflict set out an entirely solitary and 'peaceful' position for the home nation (Winkler 1995). As Minister of Defence Kaspar Villiger argued in the 1990s, looking back at Swiss Cold War foreign and security politics, neutralism defined Switzerland as a veritable 'island of peace in a sea of power politics' (Villiger 1995: 170). With their distinct ways of securitising the East–West conflict, Swiss policymakers simply did not recognise their home nation as part of an insecure community, for their home nation was not held to be directly threatened by others in the first place.

Compared to the cases of France and West Germany, where securitisation always went hand in hand with the recognition of direct threats against the respective home nation, this Swiss 'neutralist securitisation' of the East–West conflict may strike as peculiar. Regardless of this, however, neutralist securitisation is also a case of international systematisation through insecurity. As a sense-making practice, neutralism identified different kinds of actors and antagonisms in world politics and produced – by means of relating these towards each other and the self – knowledge of the home nation's position in world politics. In doing this, neutralism, too, had conditioning effects on foreign policymaking, empowering neutrality as the overarching foreign policy strategy. In the case of Switzerland, it is, however, important to note that these conditioning effects had been routinised for decades – indeed, for centuries – to the point where neutralism as a world ordering perspective evolved in intimate and almost inseparable tandem with neutrality as a foreign policy strategy. Effectively, neutralism and neutrality had been the interpretation practice and self-chosen policy in Switzerland for centuries prior to World War II. Switzerland had pursued neutralism since the sixteenth century, and foreign powers and international treaties endorsed this practice at various points throughout history. This means that by the 1940s and 1950s, neutralism as a sense-making practice and neutrality policy as its programmatic enactment had already been advanced and enacted in highly repetitive manners, with each aspect maintaining the other. By the end of World War II, neutralism had already empowered a steady and time-honoured course of neutrality policy, whereas unwavering pursuit and institutionalisation of the latter had already reconfirmed beliefs in neutralism as a valid interpretation of world politics time and time again (Spillmann *et al.* 2001: 59).

In the 1940s and 1950s, then, the *a priori* semi-contingent linkage between securitisation and foreign policymaking had become highly stabilised in the Swiss case, as both neutralism and neutrality seemed to be just plain right for that polity. Unlike the situation in neighbouring countries, where conceptions of world politics were articulated, embattled and enacted anew as time progressed, the Swiss political system simply stuck to its time-proven positions as the Cold

War unfolded (correspondingly, there are only two chapters focused on the Swiss case in this book). In the view of Swiss policymakers, neutralism produced a clear understanding of the role of others and the home nation in world politics, and neutrality policy both instantiated this understanding and helped make sure that others accepted that Swiss reading in turn. Just like countless earlier European conflicts, then, World War II was deemed to confirm the truthfulness and utilities of neutralism and neutrality. In the 1950s, neutralism had been seen to be proven a correct position to hold by Swiss policymakers, given that the nation had, indeed, not been subject to hostile framings by foreign powers during the war. Neutrality policy, too, was seen to have once again demonstrated its functional validity, for the small democratic nation remained unharmed from Europe's most bloody conflict, in spite of Switzerland's complete encirclement by warring fascist powers. Rather than providing cause for questioning and reorientation, then, World War II fitted nicely into the routinised Swiss interpretation of the basic structures of world politics and the nation's position therein (Fischer 2004).

Indeed, World War II and the emerging East–West conflict helped deepen the Swiss belief in neutralism even further. For in the 1950s – and under the leadership of politicians such as Max Petitpierre, who was Swiss Foreign Minister for no less than 16 years after 1945 – the enactment of neutralism was expanded into a doctrine of *permanent* neutrality (Trachsler 2001). Following this doctrine, Switzerland no longer merely assumed the responsibilities of a neutral country as defined by the 1907 Hague Convention, which were to refrain from assisting opposing camps in times of conflict and to not lend national territory to the activities of others. By its own choosing, the Federal Council – i.e. the Swiss Government – went further and pledged to also pursue neutrality in non-conflict settings. In practice, this meant that Switzerland sought to refrain from any act that could impair or prejudice neutrality once conflict between foreign nations had actually broken out (Möckli 2000a). Permanent neutrality, seen in this way, was considered to be both a preventive measure against possible entanglement in the future conflicts of others and a means of bolstering international support for Swiss neutrality.

In the 1950s and 1960s, this move to permanent neutrality went hand in hand with an ideological deepening of the perceived truthfulness, virtues and functions of both neutralism and neutrality. Indeed, if neutralism and neutrality had already been exempted from political debate in the late 1940s, evolving unopposed by contending interpretations and uses of world order, then these concepts became ever more dogmatically articulated and morally framed thereafter (Van Dongen 1997). By the 1960s, neutralism and neutrality were no longer merely considered most truthful and strategically useful for small state security (Freymond 1990). They were also positioned as particularly 'respectable', as anti-war frameworks and contributions to world peace even, for they did not haul the home nation into confrontational relations with others, keeping Switzerland away from engaging others in armed conflict (Galtung 1984). The validity of this assessment was unquestioned in the political arena. Commenting on the

1974 national security doctrine, for example, the lower house's Military Commission – the precursor of today's parliamentary Defence Committee – simply maintained that neutralism and neutrality were self-evident, and that it was therefore unnecessary to debate them (Schweizerischer Nationalrat [Nationalrat] 1974: 771).

During much of the Cold War, then, the key components of national foreign and security politics enjoyed truly hegemonic standing inside the Swiss polity. In society at large, too, neutralism and neutrality were essentialised and glorified during this time, and they even became considered constitutive of national identity as such. Rather than disentangling this dogmatic rendering of neutralism and neutrality, scholars played a fairly active role in their mystification. Assessing the historical trajectory of Swiss state-building and the role of neutrality in it, historian and political analyst David Lasserre, for instance, maintained: 'Neutrality is [...] a whole complex of attitudes, feelings, habits to which practice has given birth little by little. It is something living, [...] born of fortuitous circumstances' (Lasserre 1967: 229). Even in 1990, neutralism and neutrality were still presented as timeless truths in the Swiss polity and as products that had nothing to do with either a contextual analysis of short-lived international trends or even some form of proactive politics. As another academic explained the origins of Swiss foreign and security politics to his readers just before the fall of the Berlin Wall:

> As part of the very definition of Switzerland itself, neutrality is not a mere option chosen in view of particular circumstances [...], and it is not the result of a certain assessment of national interests at a specific point in time either.
>
> (De Dardel 1990: 126)

Taken together, Swiss security and foreign politics thus differed fairly radically from the other two cases presented in this book. Unlike policymakers in neighbouring countries, where a variety of enemy-identifications were articulated both after World War II and during the Cold War itself, Swiss policymakers did not recognise direct challenges to the home nation during this time. They essentially also stuck to the East–West conflict as the macro ordering paradigm of world politics when other nations shifted their focus to other regions of the world, whether to Africa, the Middle East or South East Asia. Upholding securitisation of the East–West conflict as a singular and all-encompassing ordering paradigm of world politics, the Swiss polity did not see the home nation as targeted by direct danger, but as assuming a bystander position in a tense security environment and conflict between others. By the same token, Swiss security and foreign politics was also fairly distinctive in procedural terms, since it lacked contending conceptions of world politics for most of the Cold War period. When discussed in the legislature, national security doctrines thus almost always obtained unanimous support. The doctrines' ways of assessing the state of world politics and the Swiss position therein were consistently praised as 'excellent' and 'perfectly realistic' by policymakers (Nationalrat 1966: 474–496; Schweizerischer Ständerat 1966: 324–311). Other members of the Swiss national defence establishment – the armed forces in particular – also did not consider it necessary to articulate an alternative reading of the international (Däniker 1973; Brunner 1976, 1980).

Foreign policymaking under neutralism

Between the 1940s and 1980s, the neutralist securitisation of the East–West conflict codified a simple yet nevertheless distinct imagery of world politics to Switzerland, and in doing so, it conditioned Swiss foreign policymaking. This is because the single available local truth about world politics – the Swiss securitisation of the East–West conflict – set out a specific type of knowledge about who opposed whom and how. Just like other insecurity narratives, neutralism systematised the international, making world politics intelligible to local policymakers and making their actions dependent on it. At the macro level, neutralism empowered neutrality policy. As already noted, neutralism and the choice of neutrality had become such deeply engrained world ordering and foreign policy practices after centuries of routinised instantiation that their very recursive relation is somewhat difficult to dissect analytically in the Cold War period. In the 1950s, however, neutrality had been conceptually subdivided into two more concrete types of foreign policy programmes, and these subdivisions help show how neutralism conditioned foreign policymaking. This is because according to the *Petitpierre Doktrin* – a foreign policy principle named after the long-serving Foreign Minister of the time – Swiss foreign policymaking started to differentiate between 'political' and 'technical' forms of international cooperation in the mid-1950s (Diez 1980; Schindler 1984). 'Political' forms of international cooperation, according to this doctrine, entailed a risk of national entanglement in future foreign conflict, and as such they had to be avoided. 'Technical' foreign policy programmes, by contrast, were seen as merely functional and thus permissible.

Whether a foreign policy initiative was 'political' or 'technical' in nature was, of course, repeatedly subject to debate. Yet, generally speaking, military alliances and other forms of security cooperation clearly fell into the former category, and economic agreements and membership in universal organisations into the latter (Hoffmann 1995). In practice, this meant that neutralism conditioned foreign policy in ways that prohibited military cooperation or association in military alliances such as NATO or the Warsaw Pact – since neutralism did *not* identify common security problems with others and thus did *not* present such alliances as fellows of Switzerland in the first place, and also given that the *Petitpierre Doktrin* and permanent neutrality authoritatively rejected such an association. Indeed, neutralism also denied membership in international organisations capable of deciding coercive sanctions against others, and this is why Switzerland also abstained from joining the United Nations – since unlike the League of Nations, of which Switzerland had been part, the United Nations Charter did not give neutrals the option of opting out of such sanctions (Eidgenössisches Politisches Departement 1980; Thürer 1995). In security affairs, then, neutralism disempowered any cooperative foreign policy initiative. 'Active security policy', as Swiss policymakers called such an orientation, was explicitly disqualified as mismatching the reality of world politics (cf. Schweizerischer Ständerat 1973: 722).

Neutralist securitisation, then, led to the pursuit of an isolationist type of 'self-help' approach to national security in practice. During the Cold War, and for years after, Swiss authorities emphasised the need for fully independent national defence capabilities – i.e. a national security apparatus capable of upholding the international responsibilities of a neutral power, but also an apparatus that was neither directed against a specific opponent, nor aided by any foreign ally or alliance. Between the 1950s and 1990, Switzerland invested considerably in its defence capabilities, which included the armed forces and civil protection. By the end of the Cold War, Switzerland's army ranked among the largest and technologically most advanced armies of Europe (Stahel 2006). Also by 1990, 85 per cent of the entire population had underground shelter, 1,200 underground hospitals offered treatment for more than 92,000 patients and national supplies could feed the entire army for a period of no less than three years (De Weck and Maurer 1990: 70–71).

Until the 1980s, the few security related discussions that did take place in Switzerland were thus all restricted to military topics, narrowly defined (Goetschel *et al.* 2005). In the early 1960s, for example, there had been controversy surrounding the question of whether Switzerland should develop nuclear weapons (Mark 1966), leading to two national popular referenda: one seeking to ban production and storage of any nuclear weaponry on Swiss soil and one requiring federal authorities to submit the possible production of nuclear arms to popular approval (both proposals were rejected by the electorate). In the late 1960s, different factions of the armed forces clashed over the question of whether the atomic age required abandonment of the traditional 'mass army' approach to national defence and the introduction of more mobile and dispersed defensive postures (Studienkommission für Strategische Fragen 1969). In the 1970s, policymakers and general staff officers addressed the question of whether the national civil protection efforts diluted the military's resource base (Nationalrat 1974: 765; Spillmann 1990), and they discussed the impact of electronic and urban warfare on military strategising and national defence (Nationalrat 1976; Schweizerischer Ständerat 1976).

However, the question of whether the national security environment had been assessed correctly did not form part of these discussions. Tellingly, rather than identifying a possible opponent and assessing its military capabilities, needs assessments for military defence were consequently based on abstract conceptions of possible 'forms of armed conflict'. The 1966 national security doctrine, for example, derived its calls for national military procurement from a discussion of different possible 'forms of war'. The doctrine did not conclude with a defensive posture based on an empirical analysis of an opponent's actual powers, since no such actor had been identified in the first place (cf. Schweizerischer Bundesrat 1966). As curious as such a focus on abstract 'ideal types of organised violence' – i.e. a security policy syllogism perfectly detached from concrete antagonist actors – may seem, inside the Swiss polity such programmatic reasoning was held to be fully viable and, indeed, its applicability was forcefully asserted in the political arena. As the lower house's Military Commission, for instance, defined the basic terms of discussion when introducing the 1966 national defence doctrine to the plenary: 'When designing a security doctrine, we must limit ourselves to the most probable forms of war [...]. Anything else is unrealistic and utopian' (Nationalrat 1966: 475). Rather than being considered theoretical, a conceptual focus on situations but not opponents was thus understood to be utterly realistic by Swiss defence circles, and it was maintained throughout the Cold War. In the doctrinal publications of the 1970s and 1980s, the nomenclature of this syllogism evolved, but not the broader thinking scheme as such. The national security doctrine of 1974, for instance, differentiated between 'situations of relative peace', which was defined as power politics below the threshold of armed conflict, 'indirect warfare' – i.e. subversion and agitation – 'conventional war' and 'war with weapons of mass destruction'. Still, in keeping with the neutralist non-recognition of direct antagonism between others and Switzerland proper, none of these categories of conflict was considered likely to affect Switzerland directly, and the conceptual differentiation between 'forms of war' continued to enjoy strong support in the political arena (cf. Nationalrat 1974: 764–803).

Neutralism conditioned foreign policymaking, insofar as it endangered the international environment, but designated neither opponents nor fellows to Switzerland in so doing. With this ordering of the international, neutralism worked against security cooperation with others, empowering a stringently autonomous approach to defence. Yet as the conceptual differentiation between 'political' and 'technical' forms of foreign policymaking suggested, neutrality as a general foreign policy principle not only instituted isolationism in the security domain. Neutralism disempowered security cooperation, since it did not identify fellows in a shared insecurity context; however, this does not mean that Switzerland could not have pursued other kinds of policies outside the security domain. In the economic sector, for instance, the notion of 'technical' cooperation allowed for the active pursuit of bilateral and multilateral trade agreements, as long as Switzerland was not obliged to implement sanctions, which were held to be coercive and thus dependent on, or even creative of, antagonist relations. In 1946, Switzerland became a member of the Organisation for European Economic Co-operation (OECD); in 1961, a member of the European Free Trade Association (EFTA); and in 1966, it started to participate in the General Agreement on Tariffs and Trade (GATT).

Indeed, the neutralist securitisation of the East–West conflict also enabled foreign policy activism in the areas of humanitarianism and mediation. Proactive initiatives and sustained contributions on these issues were characteristic of Swiss foreign affairs throughout the Cold War, and they included elements such as the provision of good offices to quarrelling foreign governments, the widening of international arbitration mechanisms, the safeguard and surveillance of international humanitarian law (the Geneva Conventions, of which Switzerland is the Depositary State, in particular) and projects to codify and extend international law in other domains. Materially, this strand of foreign policymaking also included the provision of significant financial support to humanitarian organisations, such as the International Committee of the Red Cross (ICRC), the deployment of peace observers, such as to the Korean Demilitarized Zone (DMZ), assistance in the airlifting of United Nations personnel in cases of non-intrusive operations, such as those of the First United Nations Emergency Force (UNEF I) in the mid-1950s and the United Nations Operation in the Congo (ONUC) in 1960, and the dispatching of medical response teams to emergency zones around the globe.

Importantly, this latter foreign policy agenda too was consistently justified by the neutralist reading of world politics at hand. This means that Swiss efforts in the areas of arbitration, mediation or emergency assistance were always presented as *solidarity* contributions. 'Active' Swiss foreign policy contributions in the realms of humanitarianism or mediation were always considered as assistance with the problems of others; they were not motivated by conceptions of challenges that were common to both others and Switzerland (cf. Spillmann *et al.* 2001: 48–57). Furthermore, such solidarity contributions were not necessarily altruistic in nature, even if some Swiss policymakers sought to present Swiss humanitarianism and mediation efforts in such terms. In part, at least, such contributions to the international community were also used strategically as a means of promoting Swiss neutrality abroad (Petitpierre 1980). This is because the more widely Swiss neutrality was accepted as valid by foreign governments, and possibly even formalised in their statements and declarations, the more confident Swiss policymakers themselves became regarding the validity of the neutralist conception of world politics on which this very same policy rested and by virtue of which neutrality policy had been made possible in the first place.

Towards knowledge of collective challenges in the 1980s

It is only towards the end of the Cold War that the Swiss security policy perspective described above started to erode. In the beginning, it was the heavy-handed emphasis on military concepts of security that provoked opposition (Fanzun and Lehmann 2000). Since the mid-1970s, Swiss policymakers had ever more authoritatively asserted the primacy of a military-centric approach to security. Speaking to critics, the government's 1979 *Intermediary Report on Security Politics*, for example, recognised that 'comprehensive defence' could be seen as 'a holistic approach to defence concerned with so-called wider challenges to the population including food and health safety'. The same government doctrine, however, also made it clear that such an approach 'must not be confused with security politics proper', which was about handling military dangers (Schweizerischer Bundesrat 1979: 4). Up until the early 1990s, non-military approaches to security policy were thus actively sidelined in the parliamentary arena (Nationalrat 1991: 905). In the 1970s, proposals for international disarmament were flatly rejected as idealist and utopian, if not outright treacherous, by the Military Commission (Nationalrat 1974: 764–803, 1980: 729ff), and even in 1990 criticisms of military-oriented security politics were heavily policed as examples of decadence and hedonism (De Weck and Maurer 1990: 79–80).

As shown in Chapter 9, this political enforcement of a military-centric security framework eventually led to a sizable extra-parliamentary backlash, including a 1989 popular initiative to abolish the national armed forces altogether. During the Cold War, however, the continuation of a military reading of international politics helped maintain the established Swiss world order perspective. Since the military vantage point was the primary analytical prism through which to interpret the international, policymakers continued to describe international relations along classic neutralist lines (Mabillard 1979; Landmann 1980). This means that even when security dynamics in new geographical regions such as Africa and Asia were recognised, they were conceptually subsumed to the military confrontation between East and West. In the late 1970s and 1980s, then, opposition between East and West had simply become known as more 'global' inside the Swiss polity, but its basic configuration remained the same, given military-centric analytics (Brunner 1980). In practice, Swiss defence budgets thus remained high until the fall of the Berlin Wall. The home nation was still seen as disconnected from the conflicts of others, and neutral non-association with foreign military alliances remained the foreign policy strategy of choice (Nationalrat 1980: 713–734).

This winning practice notwithstanding, it is important to note how the contending and subordinated conceptions of security nevertheless gradually contributed to an erosion of this traditional Swiss security imagery. The reason for this was that even if the classic Swiss syllogism of neutralist and military self-help factually continued throughout the Cold War, the emergent new insecurity discourses provided material for subtle changes in political argumentation. The 1979 national security doctrine quoted above, for instance, had forcefully asserted the primacy of military thinking about world politics. However, by virtue of relegating contending perspectives to secondary status, it had also exposed the latter as alternative possible platforms for international systematisation. As fleeting references, then, alternative ideas of national insecurity were presented, and they, too, were associated with greater understandings of international relations. In 1979, the recognition of the economic dimensions of security was the most explicit epistemic carrier of alternative international order of this kind. This was because the doctrine's secondary focus on economic insecurity suggested that revolutionary Iran – a strategically important oil producer – had embarked on an agenda of economic blackmail against the West (a practice that was even called 'terrorist', cf. Schweizerischer Bundesrat 1979: 4–8). At least as regards economics, then, the idea of Switzerland forming part of a larger insecurity community was being articulated in the Swiss polity by 1980, even if that kind of security politics had been conceptually relegated to secondary importance.

By the last decade of the Cold War, other issues also became framed in such collectivising terms. When justifying potential contributions to the Conference on Security and Cooperation in Europe (CSCE), for example, Foreign Minister Pierre Aubert no longer drew exclusively on traditional solidarity rationales to make his case (Von Tscharner 1995). Certainly, the Foreign Ministry still emphasised the solidarity line of argument and, with it, the implicit view of Switzerland as disconnected from what were seen as the problems of others. However, the CSCE's attempt to strengthen international disarmament frameworks was also recognised as beneficial to Switzerland, and as such the notion of a wider collective security system – i.e. one to which Switzerland was also party – was implicitly accepted (Schweizerischer Bundesrat 1979: 13–14). Development aid, too, was no longer only justified in moral terms of assistance to others by the 1980s. Although here, too, Swiss contributions to Third World countries were still often presented as following from a moral obligation to help the poor, the Foreign Ministry sometimes also presented development cooperation as following from the 'interdependent international system of states', and this line of argumentation again implied an emergent recognition of Switzerland as being part of some sort of larger collective (Fischer 2004: 270–282).

In the 1980s, then, the Swiss reconceptualisation of the international was very hesitant overall, and solidarity with the problems of others still provided the main justification for any 'active' foreign policy initiative. Regardless of the timid advancement of this new perspective, however, the new reading of world politics quickly gave rise to strong opposition inside the Swiss polity. Inside the Foreign Ministry, for example, Foreign Minister Aubert's statements provoked major clashes with the old generation of high-ranking diplomats. Rudolf Bindschedler, formerly the lead jurist in charge of formalising the *Petitpierre Doktrin* and the differentiation between 'political' and 'technical' forms of cooperation, but especially also Albert Weitnauer, Switzerland's first Secretary of State and thus the Foreign Ministry's 'number two' after Aubert, were adamantly opposed to the new perspectives. In 1980 – i.e. only one year after Weitnauer's promotion to Secretary of State – this conflict of diagnostics between the old generation of diplomats and the Ministry's political leadership had become so tense that the Federal Council relieved the Secretary of his duties.

The emergent new conceptualisation of world politics was also highly controversial in the political arena and society at large, as the 1986 referendum on UN membership shows. Starting in the 1970s, there had been new discussions in Swiss foreign policymaking circles about joining the United Nations. In the view of some, the accession of newly independent countries to the UN, membership of the two German states and the promotion of the People's Republic of China to the UN Security Council had turned the UN into a quasi-universal organisation. With this, UN membership became formally conceivable as a permissible type of international engagement in the perspective of the *Petitpierre Doktrin* (Hoffmann 1995: 64–65). What was more, the decision for the former Austrian Foreign Minister Kurt Waldheim to succeed U Thant as Secretary-General also suggested that the UN had become more favourable to the membership of neutrals, and there was an expectation among Swiss policymakers that the UN might tacitly accept a unilateral declaration of Swiss neutrality upon accession (Eidgenössisches Departement für Auswärtige Angelegenheiten 1991). More functionally, some also felt that UN membership was in the interest of Switzerland proper, for the country risked being seen as a blockade runner if it did not support the sanctions of an increasingly universal security organisation. Again, others supported the idea either as a means of inserting Switzerland's mediation efforts into a multilateral setting or as a way of expanding Geneva's role as host city of international organisations (Fischer 2004: 168–180, 309–328).

After long internal debates, the Federal Council decided to submit the idea of UN membership to popular vote. In its 1981 explanatory message to parliament, the Federal Council largely justified the proposal using traditional solidarity rationales – i.e. the argument that such contributions would both be a benevolent contribution to the challenges of others and a means of promoting recognition of Swiss neutrality as such. In part, however, authorities also pointed at collective security concerns as a means of explaining why UN membership was not only possible, but, indeed, also needed. The government developed further, and more squarely 'self-interested', arguments in support of UN membership:

> Our independence and security do not merely depend on whether we are exposed to direct military challenges. Political stability, the economic and social situation of our environment, and the respect and codification of international law are important factors as well. These elements influence our national and international situation, and as such they must be considered.
>
> (Schweizerischer Bundesrat 1981: 10)

Seen from this perspective, Swiss solidarity contributions were now also derived from certain collective concerns, and Swiss UN membership started to be depicted as a means of promoting the nation's reputation inside an underspecified 'international community' of which it was part. As the government suggested, moving subtly towards an understanding of world politics from whose dynamics the home nation was not spared: 'The international situation and reputation of a country are not only issues of one's own political choice or power. They also result from the quality of contributions made to the resolution of those problems facing the international community' (Schweizerischer Bundesrat 1981: 10).

When submitted to parliamentary debate, these arguments drew heavy criticism. In the view of traditionalists, the government proposal contained nothing but 'flowery words about solidarity' and not enough consideration of the role of neutrality. Challenging the authorities' assessment of world politics and the home nation's position therein, some parliamentarians even charged the government with 'not pursuing the national interest', factually criticising the Federal Council for treason. Prominent business leaders were among those who rallied to the anti-UN campaign in the course of these debates. In their view, Switzerland should not put the *Petitpierre Doktrin* at risk, as UN membership might obstruct the successful 'technical' national foreign policy agenda in the areas of international trade and business (Fischer 2004: 397, 418). When parliament finally submitted UN membership to popular vote in 1986, the proposal was rejected by a two-thirds majority. Analyses suggested that there were two main reasons why UN membership had been so clearly rejected: on one hand, the end of détente between East and West, a development that aided the more sceptical interpretations of world politics; and on the other, the failure of membership advocates to engage with the question of whether and how UN membership might be compatible with the neutralist Swiss self-positioning (Möckli 2000b). The 1986 vote on UN membership, then, illustrates again how contending conceptions of world order empowered or disqualified different kinds of foreign policies. In the mid-1980s, the emergent positioning of Switzerland as part of a larger community of nations had found insufficient support inside the Swiss political system; consequently, the need for UN membership was seen as not very meaningful by the majority of the electorate.

Conclusion

Switzerland provides an interesting case of how securitisation endangers, orders and conditions the international. *Substantively*, the Swiss ways of securitising the East–West conflict created local knowledge of a highly confrontational international context, but also an understanding of the home nation as not being directly affected by such danger. As a specific form of securitisation, neutralism subject-positioned foreign actors in antagonistic relations towards each other but not the home nation, and this means that Switzerland was hauled into a bystander position. World politics was understood organised in ways that turned the home nation into a proverbial island of peace in a sea of confrontational interstate relations. This 'disconnected' positioning of the self contrasts fairly strongly with the securitisation practices observed in neighbouring countries, and it also empowered fairly different types of foreign and defence policies – namely, autonomous defence, global trade and 'solidarity humanitarianism' (see Table 6.1 for an overview). By the same token, the Swiss case also shows how *procedurally*, security politics does not always take the form of controversial debate. For most of the time between 1945 and 1990, the neutralist reading of world politics proposed an uncontested truth about the international. After centuries of practice, the Swiss focus on neutrality had stabilised the linkage between world order description and foreign policymaking itself. For many in Switzerland, neutralism was held to 'naturally' enable neutrality policy and vice versa. Given this routine – and in stark contrast to the Gaullist period in neighbouring France, to which the next chapter turns – the political responsibilities and choices involved in producing world order perspectives and appropriating these for specific foreign policy ends were barely recognised, let alone problematised in the Swiss Confederation. Taken together, the Swiss case study thus gives further indications as to the interplay between democratic institutions and sense-making and the recursive relation between sense-making and foreign policymaking. In the first regard, it shows that security debates must not necessarily be pluralistic in a formally pluralistic polity. In the second regard, it also shows how routinised foreign policy strategies may perpetuate underlying world order concepts in themselves.

Table 6.1 Swiss constructions of international (in-)security after World War II

		1950s–1970s	1980s
East–West confrontation	Source	Regional confrontation of two blocks and alliances[D]	Global confrontation of two blocks and alliances[D]
	Target	The international – each block targets the other[D]	
	Relation	Existential relation between the two blocks, but no relation of opposition between blocks and Switzerland[D]	
	World order description	Cold War as a highly militarised conflict of two groups of states, but also as a conflict of others. Switzerland as an island of peace in a sea of power politics.	
	Conditioning effects	Fulfilment of duties of a neutral country – i.e. autonomous territorial defence against nobody specific and defence unaided by any foreign partner. Outside the military domain, global trade and business cooperation with any party. Also, 'solidarity humanitarianism' with the problems of others.	
	Policy enactment	Autonomous defence, membership in economic organisations (OEEC, EFTA and GATT), mediation and humanitarian efforts, good offices, but no UN, NATO or Warsaw Pact membership	
Economic stability/security	Source	N/A	Economics not a 'real' security issue[D] Iran[M] Poverty[M] Other unspecified sources[M]
	Target	N/A	Not a problem for Switzerland[D] Industrialised world[M] The 'international community'[M]
	Relation	N/A	N/A (not a problem for Switzerland)[D] Challenge[M]
	World order description	N/A	Secondary international challenges exist, affect everyone including Switzerland, and need to be solved
	Conditioning effects	N/A	Call for more cooperative foreign policy strategies
	Policy enactment	N/A	Attempt at UN membership, argumentative bolstering of development aid, new 'self-interested' justification for mediation and humanitarian aid

7 Gaullism as world order perspective

The Gaullist reconstruction of the United States and 'its' NATO

After World War II, a number of, at times, congruent and, at times, outright incompatible articulations of international insecurity circulated inside the French political system. Even if Atlanticism prevailed for a short period, the events surrounding the *Plan Pleven*, as shown in Chapter 4, exemplify how France lacked a stable categorisation of the world's most basic interrelations. However, it was not only the handling of Germany, the framing of the USSR and the categorisation of the world's new superpower, the United States, which was controversial. The French political system was also seriously challenged by imperial and domestic troubles. Abroad, France's empire was disintegrating at high speed. In the mid-1950s, France was forced out of South East Asia. Morocco and Tunisia left the *Union Française*, Algeria plunged into a dirty guerrilla conflict and an attempt to reassert co-ownership of the Suez Canal by military means was forcefully aborted by France's own ally, the United States (Meynaud 1962; Zartmann 1964). Domestically, French civil society was torn between the political ideologies of the time, and it also lacked effective national leadership. The Fourth Republic was a highly unstable political system in which governments succeeded each other at record speed (Furniss 1954).

In the mid-1950s, both new (post-war) and old (imperial) categories of world politics and France's position therein thus came under heavy pressure (Glardet 1960). There was no accepted vision of world order, and no individual political groupings were strong enough to authoritatively advance their vision at the expense of others (Vernant 1963). This situation changed in the years following 1958, when a military coup forced Prime Minister Pierre Pflimlin out of office, bringing General Charles de Gaulle back to power and leading to the adoption of a new constitution and republican system, the Fifth Republic. The Fifth Republic instituted a strong presidential system. Its design stabilised French politics, but it also restructured national foreign and security policymaking. Under the new constitution, the government was no longer obliged to justify any minor policy issue to the legislature, and parliamentary debates themselves were reorganised in ways so that not as many speakers – usually only the party leaders – could now comment on security and foreign affairs. Practically, this specific rearranging of formal powers helped the ruling Gaullists significantly in advancing and implementing their distinctive views. And, indeed, the Gaullist circles' interpretation of world politics gained much epistemic currency in France after the institution of the Fifth Republic, exerting lasting influence over national foreign and security affairs.

As a distinct reading of world politics, Gaullism encompassed a variety of positions. One of its key components was an adversarial reinterpretation of the United States and NATO and thus also a reordering of their relations with France. Importantly, the Gaullist endangering of the United States and NATO differed substantially from the French communists' characterisation, which centred on capitalist ideology and was also much more radical in its opposition. Also, contrary to popular externalist accounts of French Cold War politics, the emergent Gaullist reading of world politics had fairly little to do with simple envy of US power or an emotional quest for honour and *grandeur* – even if solemn calls for heightened national independence can also be found in the French political system of the time. On the contrary, archive work shows that Gaullist circles' adversarial rereading of the United States – a crucial and long-term ally of France – derived directly from their articulation of a differentiated and alternative conception of international (in-)security.

This articulation departed from French discontent with the kind of insecurity community recognised by the Atlantic Alliance. Starting in the early 1950s, an understanding crystallised inside France that its allies did not see the Mediterranean space as a shared security concern. Not only was Algeria, which was part of metropolitan France, excluded from the alliance's cover, but French politicians also felt that the allies were actively obstructing their efforts to manage that region. In 1956, the United States stopped a Franco-British intervention in Suez. When violence erupted in Algeria, French requests for an extension of the allied operations theatre across the Mediterranean Sea and French command of NATO's Mediterranean fleet, 'the vital link to North Africa' (Assemblée 1962: 55/Pierre Pflimlin), were also flatly rejected by the United States (LeM 1964, 1966a). Indeed, the United States, together with the United Kingdom, refused French demands for exclusive arms shipping rights to Morocco and Tunisia – a means by which France had sought to prevent arms trafficking into Algeria (Vernant 1963). With this series of refusals, the view emerged that the US, in particular, did not actually share the same conception of insecurity as France (Assemblée 1959d: 3670/Foreign Minister Maurice Couve de Murville, 1964b: 1005/Foreign Policy Commission President Maurice Schuman). For Gaullists, US actions towards North Africa showed that the US did not subscribe to the view of this region as a shared security concern – a failure that was all the more incomprehensible given that French politicians had accepted Cuba in such terms on their part (Assemblée 1962: 55/Pierre Pflimlin).

The emergent Gaullist description of the US as a 'problem of sorts' was soon also driven by new strategic syllogisms. In the view of French strategists, the USSR's development of intercontinental strike capabilities had a tremendous impact on the security of France. Not only did this arming bring a general fear of a global nuclear holocaust, as witnessed during the Cuban Crisis. It also gravely impaired French trust in America's readiness to defend Europe from Soviet attack (De Bavière 1968). Despite the controversy surrounding the question of whether nuclear parity of the two superpowers was a situation still to come or already reached (Erler 1964; Gallois 1966), it became an accepted fact in France that the very existence of Soviet nuclear weapons as such had factually impaired America's willingness to protect Europe. As the former head of France's delegation to NATO's Parliamentary Assembly argued:

> Since the moment when the USSR found itself capable of threatening massive retaliation against the United States, the very nature of the Atlantic alliance had been modified. The United States are now directly threatened. It cannot accept, for reasons that seem secondary to the American people, to be implicated into a conflict that, for the first time in America's history, could risk the almost total destruction of its territory.
>
> (Palewski 1964: 119)

By the 1960s, the United States was thus not only seen as failing to endorse the French establishment's conception of North Africa as a shared security concern. Nuclear syllogisms also seemed to stratify the very insecurity community that had motivated North Atlantic cooperation in the first place. In the 1960s, *le monde atlantique* was no longer understood to be as uniformly threatened by the East, and thus aligned, as it had been earlier. The US adoption of a doctrine of flexible (nuclear) response seemingly confirmed that understanding. The US renunciation of massive nuclear retaliation in case of war, according to French strategists and Gaullists, directly exposed Europe and France to conventional attack from the East (Beaufre 1962; Assemblée 1966b: 781/Diomède Catroux). As a consequence of technological developments and US strategy, then, the US had come to be viewed as an unreliable ally and something of a source of European insecurity. With this, the question of whether France, Europe and the US still formed part of exactly the same insecurity community was also raised on a global scale – i.e. beyond French concerns with North Africa.

NATO was gradually compacted into this view. In the beginning, NATO was merely seen as helping to execute US nuclear strategy, imposing a defunct defence doctrine onto European allies (Gallois 1966). Soon, however, NATO was also being criticised for reproducing the block system and the partition of Europe itself. Because it aligned the Western allies increasingly closely with each other and against one common danger, the organisation was accused of blindly institutionalising the 'American division of the world' into two antagonist blocs. This systematisation of world politics was not considered adequate to overcome the danger of global nuclear war. Worse still, it was also considered to be a direct problem for France, for it was seen as turning France into a co-target of any action directed against the West. 'The American organisation', as de Gaulle eventually called NATO (LeM 1966d), risked entangling France and

Europe in the US's own agenda and problems, such as Vietnam (Assemblée 1966b: 777/René Capitant, 1966a: 624/Prime Minister Georges Pompidou). For France, this was a particularly dangerous position. NATO headquarters were located just outside Paris, and arguably they offered a prime target for any retaliatory action against Western policies, no matter whose (Assemblée 1966a: 689/ Foreign Minister Maurice Couve de Murville).

Taken together, the Gaullist rereading of the United States and NATO was thus fairly strongly driven by differential conceptions of the organisation of international (in-)security. It was now up for debate whether France's, the United States' and NATO's views of world politics were still as well-aligned as in the late 1940s and early 1950s, and Gaullists claimed that they were, indeed, becoming ever more incongruent. In their view, France's Mediterranean perspective had not been reciprocated by its allies, the Atlantic community had become stratified in itself and the 'American' systematisation of the world into two radically opposing blocks was insufficiently differentiated. With time, the latter 'American view of the world' also came to be portrayed as a totalising and hegemonic knowledge project – i.e. as an attempt at comprehensive world ordering that was being imposed on France and Europe (Aron 1986; Bozo 1995). NATO was held complicit in this process, since its integration of allied armed forces solidified the binary division of the world in practice. It was based on this awareness of differential world order perspectives that Gaullist policymakers then developed a vocal agenda for national emancipation and heightened independence. Rather than to submit to the 'American' ordering of the world, and thus also of France's relations with others, they called ever more overtly for the articulation and enactment of France's own reading of world politics (Assemblée 1962: 42/Prime Minister Georges Pompidou).

The Gaullist endangering of the US and 'its' NATO was not uncontested locally, on the contrary. Leftist politicians, for instance, continued to advocate for an even more adversarial – and, indeed, outright existential – securitisation of the United States. Presenting the US as the prime enemy of workers worldwide, they criticised the Gaullists for failing to comprehend the true dangerousness of the US and 'its' capitalist system (Assemblée 1962: 60/Guy Ebrard). Atlanticists, too, put up ardent opposition, although for very different reasons. In their view, the very endangering of the United States was completely unfounded (Assemblée 1966a: 684/René Pleven). Atlanticists disqualified the government's push for French nuclear armament as untenable nationalistic self-positioning (Assemblée 1968: 5129/Jean Montalat) and later even criticised the Gaullist framing of the United States for having facilitated the Red Army's invasion of Czechoslovakia (Sauder 1996). Atlanticist politicians, then, upheld the securitisation of the USSR as an existential problem common to the entire Atlantic community. At the same time, they rejected the view that one of France's co-victims of that very danger – i.e. the United States – had become a source, of sorts, of French insecurity itself.

Despite these sustained criticisms, the Gaullist rendering of the US became ever more influential inside the French political system in the early 1960s

(Hassner 1976). Scholars (Vernant 1963, 1970), journalists (LeM 1966b, 1966c) and a powerful coalition of politicians (Assemblée 1966a: 641/Pierre Comte-Offenbach) subscribed in large numbers to the differentiated endangering of the US and NATO, and the coming-to-power of this distinct perspective then guided various French foreign policy initiatives. Initially, the Mediterranean focus gave way to diplomatic efforts to align the alliance with France's conception of North Africa as a shared security concern. Strategic syllogisms were then followed up with attempts to prevent NATO from adopting a flexible (nuclear) response as official doctrine, as well as proposals for a new institutional arrangement of Western leadership itself. Later, the apprehension of incongruent worldviews enabled a vocal agenda for national and European emancipation from US foreign policy and hegemony (De la Serre 1982), as well as costly efforts to develop an independent nuclear arsenal (Centre d'Etudes de Politique Etrangère 1959: 129–130). Most spectacularly, perhaps, the Gaullist reconstruction of the US and 'its' NATO also empowered France's abandonment of the latter and the expulsion of NATO from French territory in 1966.

Importantly, however, the Gaullist perspective did *not* empower, and did *not* lead to, rejection of the Atlantic Alliance itself. As a result of the Gaullist perspective, France left NATO, but did not withdraw from the 1949 Washington Treaty and also pledged full military support to its allies in case of unprovoked attack from abroad (Assemblée 1999). Gaullists conceptualised the United States as an *adversaire-partenaire* (Touraine 1993), hence as adversary and partner at the very same time. The endangering of America – its interpretation as an actor causing insecurity by virtue of imposing an unwarranted, partially incongruent and partially defunct view on the world – led France to take critical distance from the US through foreign policy. But this did not imply the converse argument, according to which the US was no longer threatened, together with France and others, by the Soviet Union. Confronting local opposition, Gaullists did not accept the view that it had to be either the US or the USSR that caused existential danger. Instead, they maintained that *both* superpowers were sources of national and international insecurity (even if the USSR was held to be more threatening overall). As regards France's relations with the US, this 'dialectical' perspective led to a critical distancing from, but not an outright refutation of, the US. As Louis Terrenoire, parliamentarian and former speaker of General de Gaulle, explained France's foreign policy agenda towards the United States, NATO and the co-signatories of the Washington Treaty:

> While remaining fully truthful to the Atlantic Alliance, which will remain as solid in its foundations and obligations as long as the danger to which it corresponds remains what it is, the government of France has shown that its faithfulness to her allies must not necessarily be accompanied by its *satellisation*.
>
> (Assemblée 1964a: 981; *satellisation* denotes the process of becoming another power's satellite)

Re-engaging the USSR

The Soviet Union, then, was upheld as the primary source of danger by the Fifth Republic's ruling circles, despite their paralleling securitisation of the US and NATO. But this does not mean that the 'communist danger' signified the same thing to Gaullists as to other factions in France or was understood in the same way that it had been years earlier. Indeed, just as Gaullists demanded ever more confidently the pursuit of 'France's own vision of the world', they also called for re-engagement with the concept of the 'Soviet threat' that Atlanticists had earlier promoted so successfully. In their view, the very dangerousness of the Soviet Union had to be pondered anew and outside the binary 'American' framework of world politics. This also meant that the USSR in its entirety – its economy, people and culture – had to become much better known (Assemblée 1959c: 1962ff/Arthur Conte), for the USSR was still deemed a fairly 'mysterious' and unknown entity by many in France. Starting in the 1950s, study delegations were thus sent to the East with a view to providing comprehensive assessments of the Soviet Union, its composition, intentions and concerns. Later, high-level meetings between French and Soviet leaders were promoted. Nikita Khrushchev, for instance, was invited to Paris, and in 1966 – the same year that France left and expelled NATO – President de Gaulle visited Moscow.

As part of a longer process, Gaullists re-engaged the prevailing securitisation of communism and developed a differential – and, in their syllogism, also an 'independently French' – view of it. This process evolved in tandem with Khrushchev's policy of pacific international coexistence (Doly 1978). For Gaullists, that declaration – as well as the critical findings of the various study delegations – confirmed the view that France's relations with the USSR were tense, yet non-violent (Assemblée 1960, 1966c, 1967). The term 'coexistence', in the understanding of commentators close to the French ruling circles, represented an acknowledgement of a basic right to exist. It included the possibility of any type of exchange short of interference into domestic affairs, but it did not exclude rivalry and peaceful competition (XXX 1960: 221). Taking into account the Soviet agenda for world revolution, Gaullists claimed that strong rivalry was an accurate description of Europe's relations with the USSR. This meant the USSR was securitised as a collective and fairly important source of danger to the West, but not as a totalising and existential danger. Whereas the United States had become framed as an *adversaire-partenaire*, the USSR came to be considered an *adversaire-rivale* – i.e. something between an outright hostile adversary and a more peaceful rival (Touraine 1993).

As could be expected, this rendering of the Soviet danger was not uncontested in the Fifth Republic, and various world events and global developments were seized by different political factions, in order to make a case for alternative characterisations. For some, the Soviet Union's alleged achievement of nuclear parity with Washington had turned the former hyper-confident and utterly unpredictable, rendering it more aggressive and dangerous than ever (Erler 1964: 435). In the view of such politicians, the USSR remained a revolutionary *marrée montante* – an excessively armed nation destined to seize any opportunity for aggression and subversion worldwide (Doly 1978: 275). Accordingly, it was in intimate response to communist existential global danger that all French foreign policy had to be conceptualised. Others challenged *any* endangering of the East. Members of the French Communist Party in particular stressed the Soviet Union's pacifist orientation. Focusing on capitalism and German militarism, these representatives sketched the US as a hostile power and the Federal Republic as a dangerous, fascist and revanchist regime (Assemblée 1959b: 380ff/Billoux, 1975: 4940/Raymond Rhétoré). Socialists proposed yet another organisation of international insecurity. Presenting the USSR as 'a bigger threat than Germany', this party denounced the erection of 'Soviet protectorates' in Eastern Europe as much as it recognised adversarial relations with the Federal Republic (Assemblée 1959b: 379ff./Arthur Conte).

These contending renderings notwithstanding, the Gaullist method of securitising the USSR prevailed, and it thus had the most direct influence on the structuring of French foreign policymaking. It allowed France to maintain its commitment to Western security cooperation, but it also enabled it to promote treaty-based cultural, political, technical and economic exchanges with the East (Assemblée 1960, 1966c, 1973: 2261/Foreign Minister Michel Jobert). Conversely, it disempowered more exclusionary foreign policy agendas, whether all-out integration into the Western camp or all-out withdrawal from it. Closer to the 1970s, numerous politicians then also connected the two above actors with each other. Developing the notion of the 'superpower condominium', they argued that neither great power actually sought to overpower the other. Current events were seized on to substantiate this reading, and history was reinterpreted in this light as well. America's assurance to the East that West Germany would not be permitted more substantial armament (Vernant 1973), for instance, its acceptance of the Brezhnev doctrine (according to which the USSR claimed the right to sort out things in Eastern Europe as it pleased), shipment of grain to the East ('sustaining communism in its home country') and alleged tolerance of the Soviet smashing of the Hungarians (Assemblée 1966a: 637/Pierre Clostermann) were all seen to prove this view. This meant that the two-block system became increasingly widely seen as having evolved into an unholy alliance between Washington and Moscow – i.e. a collaborative organisation of world politics that allowed each to impose leadership over their respective region. The continuing partition of Europe, Korea and Cyprus (Centre d'Etudes de Politique Etrangère 1967; Assemblée 1978: 2685/Michel Debré), the earlier US abortion of the Franco-British adventure in Suez, the exclusion of European powers from the US-Soviet nuclear arms limitation talks (Heisbourg 1988; Silvestri 1988) and the eventual US-UK proposal for Europe's denuclearisation were all seen as attempts to keep Europe vulnerable and hostage to the superpowers (Assemblée 1973: 2261/Foreign Minister Michel Jobert; Weisenfeld 1975; Gallois 1977). As Maurice Couve de Murville polemically exclaimed in parliament: 'The Cold War is over! The armistice had been concluded between the Russians and the Americans in 1962, after that strange Cuban crisis' (Assemblée 1973: 2268).

The 'superpower condominium' is fundamental to an explanation of French foreign policymaking during the late Cold War years. It codifies the view that the USSR and the US were no longer threatening each other, but that they were both important sources of insecurity in Europe at large. The Gaullist securitisation of the two superpowers, then, created mutually supportive imageries of collective danger on the continent. Even if the identified threats differed in their intensity and reach (the East was considered more threatening overall, in spite of the securitisation of the US, and it was also held by some to be more problematic to the US than the US was to the USSR, although for others both superpowers had stopped challenging each other altogether), the ways in which Gaullists securitised East and West in practice meant that France was positioned unmistakeably in a pan-European insecurity community. As has been shown, this reading was not the sole perspective available inside France, and contending securitisations of East and West proposed fairly different positions for France and Europe in world politics. Given the dominance of the Gaullist interpretations, however, the view that France and Europe had become inescapably caught up in a common insecurity context prevailed in France, and this enabled a distinctly 'European' foreign policy agenda in return.

The creation and expansion of 'Europe'

Indeed, the construction of Europe as an insecurity community represents a third key element of Gaullism. Certainly, 'Europe' had been used in collectivising terms earlier in history, as a signifier for imperial global power, for example, or as a loose reference to Western thought and values, some of which had also been held to be in danger by various authors at various points in time. After World War II, however, the rendering of Europe as a collective of similarly threatened societies was articulated in new and much more consistent terms. During the Fourth and Fifth Republics, the communitarian construction of Europe advanced gradually, and it followed partially complementary and partially contradictory interpretations of world politics advanced by different epistemological camps. In the view of nationalists, for instance, the German nation created a community of threatened states that was very Western in shape, including all Western European countries and France. Europe also signified a Western entity to Atlanticists, in whose view communism posed a danger to all of Western Europe, including France *and* West Germany, and beyond that also to North America. For Gaullists, Europe meant something subtly different again. In their view, it was US *and* Soviet danger that turned Europe into a common political entity. Europe's subordination to the whims of both superpowers, de Gaulle believed, transformed the continent but not the North Atlantic space into a *communauté de destin* (Doly 1978: 280).

In each of these cases, a certain kind of Europe was seen as united in some form and as a result of some distinct configuration of international insecurity. Different conceptions of this kind enabled different foreign policy strategies, and Chapter 4 showed how this occurred for nationalists and Atlanticists. Yet, the

Gaullist conception of Europe had the most direct influence on foreign policy-making during the years of Gaullist rule. Placing France, Western Europe and West Germany – but not the superpowers, Eastern Europe or the rest of the world – in one group, it laid the basis for an active foreign policy agenda aimed at organising and integrating European power (Kawalkowski 1964). In the view of Gaullists, this was necessary for Europe to liberate itself from the superpowers' division of the world, the partition of Europe and hyper-militarisation of the continent. Given divergent conceptions of 'insecure Europe', this agenda was met with various degrees of support or criticism at home. Atlanticists and communists challenged the exclusion of one or the other superpower from European organisation (LeM 1970, 1973). Other political camps cared less about the 'external' borders of the Gaullist notion of Europe and more about its inner composition. National-conservatives, for instance, criticised the equation of France with Europe, irrespective of further superpower dimensions. In their view, any idea of a 'common Europe' was *un phantasme des théologiens d'une petite Europe fusionnée* – an idealistic projection of cosmopolitanism and transnational destiny (Debré 1953; LeM 1978). By the same token, the quest for European institutions was also denounced as aiding revanchist Germany in its quest for continental hegemony (Armengaud 1960).

While there had been significant agreement on the positioning of 'Europe' as a community of nations with collective security concerns, then, its precise inner and outer boundaries – the question of who shared what kind of insecurity with whom and without whom, but also the question regarding what or whom Europe had to protect itself from in the first place – remained a subject of debate. Furthermore, the practical promotion of European cooperation was controversial, though more so for international interlocutors than for French politicians themselves. This was so because for the ruling Gaullists, the prevailing situation was not merely seen as requiring the unification of Europe. More than that, it was also held to demand integration of European power under sovereign French leadership. As Gaullists saw France as being in need of active emancipation from the world ordering politics of the superpowers and Europe as being put into harm's way by them, their representatives did not hesitate to combine these two rationales and call for a *French* lead on European organisation. In few instances was this claim to regional management expressed more clearly than in the French strategic debates. As Jean-Paul Palewski succinctly argued in one such debate: 'Is an integrated European strategic force possible today? No. Does Europe need to obtain its nuclear independence? Yes. Which country can give Europe her strategic independence? France.' (Palewski 1964: 130).

Unsurprisingly, perhaps, this view received only limited support from the very European nations that France sought to organise. By the 1960s, French politicians had already realised that, contrary to expectations, continental integration was not proceeding as readily as they had foreseen (cf. Assemblée 1980: 483/Robert Montdargent). European governments, they realised, only half-heartedly supported the European project envisaged by France. The UK, in particular, was seen as slowing down France's European agenda

(Assemblée 1964a: 983/Louis Terrenoire) and accused of upholding an 'Anglo-Saxon' organisation of international politics. As a result, de Gaulle began promoting a much more continental conception of Europe, rejecting the United Kingdom's accession to the European institutions (Vernant 1970: 624). A differential and problematic framing of the UK endured for years in the Fifth Republic. Only after de Gaulle left power and a dispute deepened between British and US policymakers over nuclear armament (the Skybolt Affair) did French politicians become more favourable again to the inclusion of the UK into 'Europe' on both the epistemological and institutional levels (Hassner 1976).

These tensions with the UK are indicative of the opposition with which the Gaullist claim to regional leadership was confronted internationally. Domestically, it assisted in the reformulation of that claim. On the one hand, politicians started to sketch European integration more broadly as a means of creating a pole of economic, political and social attraction, as opposed to an integrated power (Harmel 1971: 114–115). On the other hand, it also led to the more active and cooperative recruitment of partners for the purpose of European integration. In practice, this meant that French politicians were also set to re-engage their historical enemy, Germany. As shown earlier, Germany occupied an increasingly ambivalent position in French security debates – namely, both as a source of danger and as a partner against common insecurity. This tension also continued under the Gaullist governments. In their view, Germany still had significant potential to impair the security of France. At the same time, however, there was also an understanding that France had to work with the demographic and economic power of its neighbour if it was to counter communism, prevent Germany's independent reconstitution and liberate Europe from the superpowers.

Again, Gaullists rejected the binary choice of seeing Germany either as an ally or as an enemy. However, the adversarial component of their conception of Germany was nevertheless re-evaluated at lower levels over time. As concerns with the 'superpower condominium' gained importance, Germany became ever more crucial for integrating Europe. In the early 1960s, de Gaulle personally jump-started the improvement of bilateral relations. At his initiative, the Elysée Treaty of 1963 instituted regular high-level visits between the respective heads of state. In parallel, a number of remaining territorial disputes were solved by plebiscite or negotiation. The *Saarland* had already been returned to West Germany in 1957. In 1962, new proposals were made to resolve further border disputes, such as the Mundat Forest (Assemblée 1963). With time, the bilateral process thus initiated led to ever closer consultation on a variety of topics and a gradual de-emphasis of the German danger. This process of measured bilateralism, the first French White Book of 1972 makes clear, was deliberately driven by the quest for European integration and continental emancipation (Gouvernement Français 1972).

Non-adversarial framing of Germany, then, had been in the making in the 1960s and 1970s, but it was far from instantaneous. Germany had *not* been instantly de-securitised by French politicians, on the contrary. Like others in France, Gaullists, too, kept a watchful eye on their eastern neighbour, although for different reasons. For some, Bonn seemed too 'American' in orientation, and this raised the question of whether bilateral cooperation truly helped the European project or whether it would, in fact, produce a 'bigger American Trojan Horse in Europe than the UK' (Assemblée 1964a: 966/Foreign Minister Maurice Couve de Murville). For others, Germany was still too risky to work with. This view was supported by politicians from various camps, who insisted on the inherent dangerousness of the German population (LeM 1976; Hoffmann 2000) and also argued that fear of Germany had been the Elysée Treaty's sole rationale (Weisenfeld 1975). Franco-German relations hence remained highly ambivalent for a long time. The Ailleret-Lemnitzer Accords of 1967, for instance, which – at Bonn's request – guaranteed that French troops could continue to be stationed in the FRG even after France's withdrawal from NATO, were seen both as a means for countering the common communist challenge and as a French show of force toward Germany. In the 1970s, it was still possible to find explicit justifications of French military spending that make watchful reference to the defence budget of West Germany (LeM 1976).

It was not until the 1980s that the adversarial framing of Germany reached a veritable low point. At this point, the Afghan War and the *Euromissiles* crisis lent much weight to the Gaullist analysis of European insecurities being produced by the two superpowers (Adrets 1984). By the same token, West German politicians' own attempts to transcend the division of Europe (by virtue of *Ostpolitik*), their pledge to honour international treaties and to accept Germany's post-war borders to the East (Erler 1964), their endorsement of North African stability as a common European task (De Bavière 1968) and their more recent proclamations of Europe as a collective of similarly placed and threatened nations (Rühe 1988) helped sustain the gradual reframing of Germany in France. In the 1980s, this situation allowed for an expansion of the Elysée Treaty – i.e. the adoption of bilateral consultation mechanisms in the event that French nuclear weapons were targeted at objects on German soil – and the planning of a joint military battle group, the French-German Eurocorps (Bertram 1979; Heisbourg 1995).

After the initial construction of Europe, and in parallel with a certain delay in its more 'cooperative' reformulation, the issue of Eastern Europe was finally also addressed. Starting in the 1960s, the view was revived that Eastern European countries were not merely dangers to the West, given their membership in the Warsaw Pact, but that they were threatened by Moscow themselves. Indeed, such a conception of Eastern Europe had already been in circulation at an earlier date. In the late 1940s, Raymond Aron had forcefully argued that the Soviets used East Germany to threaten the Poles into submission, since they could always make East Germans demand the return of the former German Eastern Territories – i.e. the territory on which post-war Poland was founded (Aron 1949). In the 1960s and 1970s, this theme was renewed following the Chinese-Soviet split, which itself helped question the presentation of communism as a monolithic block (LeM 1970; Hermet 1980). With it came a constituent denunciation of the Soviet repression of the Poles, Czechs, Bulgarians, Romanians and East Germans (Windsor 1982; Beltran 2000) and a re-articulation of Eastern Europe as co-victims of communist danger and 'friends of France' (Assemblée 1976: 2697/Foreign Minister Jean Sauvagnargues). As scholar Pierre Hassner summarised this epistemological re-ordering of European security relations:

> Similar to the fact that the Cold War has not disappeared but a multiplicity of Cold Wars had emerged, and so in some sense put the old one into perspective, also the monolithic blocs had been replaced not by non-alignment but by a multiplicity of alignments, alignments which do not eliminate the old ones but which put them into perspective as well. A country such as Romania remains aligned with the communist states against the non-communists, but it is also aligned with France against bipolarity.
>
> (Hassner 1976: 1034)

This 'second' Gaullist reconstruction of Europe is central to explaining French foreign policymaking during the final years of the Cold War. It distinguished between Eastern European nations and the USSR conceptually, and it also defined their interrelations in antagonistic terms. In doing so, it catered to a much more 'continental' definition of the European insecurity community, which was seen as created by Soviet danger. This new knowledge of the organisation of European insecurity motivated the French foreign policy initiatives of the time. With regard to West Germany, it enabled forceful support for *Ostpolitik*. More than that, it enabled veritable demands on Bonn to recognise the inner-German frontier and launch a reconciliation process with East Germany (Harmel 1971). Commentators made clear just how intimately this demand was connected with the creation of a broader European community and the liberation of Europe (broadly defined) from the superpowers:

> By recognising its current eastern frontiers, Germany could eliminate the fundamental obstacles to its unification and contribute to the extension of Europe to its historical limits [...]. There is no doubt that a quick German adoption of the French idea of Europe could diminish the scepticism of the Eastern nations, accelerate their rapprochement to the Community, open up perspectives for their own emancipation and so prepare the reunification of all of historical Europe, this is to say: the return to Europe of East Germany, Poland, Hungary, Romania and Czechoslovakia.
>
> (Kawalkowski 1964: 275, 276)

With regard to Eastern Europe, the same perspective enabled French assistance to the Helsinki Process and collaboration on the establishment of a pan-European security organisation (Smouts 1974). Taken together, then, France's conception of 'Europe' as an entity united by common insecurities had been actively constructed and was then reformulated into subtly different systematisations of world politics over time. Moving from a French-led and fairly sovereign conception to a 'Europe of equals', including West Germany (and temporarily excluding the United Kingdom), it had been expanded into a much more 'continental' concept by the 1980s. These evolving Gaullist conceptions were always paralleled by other local truths about the organisation of international insecurity. Atlanticist, nationalist, communist and others – indeed, also factions of the Gaullist movement itself – all advanced more or less contending conceptions of the European insecurity community (cf. Laux 1973; Baillot 1983). As was the case with the US, NATO and the USSR, however, the particular perspective on Europe described above prevailed in policymaking circles. It is on the basis of that knowledge of international insecurity that European integration was made possible and was pursued in the distinct way it was – namely, as a westwards-oriented agenda first, accompanied by a more intimate bilateral agenda with West Germany second and as a pan-European project third.

The late Cold War years – towards global insecurities

The US, NATO, the USSR, Germany, the UK, North Africa and Europe clearly represent the most central components of French security thinking and world ordering between the late 1950s and mid-1980s. The specific securitisation of these key elements was often subject to debate. Overall, however, their 'Gaullist' rendering prevailed fairly clearly until the end of the Cold War. This meant that the end of détente between the US and the USSR had surprisingly little effect on French foreign affairs in the 1980s (De la Serre 1982). It also meant that the Gaullist thinking scheme was continued by the first socialist President of France, François Mitterrand (elected to the presidency in 1981), and his cabinet of socialist and communist ministers. Instead of bringing France into the closer orbit of the East, as critics feared (Weisenfeld 1986), and instead of disbanding the French nuclear forces, as Mitterrand himself had pledged earlier (Klein 1978), once in power the leftist parties continued with Gaullist views and policies. Their strategic doctrine of *dissuasion tous azimuts* or omnidirectional (nuclear) defence was – with the exception of minor deviations (Moïsi 1985) – a quasi-perfect continuation of the Gaullist perspectives formulated in the 1960s (Klein 1983: 329). A quote from 1975 indicates that the French political left professed a very 'Gaullist' view on the international itself, and thus how strongly Gaullist thinking about world politics had become dissociated from its original party label:

> Nobody imagines a conflict with our neighbours; nobody keeps the hypothesis alive according to which an aggression could be targeted at France and at France only outside any universal conflict that departs from either the USSR or the United States.
>
> (Assemblée 1975: 4930/Francois Mitterrand)

In the final years of the Cold War, then, the now well-known lines of argumenta-tion were advanced and reproduced inside France. As had been the case earlier, opposition forces continued to question the appropriateness of the Gaullist diagnosis of world politics, suggesting contending securitisations, while the dia-gnosis was defended by its advocates (Cohen 1989). Whether it was the station-ing of Soviet SS-20 missiles in Eastern Europe (Boyer 1985), the Soviet downing of a Korean airliner (Assemblée 1983) or sense-making of any other current event – the ruling politicians continued to articulate and enact a Gaullist analysis of world politics, although they were criticised for being either too close to the USSR, too close to America or insufficiently aware of German danger (François-Poncet 1985). When in power, they also defended this perspective on world politics, regardless of whether they were socialists or members of the Gaullist party.

Nonetheless, it is important to note how further – secondary – types of inse-curities were introduced into the French debates during the second half of the Cold War, and how these began to depart from the established lines of French world ordering described above. A new insecurity discourse premised on 'insta-bilities in the Global South', for instance, rationalised conflicts in places such as Nicaragua, El Salvador, Angola, Ethiopia, Yemen, Afghanistan and Cambodia (De la Gorce 1981; Windsor 1982). Following predominant interpretations, these conflicts were widely considered to be 'lesser problems' in comparison to the above issues. Who or what caused those conflicts, however, was less consensual: for some politicians, it was France's post-imperial withdrawal from the Global South that had caused the observed conflicts (Assemblée 1973: 2262/Foreign Minister Michel Jobert); for others, the problem was self-propelled (De la Gorce 1981; Boyer and Palmer 1989). Characterising the Iranian turmoil of 1979, for instance, Maurice Couve de Murville explained:

> The Iranian revolution is [...] a spontaneous uprising of a still medieval and deeply religious people against a regime that sought to enforce a precipitous modernisation in the midst of a general misery that was marked by outrages excesses of the elites.
>
> (Assemblée 1980: 481)

Another group suggested that the southern instabilities were driven by the two superpowers. In their view, the unrestrained dissemination of weaponry by the latter had introduced a North–South dimension into the East–West conflict (Eylau-Wagram 1981). The question of what precisely was known to cause conflicts in the Global South – and thus the question of who or what had to be countered by foreign policy so as to mitigate this secondary challenge – was not, then, fully settled in French politics. Interestingly, however, parliament-arians agreed very broadly with the characterisation of those secondary chal-lenges as problems for the 'entire international community' (Devillers 1974; Assemblée 1982; Loescher 1994). With this, the securitisation of Third World conflicts diverged from the more traditional French concerns with East, West and Europe. Instead of reproducing these established container concepts, 'southern instabilities' pointed to the presence of a much larger community of threatened actors instead.

In the 1970s and 1980s, emerging concerns with energy supplies also broke with the established grand systematisations of world politics. The oil crises, for example, were directly attributed to a coalition of Arab governments and explained as retaliation against Western support to Israel (Leveau and Rifaï 1974; De Rosé 1980). Later, the war between Iraq and Iran was also used to securitise the region and Western reliance on oil, although this time, and in contrast to the oil crises, its negative effects were held to have been produced inadvertently, rather than deliberately. In both cases, a rapid characterisation of oil supplies as a global challenge is evident. Introduced into French debates as a European problem under the presidency of Georges Pompidou, energy security quickly became defined as an outright 'global' concern with the presidency of Valéry Giscard d'Estaing (Zorgbibe 1976). Even if some politicians at times linked Arab nationalism with the danger of communism (Assemblée 1986c), the securitisation of energy supplies shows that new notions of insecurity helped articulate new ideas of threatening and threatened actors in world politics.

Lastly, by the late Cold War years, French security debates were also enriched with new syllogisms following the intertwined securitisation of terrorism and migration. Terrorism became an important insecurity narrative with the hijacking and bombing of civilian airliners worldwide (LeM 1980). In France, this category became particularly salient in 1985–1986, when Paris was hit by a number of bloody attacks – blackmail attempts to force the release of imprisoned criminals (LeM 1986). The question of who exactly was causing danger, however, was not fully determined in this novel threat narrative either. For some, terrorism was a state-driven problem. According to some political factions, it was either Iran (LeM 1986), Libya, the USSR or the US that sponsored terrorism, and consequently French counterterrorism policies had to be directed against these actors (Assemblée 1986b). For others, such as Prime Minister Jacques Chirac, terrorism was driven by individuals and groupings unconnected to state agency. In his view, counterterrorism had no foreign states as object of action, yet its origins could nevertheless be ascribed to a specific geographical region – namely, North Africa (Assemblée 1986a). It was from this region that terrorism emanated, creating a danger to France in particular, but also to Europe at large (Boyer and Palmer 1989).

National-conservatives developed this non-statist rendering of terrorist agency further. Connecting terrorism, crime and foreigners in general, they argued that immigrants were 'escaping' the national security apparatus. In their view, migrants supported terrorist acts on French soil or they even committed those acts themselves (Assemblée 1986b: 4451–4453/Jean-Marie Le Pen; Weil 1994). In terms of foreign policymaking, this emerging debate on terrorism initiated a two-pronged agenda. On the one hand, it enabled an expansion of international counterterror cooperation efforts, such as through United Nations frameworks.

On the other hand, it laid the foundation for ever closer police cooperation in Europe (Palmer and Boyer 1989).

'Southern instabilities', energy security and terrorism/migration thus enriched the French security debates of the late Cold War years with new insecurity themes. But their introduction into the local discussions did not merely add new 'threat topics' to the polity. Compared to the traditional lines of world ordering described earlier, the new insecurities also advanced new knowledges of the organisation of international insecurity. The new dangers were deemed to be caused by a regional collective of states outside the conventional East–West divide (such as in the case of energy security) or they were held to be driven by non-state actors (such as terrorists and migrants). At the same time, they were considered to threaten not only France and Europe, but – depending on the threat in question – also the industrialised world or the 'international community' *tout court*. These new insecurities of the late Cold War years are indicative of a larger upcoming shift in world ordering through securitisation in Europe. These new dangers may have been categorised as secondary in comparison to concerns with the US, the USSR and Germany, but as the subsequent chapters show in more detail, they heralded a time in which non-state actor-centric conceptions of international insecurity, but also more expansive notions of threatened collectives, became recognised and enacted.

Conclusion

Did French politicians securitise the US, although the two nations were allies? Was the USSR considered a primary threat to national security in the Fifth Republic? Was Germany deemed dangerous during the Cold War, European integration notwithstanding? These entities had, indeed, been securitised by many inside the French political system, yet not everyone accepted their basic endangering, and many debated whom and how these dangers threatened precisely. A positional/relational perspective on French insecurity politics helps in assessing these observations and to understand how specific such conceptions of national insecurity empowered certain courses of action, such as the expulsion of NATO from France and the quest for European integration, but not others, such as all-out withdrawal from the West or a harsher countering of West Germany (for a schematic overview, see Table 7.1). What is more, the same perspective allows recognising how patterns of such ordering evolved over time. The emergent focus on 'new threats', for example, points to a deeper shift in world ordering through notions of insecurity, and one that defies the state-centric frameworks of world politics advanced by grand IR theory. And, indeed, a similar movement in world ordering through insecurity can be witnessed in neighbouring West Germany around the same time, the next chapter shows, even if that polity had been concerned with a more restrained perspective on national insecurity in the beginning.

Table 7.1 French constructions of international (in-)security during the Cold War

		1950s/1960s	1970s/1980s
US/NATO/ capitalism	Source	Blockade of France's Africa policy^W; Entanglement of France^W; NATO headquarters near Paris^W; Capitalist economy^M	Doctrine of flexible nuclear response^D; Mutually assured destruction^D; Capitalist economy^M
	Target	French imperial interests^W; European independence^W; Workers worldwide^M	European independence^D
	Relation	Challenge^W; No threat^W; Existential^M	Challenge^D; No threat^W
	World order description	US foreign policy as source of danger to France and French imperial interests in particular, but also to Europe	US foreign policy as source of insecurity to all of Europe
	Conditioning effects	Emancipation of France and Europe from US foreign policymaking, but no rejection of the US as an ally jointly opposed to communism (US as *adversaire-partenaire*)	
	Policy enactment	Efforts to have NATO recognise North Africa as a common interest, proposal for new Western leadership (directorate), efforts to prevent NATO from adopting a new nuclear doctrine, development of national nuclear arsenal, expulsion of NATO from France, vetoing of British accession to European institutions	Continuing signatory of the Washington Treaty (but no longer a member of NATO), European integration
Communism/ USSR	Source	USSR/Warsaw Pact^D	USSR (not Eastern Europe)^D; Warsaw Pact^W
	Target	North Atlantic nations^W; Europe (incl. West Germany)^M	Europe (incl. West Germany)^D; North Atlantic nations^W

Relation	Challenge[W] Existential[W] No threat[M]	Challenge[D] Existential[W]
World order description	Persistent major threat to West in general and Europe in particular	Persistent challenge by USSR (and less so by Eastern European countries) to Europe
Conditioning effects	Collective Western and European countering of the East (USSR as *adversaire-rivale*)	Collective Western and European countering of the East, but also coexistence and bilateral contacts with the East (USSR as *adversaire-rivale*)
Policy enactment	Continuing signatory of the Washington Treaty, pledge to defend West Germany in case of unprovoked attack, development of national nuclear arsenal, bilateral visits and exchanges with the Soviet Union	Continuing signatory of the Washington Treaty, pan-European security cooperation, European defence efforts
Superpower condominium		
Source	N/A	US/USSR collaboration[D]
Target	N/A	Europe[D] The hemisphere of each superpower[D] Korea, Africa, Latin America, etc.[W]
Relation	N/A	Challenge[D] Existential[W] Not a threat[M]
World order description	N/A	An unholy alliance of two ideologically opposed superpowers attempting to keep the world dependent on their preferences and political agreements
Conditioning effects	N/A	Emancipation of France and Europe from both superpowers
Policy enactment	N/A	European integration, extension of contacts to Eastern Europe, support for pan-European security, demands for West German *Ostpolitik*, founding of Eurocorps

continued

Table 7.1 Continued

		1950s/1960s	1970s/1980s
(West-)Germany	Source	Culture of militarism[D] 'Bonn' as Fourth Reich[M]	Culture of militarism[D]
	Target		France (German *revanche*)[W] Europe (continental hegemony)[W] Everyone (incl. USSR)[M]
	Relation	Challenge (less than USSR)[D] Challenge (on par with USSR)[W] Existential[W]	Diminishing challenge[D] Existential[M]
	World order description	A persistent challenge to France and Europe at large	A diminishing challenge to France and Europe at large.
	Conditioning effects	Continuing 'cooperative containment' of West Germany through bilateral cooperation, continental and North Atlantic integration and French nuclear forces	
	Policy enactment	Friendship treaty with West Germany, resolution of territorial disputes, Ailleret-Lemnitzer Accords, European integration	Support to/demands for West German *Ostpolitik*, expansion of Elysée Treaty provisions (consultation on use of nuclear weaponry), Eurocorps
'Southern instabilities'	Source	N/A	Superpower politics[W] Local politics (self-propelled)[W] Lack of French tutelage[M]
	Target	N/A	International community[D]
	Relation	N/A	Challenge[D]
	World order description	N/A	Emergent challenge from the Global South, with unclear sponsorship, but affecting the entire world
	Conditioning effects	N/A	Emancipation of third parties from superpower politics
	Policy enactment	N/A	N/A, secondary security agenda

Energy security	Source	N/A	OPEC/Arab world[D] Western dependence on oil[M]
	Target	N/A	Western world[W] Industrialised countries worldwide[W]
	Relation	N/A	Challenge[D]
	World order description	N/A	Emergent challenge emanating from a distinct world region and driven by states, affecting either the West or all industrial nations
	Conditioning effects	N/A	N/A, secondary security agenda
	Policy enactment	N/A	N/A, secondary security agenda
Terrorism/ migration	Source	N/A	Non-state actors[D] North Africa/Middle East[D] Migrants living in France/Europe[M] Iran, Libya, USSR or US[M]
	Target	N/A	Europe[W] Every nation[W]
	Relation	N/A	Challenge[D]
	World order description	N/A	Emergent challenge emanating from across the Mediterranean Sea, with mixed statist/non-statist origins and affecting all nations (hijacking) and Europe (bombings) alike
	Conditioning effects	N/A	Promotion of global and regional law enforcement capabilities
	Policy enactment	N/A	Participation in international counterterrorism frameworks, promotion of European policing

8   The West German *Ostpolitik* years

Ostpolitik and its critics

As Chapter 5 showed, West German security politics had in the 1950s become restricted to *Westbindung*. According to this perspective and policy, 'East' and 'West' were conceived as two homogenous blocs, with the former existentially threatening the latter. In the mid-1960s, this rendering of the 'communist danger' was subtly challenged. In the view of increasingly powerful factions, Eastern European nations were held to threaten the West, because of their membership in the Warsaw Pact. With the exception of the more problematic case of East Germany, however, these nations also came to be characterised as entities threatened by the USSR themselves. At the same time, the 'Eastern danger' was differentiated into a multiplicity of interlocutors and relationships. Some Eastern nations were considered to have a highly antagonistic relationship with West Germany and the West at large, whereas others were considered less hostile. Conceptually speaking, select Eastern European nations were thus projected into a larger insecurity community together with the FRG and other Western nations, notwithstanding their complicity in threatening several of the latter. In the grand coalition government of Kiesinger and Brandt, the co-presence of these two interpretations of world politics empowered a transition from the traditional *Politik der Stärke* to the more differentiated *Politik der kleinen Schritte*. This latter foreign policy doctrine upheld West German membership in NATO, but it also enabled limited improvement of relations between the FRG and select nations in Eastern Europe.

In the late 1960s, the differentiated reading of 'Eastern danger' was advanced ever more forcefully by social democrats and liberals. In the view of such politicians, the international security context was yet not only organised differently to what conservatives argued. Contrary to earlier times, there was also an emergent understanding that the international security context could be actively changed by means of Germany's own foreign policy strategy (Kaiser 1969; Bundestag 1973c: 543/Wehner SPD). Instead of foreign policy being portrayed as a mere reaction to the international security context, then, there was a new sense that the latter also had to be construed as the result of Germany's own policies (Brandt 1964). International authorities were invoked in confirmation of this view. One analysis that was commonly used to aid this perspective over the years was NATO's 1967

Harmel Report (Bundestag 1970: 2751/Minister of Defence Schmidt SPD, 1973e: 2741/Foreign Minister Scheel FDP). The Nobel Peace Prize, awarded to Willy Brandt in 1971 for his efforts in normalising relations between East and West, became another such authority (Bundestag 1972b: 9836/Minister for Inner-German Relations Franke SPD). At times, even neighbouring France's dominant Gaullist perspective on world politics was mobilised in support. Like the Gaullists, West German politicians, too, began arguing that integration into NATO entailed a certain loss of agency in national foreign policymaking. Unlike in France, however, this loss of agency was not attributed to US foreign policymaking, but to West Germany's conservative governments of the 1950s (Frank 1970: 867). Also, it was diagnosed a good decade later than in France.

In 1969, the grand coalition of the CDU/CSU and SPD then broke apart, giving way to a new coalition between social democrats and liberals, which following the 1972 elections became even more powerful. After this redistribution of formal political power, the differentiated perspective on the 'Eastern danger' was advanced more forcefully by its advocates. At the same time, however, it was also criticised ever more harshly by the opposition. Indeed, conservatives had already challenged alternative assessments of Eastern Europe as 'excessively optimistic' during the grand coalition years (DZ 1966a). When relegated to the opposition for the first time in the history of the FRG, they then radically negated any contending conception of world politics. Manfred Wörner, for instance, later Minister of Defence and NATO Secretary-General, accused the government – and after the 1972 elections, also the general electorate – of being unable to grasp the 'reality of international politics' (Bundestag 1971d; DZ 1972). Rainer Barzel, another influential CDU politician and twice candidate for the West German Chancellorship, went further. Relations between East and West, in his view, were, 'in fact', so tense that World War III was imminent (Bundestag 1973c: 538). In the view of highly agitated conservatives, any differentiating perspective on the East was destructive to national security (Bundestag 1970: 2763–2764/Zimmermann CDU). It equalled an 'abandoning of Europe' (Bundestag 1974: 5914/Wörner CDU), a 'switching of sides' from West to East and a 'renunciation' of national sovereignty (Bundestag 1971a: 9791/Kiesinger). Leading conservatives even proclaimed that Chancellor Brandt was a 'European Mao Zedong', who was deliberately bringing West Germany under Soviet control (Bundestag 1972a: 9797/Barzel CDU, 1974: 5914/Wörner CDU).

In the heated debates of the late 1960s and early 1970s, this epistemological controversy was then also enmeshed with further lines of criticism. The government's argument that relations with the East could be improved proactively – i.e. that their nature also depended on the active foreign policy choices of the FRG itself, for example – was rejected as outright utopian. This view held that West German foreign policymaking should aim to counter the current international reality – it should not be premised on a possible future of world politics (Schulz 1971; Bundestag 1973c: 566/Abelein CDU). The new government's ways of conceptualising national foreign and security policy were also challenged. According to this critique, the very methods by which new foreign policy initiatives were decided were deemed hectic and premature. Governmental communication on national security and foreign affairs was considered 'disastrously contradictory', inviting misinterpretation by allies and enemies alike (e.g. Bundestag 1971b: 5073/ Gradl CDU, 1971c: 5127ff./Marx CDU). Finally, after Brandt was awarded the Nobel Peace Prize, conservatives also took great offence at the Social Democrats' self-presentation as the national 'peace party' – i.e. their alleged claim to moral superiority in world politics (Bundestag 1971c: 5128/Marx CDU).

Such harsh criticism notwithstanding, the differentiated securitisation of the Eastern danger was maintained by government circles in particular. Brandt and his colleagues insisted on a differentiated rendering of Eastern Europe, as well as the understanding that dialogue with West Germany's eastern neighbours would eventually help re-evaluate interstate relations at lower levels (Bahr 1991). In terms of foreign policymaking, this perspective then gave rise to *Ostpolitik*, a series of diplomatic gestures towards the East. Under its umbrella, the federal government organised state visits to Eastern capitals and factually abandoned the *Hallstein Doktrin* (DZ 1969b). It accepted the partition of Europe as the result of World War II and Nazi warmongering. Chancellor Brandt personally apologised for the fascist war crimes, including by means of his famous *Kniefall* at Warsaw's Ghetto Memorial. Most importantly, on the formal level, a number of international treaties – the *Ostverträge* – were designed to regulate West Germany's relations with the East in new ways.

The Moscow Treaty (*Gewaltverzichtsvertrag*) of 1970 was the first of the *Ostpolitik*'s five treaties. It pledged the renunciation of physical violence as a means of conflict resolution between the FRG and the USSR, while also demanding further diplomatic normalisation between the two states. The agreement, Minister for Inner-German Relations Franke made clear in the *Bundestag*, did not imply that bilateral relations had suddenly become non-antagonistic. However, the treaty set out a basis for the transformation of these relations from 'a mode of opposition into a less hostile mode of concurrence' (Bundestag 1972b: 9837/Franke). In the same year, the Warsaw Treaty addressed relations with Poland. Recognising the need to 'accept the realities of 25 years of European partition', it described Poland as the first victim of Nazi aggression – although in the *Bundestag* politicians also went further, presenting Poland as a victim of totalitarian regimes more generally, thus including the notion of Soviet repression within the ambit of their discussions (Bundestag 1971a). More importantly, perhaps, this second *Ostvertrag* also recognised the *Oder-Neisse* as Poland's inviolable Western frontier. With this, the government of the FRG effectively ceded claims to Germany's former Eastern Territories.

Several treaties dealt with the City of Berlin, East Germany and Czechoslovakia. The 1972 Four Power Agreement, enacted by the Allied Control Council on behalf of West Germany, facilitated access and supplies to West Berlin. Regulating West Berlin's special relationship with the FRG, it forbade official functions of the latter in the city, but also allowed West Berlin to be represented by the FRG internationally. Overall, this third multilateral agreement thus helped West Germany to protect the existing *modus vivendi* in West Berlin from Soviet pressure (Mahnke

1971). The 1972 Basic Treaty (*Grundlagenvertrag*) then addressed relations with the GDR. It recognised the inviolability of the respective countries' external frontiers and denied each the ability to represent Germany as a whole internationally. This fourth *Ostvertrag* stopped just short of full recognition of the GDR by West Germany, and it led to the setting up of 'permanent representations' – but not embassies – on each other's territory. Lastly, the 1973 Treaty of Prague recognised the inviolability of frontiers between the FRG and Czechoslovakia. It established bilateral diplomatic relations and cooperation on technical and economic issues. Importantly for the long-term improvement of bilateral relations, this fifth *Ostvertrag* also nullified the 1938 Munich Agreement, which had dismantled Czechoslovakia and attached the *Sudetenland* to the German Third Reich.

Further factors are, of course, important in explaining why these five treaties were endorsed by *all* of their signatories. East Germany, for instance, had arguably been pressured fairly forcefully by the USSR into accepting the FRG's *Ostpolitik*. The USSR, by contrast, apparently sought to capitalise on the West's recognition of the *Oder-Neisse* frontier and to safeguard its own strategic arms limitations talks with the US (Frank 1970; Von Baudissin 1970). The actions of Western allies, too, were driven by distinct contextual, managerial and epistemological rationales, such as the Gaullist reading of world politics. As important as such further factors are for a global account of *Ostpolitik*, West Germany's own foreign policy agenda can only be explained by the conception of world politics propagated by its ruling parties. This dominant conception suggested that the 'Eastern danger' was organised in a manner quite different to that which might be suggested by the bloc perspective. It was the differential rendering of the East that allowed a basic renunciation of armed force in the relations with the USSR, and that permitted limited and mostly technical cooperation with the GDR, but also more comprehensive cooperation schemes with Poland and Czechoslovakia. It was on the basis of this perspective that the *Hallstein Doktrin* could be terminated, relations with further Eastern European countries – Bulgaria and Hungary especially – could be normalised (Scheel 1973) and, later, the Helsinki Process could be supported and sustained by Bonn (Genscher 1980). And, of course, it was also on the basis of the collective rendering of the Soviet danger that West Germany maintained its commitment to West European institutions and NATO in particular.

Conversely, the dominant reading of the national (in-)security context also disempowered the adoption of alternative foreign policy proposals. On the basis of their own understanding of the threats faced by West Germany, conservative politicians continued to advocate for the traditional *Politik der Stärke* throughout the early and mid-1970s. In their reasoning, the East as such would eventually be exhausted or overpowered, if only it was countered forcefully enough (Bundestag 1972c: 9941ff./Zimmermann CDU). It was on the basis of this perspective that the CDU/CSU opposed the government policy ardently, its opposition ranging from verbal criticisms to outright boycotts of foreign affairs meetings in both the *Bundestag* and at NATO headquarters. It was on the basis of their particular vision of world politics as a hostile confrontation between East and West that these parties advocated for Western integration, declined all five

Ostverträge and, a few years later, rejected the Helsinki Final Act (Bundestag 1972c, 1973a, 1973b, 1973c). The only other groups in Europe to reject that Act were the Albanian communists and the Greek neo-fascists.

In the face of such consistent criticism, the differentiated re-securitisation of the 'Eastern danger' proposed by social democrats and liberals had to be actively defended (Joffe 1979). And, indeed, in the 1970s the government felt compelled to communicate its reading of world politics much more effectively to the public (Bundestag 1970: 2767/Buchstaller SPD). One way of doing so was the conceptualisation and release of biannual *Weissbücher* – a very high frequency for the publishing of such documents by any international standard. In these national security doctrines, the government posited, in most explicit terms, the Soviet military arsenal as the biggest threat to international security. Communists, the various *Weissbücher* of the 1970s authoritatively proclaimed, had been engaged in hostile actions against the West ever since the late 1940s. The communist danger appeared with the annexation of Eastern Europe, Eastern Germany included, and it expanded further with the Korean War and the various Berlin crises. The government publications also emphasised that the USSR sustained an awe-inspiring military arsenal, that these capabilities were being reinforced on all fronts for no apparent reason and that the Red Army had adopted a highly dangerous 'surprise attack posture' along its Western front. Following from this assessment of the international security context, all *Weissbücher* stressed the Republic's commitment to NATO and the European Communities, and they also emphasised a need to reinforce West Germany's own military defences. As the Ministry of Defence succinctly argued: 'It would be irresponsible to depart from *détente* and so to neglect the protection of the own existence, or to underestimate the continuing arms race' (Bundesminister der Verteidigung 1970: 1). Indeed, West German defence spending increased in the 1970s, despite the new government's differentiated and less categorical perspective on the 'Eastern danger'. Despite the harsh criticisms that opposition forces levelled against the centre-left government, federal authorities dedicated more public funds to military defence than any preceding government (Bundestag 1976a: 18105/Minister of Defence Leber SPD). If the *Weissbücher* defined a strong – and collectively Western – deterrent position vis-à-vis the Soviet Union, however, they also maintained that not all Eastern nations could be equalled with that power in practice. The East no longer presented a monolithic bloc, the doctrines argued. Consequently, foreign policy strategies had to be adapted to this situation. The *Ostverträge*, the doctrines and its proponents argued, recapitulated and reiterated over and over again throughout the decade, did not derive from sudden amity between the FRG and the East, but from a 'realistic', differentiated and forward-looking view of world politics. Referring to the Basic Treaty with Eastern Germany, for instance, social democrats maintained:

> The treaty does not solve the German question, but keeps it open. It provides a real chance that the hardened relationship between the two German countries can loosen up and that the current situation of opposition can be turned into a situation of coexistence and future togetherness.
>
> (Bundestag 1973d: 1428/Heyen SPD)

Towards 'pacifism' and anti-Americanism

In the mid-1970s, the Federal Republic's ruling parties were obliged to consistently defend their differentiated conception of world politics from alternative interpretations. As a dominant understanding of international politics, however, their conception of the international laid the basis for a lasting foreign policy strategy of combined deterrence and dialogue (Genscher 1980). The conception enabled a particularly active foreign policy agenda towards Eastern Europe, where diplomatic successes often validated the foreign policy's underlying epistemological premises in return. In the 1970s, the FGR was, indeed, able to multiply high-level contacts with its Eastern interlocutors. With Poland, Czechoslovakia, Hungary and Romania, it even managed to conclude agreements on trade, tourism, youth exchange and scientific cooperation. In the late 1970s, the West German Government praised the 'enduring friendship' and 'excellent cooperation schemes' between the FRG and these countries, and it also publicly commended Romania's initiative for a general conference on security and cooperation in Europe (Bundestag 1978: 4962/Chancellor Schmidt SPD). Looking back at the results of *Ostpolitik*, the 1979 *Weissbuch* maintained that relations with Czechoslovakia, Hungary and Romania had evolved ever more positively in recent years. Relations with Poland, the doctrine even argued, had been 'fully normalised' (Bundesminister der Verteidigung 1979).

West Germany's conceptions of other Eastern interlocutors, however, did not evolve as positively. For its part, the government had viewed relations with the GDR as improving at the beginning of *Ostpolitik*. There had been a significant relaxation of travel and communication restrictions between the two German states, and the replacement of Walter Ulbricht by Erich Honecker as leader of the GDR had raised hopes for further political liberalisation in East Germany (Bundestag 1973d: 1445/Schütz SPD). Soon, however, the GDR was seen to distance itself again from West Germany. East Germany's repeated increase of the *Reisepauschale* – i.e. entrance fees levied on West German visitors – and, in particular, its crackdown on West German journalists in East Berlin were widely construed as hostile actions in Bonn. Although *Ostpolitik* was construed as having loosened Moscow's grip on the GDR, many analysts and politicians saw relations with the GDR as having become highly tense once again (Joffe 1979). Although advocates of *Ostpolitik* were quick to denounce this view as 'political warmongering' (Bundestag 1977b: 2999/Neumann SPD), stressing that the improvement of inner-German relations represented a long-term project (Bundestag 1977d), even influential social democrats eventually endorsed the opposition's argument that the GDR was firmly anchored in the Warsaw Pact, that it remained a highly repressive and militarised state and that it engaged in highly hostile relations with West Germany again (Bertram 1979; Apel 1984; Mantzke 1990).

Epistemological disagreements between the major political camps in the FRG then gradually diminished towards the end of the decade. Perspectives on the Soviet Union also began to converge, especially after the latter's deployment of new nuclear missiles in Eastern Europe. The new weapons – the SS-20 – were capable of targeting smaller installations much more precisely. This led West German strategists to fear that the American grand deterrent had been weakened. In their view, the US could not be expected to retaliate any longer against dense cities – as it threatened to do – if the East 'merely' attacked military installations. The 1979 Soviet invasion of Afghanistan, too, was seen by many as a confirmation of the USSR's existential hostility (Wagner 1980; Von Braunmühl 1983). By the turn of the decade, then, the Federal Republic's largest political parties advanced fairly similar assessments of Moscow's true dangerousness. Unlike in neighbouring France, where there was a local communist party that advanced a different perspective on the USSR, no major faction in Bonn had deemed the political endangering of the USSR inappropriate. Instead – and also unlike the Gaullists' less antagonistic reading of the USSR – a strong coalition of West German political forces categorised relations between Moscow and Bonn as deeply hostile.

This said, disagreements as to the 'true nature' of that danger emerged in another dimension in Bonn. In the late 1970s, politicians began to disagree on the very targets that the Soviet danger threatened. For many conservatives and a sizable group of politicians around Chancellor Schmidt, the Soviet threat was still construed as a transatlantic challenge. In their view, the USSR threatened the West in its entirety, and thus this threat could be countered collectively. Another group, however, suggested that Europe was threatened more strongly by the USSR than the US and Canada, and that the latter might, indeed, no longer be threatened by Moscow at all. Similar to what French strategists had argued, this group felt that Soviet intercontinental capabilities had rendered dysfunctional the US grand deterrent along NATO's eastern front. The risk of mutual destruction had made conflict between the USSR and North America impossible, they argued, and this permitted Moscow to use its regional nuclear superiority on the European continent much more freely (Weidenfeld 1987). A third group went even further, suggesting that the Soviet threat now targeted West Germany exclusively. The Red Army's new intermediate-range nuclear missiles, these analysts argued, posed a problem to the FRG, but not to its allies, given intercontinental deterrence. In the 1980s, the question of whether this radically self-centred perspective on the organisation of communist danger could be considered truthful or not was aptly called the *Sonderbedrohungsdebatte* – i.e. the 'special threat debate' (Enders and Siebenmorgen 1988).

In the late 1970s and early 1980s, conceptions of Eastern danger had hence subtly evolved inside the West German political system. After years of polarised debates, they gradually converged along new lines. There was an increasingly broad sense that relations with the USSR and the GDR remained – or had once again become – extremely tense. As shall shortly be shown in more detail, there was also a gradually increasing consensus among West German politicians that, irrespective of this situation, the East consisted of multiple actors, and that relations with some Eastern European countries were, in fact, less hostile than had been proclaimed earlier. However, conceptions of the *West* also evolved inside the FRG. Given continuing tension between Greece and Turkey, but also a perception of increasing American unilateralism both in regard to European defence and in South East Asia, NATO was also decreasingly seen as a homogenous bloc (Mates 1976; Kaiser 1986). Doubts emerged as to whether the West could still be described as a community sharing similar dangers. In the view of some in Bonn, the communist danger had recently been delimited to continental Europe. For others, it no longer produced an international insecurity community as such, given that the Soviet Union had become a 'special threat', exclusively aimed at West Germany. Depending on who else was seen as affected by Soviet danger, unevenly powerful political camps thus advocated for different West German foreign policy strategies, whether transatlantic responses, continental initiatives or more unilateral self-defence (Enders and Siebenmorgen 1988).

Eventually, the critical examinations of the Western community gave way to a questioning of whether Western actors themselves were complicit in causing West German insecurity. Contrary to what might be expected, this emergent discourse did yet not replicate the French Gaullist view of world politics. Even if West German politicians were worried about the effects of strategic arms limitation talks for Europe, they usually did not identify the US or the 'superpower condominium' as outright sources of insecurity to the FRG and others. Exceptions notwithstanding, it was the general dangerousness of armed forces as such that turned into a salient issue. This new focus also evolved from West Germany's very own disarmament agenda. With *Ostpolitik*, Bonn had been forcefully calling for international arms control mechanisms (Brandt 1971). Irrespective of the FRG's own increase in defence spending, social democratic circles and a gradually more powerful extra-parliamentarian peace movement began to criticise the international arms race ever more aggressively. In this process, militarisation in general and nuclear weapons in particular became seen as key sources of international insecurity in the Federal Republic. And, of course, both German states had been exposed particularly strongly to these elements. In the late 1970s, the inner-German border was highly militarised, and NATO and the Warsaw Pact nuclear weaponry was deployed in great numbers on the territories of both German states.

In the 1980s, this securitisation of military means of violence gave way to two new perceptions of international (in-)insecurity. On the one hand, 'pacifism' re-emerged as a strong guiding rationale. Contrary to the way in which this perspective had been specified in the immediate post-war years, it was not directed against Germany's own 'militarist culture'. Instead, it was largely directed against nuclear weaponry. In the late 1970s and early 1980s, this securitisation of strategic arms drew on a variety of local, national and international elements. Locally, it responded to repeated transport and handling accidents involving allied nuclear weapons, by allies, on West German soil. Nationally, the extra-parliamentarian peace movement became stronger following NATO's 1979 *Doppelbeschluss*. According to this 'twin track strategy', NATO continued its dialogue with the Warsaw Pact, but also pledged to substantially reinforce its own military deterrent. Despite heavy criticism from his own party and the peace movement, Chancellor Schmidt endorsed this decision, which implied an upgrade of allied nuclear capabilities on West German territory (Bundestag 1981: 1542/Chancellor Schmidt SPD). On the international level, finally, the securitisation of nuclear arms also drew on terrifying nuclear incidents and accidents, the 1962 Cuba crisis and the 1986 Chernobyl catastrophe especially. In the 1980s, the epistemological validity of this endangering of strategic weaponry as a threat to European well-being and global peace – but also the political power of the peace movement and other partisan factions endorsing this discourse – was considerable. In 1987, the Prime Minister of the *Saarland* Oscar Lafontaine drew on it to demand West Germany's withdrawal from NATO and a complete denuclearisation of the country (Weidenfeld 1987: 260).

On the other hand, the endangering of nuclear weaponry also gave way to an eventual securitisation of the United States. By 1980, US foreign policymaking was considered unpredictable by some, even an attempt to 'decide German affairs above German heads' (Bialer 1983; Weidenfeld 1987: 295). The Green party, which entered the *Bundestag* for the first time in 1983, advanced this antagonistic rendering of West Germany's powerful ally most explicitly. Unlike the Social Democrats, whose leadership endorsed NATO's *Doppelbeschluss* despite criticism from within their own ranks, the Greens openly opposed US grand strategy. Presenting the United States as a veritable source of West German insecurity, they vocally denounced the stationing of American strategic arms on German soil, and they also rejected US interventions in Nicaragua and El Salvador, characterising them as major sources of international instability (Bundestag 1983b: 693ff./Schily, 1985, 1986). In the 1980s, the endangering of the US thus offered yet another systematisation of the international security context. In this view, West Germany was located in a different insecurity community than what had previously been suggested. This insecurity community had a fairly global 'reach', and its causes were located in North America. Accordingly, foreign policymaking had to be oriented much more directly against the US.

The emergent anti-American reading of international affairs, however, never became a dominant method of systematising the international in the West German polity. Although influential outside parliament, environmentalist circles remained marginal overall in the formal political sphere in the 1980s. Also, conservatives and liberals strongly opposed the Greens' foreign affairs perspectives as excessively sceptical or negative (e.g. Bundestag 1982b: 8026/Rühe CDU). Social democrats, for their part, officially rejected the anti-American threat frame as well. Following the 1979 *Doppelbeschluss*, however, that party effectively split into different factions. Some social democrats – such as Chancellor Schmidt – upheld intimate collaboration with the West, and thus notably also the US, against the East. Other social democrats, however, associated themselves more closely with the arguments made by the peace movement. In doing this, social democrats emphasised increasingly stronger 'pacifist' views against nuclear weaponry, but they did not become outright anti-American. Following this shift and internal split, however, Schmidt's coalition government of social democrats and liberals became highly unstable in the late 1970s (DZ 1982). Its emphasis on arms reduction and dialogue with Eastern interlocutors, observers argued, was in irreconcilable contradiction with its official support for the expansion of nuclear armament in Europe (Ruth 1982).

In 1982, following a dramatic reversal of political alliances, the Social Democrats then lost power to a new coalition of conservatives and liberals (DZ 1983). The new government, led by Chancellor Helmut Kohl, immediately set out to 'objectively identify and assess the military potential of the GDR and Eastern Europe' (Bundestag 1982a: 1). Interestingly, however, this process did not lead to a radically new foreign policy agenda. Instead of bringing about such a break in foreign policymaking, as the call for 'objective assessment' seemingly implied, the new government continued with the policies adopted in the 1970s. A closer analysis of the conservative perspectives on international security shows that conceptions of world politics had, indeed, been converging in the late 1970s, the earlier epistemological controversies notwithstanding. Certainly, in 1975, conservatives had rejected the ratification of the Helsinki Final Act. In their view, the East confronted the West in much more of an existentialist manner than that which the document had suggested. Also in 1976, the then opposition politician Helmut Kohl was radically negating the government's reading of world politics. As he succinctly replied to Chancellor Schmidt's assessment of the *Lage der Nation*: 'Your elaborations on foreign and security policy are not doing justice to the seriousness of the situation!' (Bundestag 1976b: 63).

In the 1970s, conservatives had thus continued to stress the existential nature of the communist danger. In their view, Western defences were so poor that 'the Russians could be standing on the boards of the Rhine' – and thus could conquer most of West Germany – 'within 48 hours' (Bundestag 1977b: 2990/Wörner CDU). Irrespective of the fact that West Germany was spending more on national defence than ever, they accused the government of spending too much on welfare and too little on the military (Bundestag 1977a: 613/Damm CDU). By the end of the decade, however, conservatives had begun to adopt foreign policy perspectives that were not too dissimilar from those advanced by the parties in power. Despite their earlier rejection of governmental views on world politics, conservatives, too, now gradually endorsed a differentiated reading of the FRG's eastern relations (Bundestag 1980b: 47/Kohl CDU). By the early 1980s, the new coalition government's first declarations and defence doctrines show, conservatives had come to endorse both the foreign policy perspectives and foreign policy strategies adopted by their predecessors in government (Bundesminister der Verteidigung 1983: 4–6, 1985: 3ff. and 20ff.). Conservatives, too, had come to accept the differentiation of the East into different actors, some of whom had a less antagonistic relationship with the West than others (Rühe 1988; Schöpflin 1990). Following this, the new centre-right government not only reiterated its commitment to NATO and other West European institutions. It also maintained those *Ostverträge* whose ratification the conservatives had opposed earlier. Most spectacularly, perhaps, the new coalition even lent its full support to the Helsinki Process by the late 1980s. Assessing the importance of the Conference on Security and Co-operation in Europe (CSCE) – whose founding document conservatives had rejected 10 years earlier – Chancellor Kohl argued: 'The CSCE is an indispensable instrument to safeguard peace in Europe, to overcome the partition of Europe, to promote cooperation on all issues, and to bring people closer to each other' (Bundestag 1987: 69).

Terrorism, economics and global risks

It is no exaggeration to state that preoccupation with the Warsaw Pact in general, the GDR and the USSR in particular, but also Eastern Europe and – starting in the 1980s – the Western alliance and nuclear weaponry represented the main themes of West German security politics during the period covered by this chapter. It is via these insecurity themes that West German politicians systematised and enacted the international in specific ways, empowering collaborative Western responses against common Eastern dangers. The dominance of these narratives notwithstanding, it is nevertheless instructive to also address the articulation of new, secondary (in-)security rationales in West Germany in the 1970s and 1980s. Indeed, a careful analysis of the security and foreign policy debates of the time shows that terrorism, concerns with international economic relations and an emergent notion of global interconnectedness and risk gradually joined the predominant systematisations discussed above. Although these new narratives were still considered secondary in the Cold War, they pointed to fairly new ways of ordering the international. These new ways of systematising world politics would then become considerably more salient in the 1990s, as Chapter 11 shows.

The danger of terrorism for its own sake was identified in the 1970s. At that time, the daring activities and violent attacks of the *Rote Armee Fraktion* gained significant attention. Importantly, however, the West German securitisation of terrorism in the 1970s and 1980s evolved very differently from the securitisation of terrorism witnessed in the early 2000s. Indeed, terrorism was not even addressed by the national security doctrines of the 1970s. Instead, it was (dis-)qualified as 'ordinary crimes' (Wiegreffe 1976; Bundestag 1977c: 3166/ Chancellor Schmidt SPD). Even if select conservatives suggested that the government 'spiritually favoured' the Red Army Faction, as a result of their 'lax attitude to education and neglect of family structures' (Bundestag 1978: 4986/Kohl CDU), there was a general understanding that terrorism was driven by a small set of radicalised local individuals. Indeed, the terrorist acts of the *Rote Armee Fraktion* were not portrayed as a transnational phenomenon in the FRG (Kreis 1976; Lange 2003). The Red Army Faction's various crimes were considered a danger to the FRG as a democratic society, but their reach was not collectivised beyond borders (Bundestag 1977c: 3169/Wehner SPD). Only in 1985 – after several bombings in the French capital – was terrorism finally addressed by a West German national security doctrine. Even then, however, its discussion was cursory. The problem of terrorism was literally introduced on the document's final page, where it opened up an exploratory discussion on the possibility of police contributions to national security (Bundesminister der Verteidigung 1985: 64). Terrorism, then, remained a secondary security theme during the 1980s and, as an organising principle, it contributed a highly self-centric 'domestic' insecurity theme for the FRG. Unlike in the 2000s, the endangering of terrorism was not meaningfully expanded to the international level during the Cold War. It was neither considered pressing enough, nor was it held to imply other actors in world politics, whether as sponsors or as targets of terrorism.

Economic factors were endangered, too, in the 1970s and 1980s. Indeed, anxieties revolving around economics became increasingly prominent in the West German public policy debates of the time. Grand concerns with NATO and the Warsaw Pact – unquestionably the primordial topics of public discussion in the early 1970s – were paralleled by lively discussions about unemployment, job security and pensions (DZ 1974a). Concerns regarding economic well-being also slowly turned into a secondary type of security issue. The *Weissbuch* of 1974–1975, for instance, made such a connection when linking the morale of the *Bundeswehr* to the challenge of civilian job security. However, economic issues also gained international dimensions. The *Weissbücher* of the early 1970s had already problematised the currency exchange compensation scheme between the FRG and the US as excessively burdensome. The *Weissbuch* of 1975–1976 then relaxed the traditional military-centric conception of national security correspondingly. Arguing that security was not only about military force, but 'also about all other factors that an attacker and a defender could use: geography, geo-strategy, economic power, human and technical capacities', the doctrine argued that national security policy was 'now having both a military and an economic function' (Bundesminister der Verteidigung 1976: 39ff., 24, 47).

As a national concern, economic security gradually developed further. The oil crises, conflicts in the Middle East and, later, economic competition and 'trade wars' between North America and Europe all added to this process (Czempiel 1984). In the 1980s, the presentation of economics as a challenge of sorts was then expanded to the notion of globalisation (Bundestag 1983a: 525–533/Chancellor Kohl CDU). With this, the notion of economic insecurity moved away from preoccupations with select state actors – such as the US – and turned into the broader idea of a 'global challenge'. This 'global challenge' was increasingly seen as driven by private companies and not foreign governments. By the same token, this challenge was also linked to a suggestive notion of global interdependence. With this subtle reformulation, concerns regarding economic security became ever more strongly depicted as problems for 'everyone' worldwide, not just Germany (Genscher 1980: 372ff.). Under the umbrella of the securitisation of economics, then, an unprecedentedly larger insecurity community had been projected abroad, and the sources of that community were increasingly directly attributed to a new, private type of actor category.

The Global South was compacted into this emerging discourse on globalisation and 'shared risks' (DZ 1976). Contrary to how it was conceived in neighbouring France, however, the Global South was not usually defined in antagonistic terms in Bonn. The 1979 *Weissbuch*, for instance, recognised decolonisation and the multiplication of states in the Global South. However, it also differentiated East–West and North–South qualitatively into different kinds of relations. In its view, relations between East and West were governed by 'military security issues', whereas relations between North and South were characterised by 'economic concerns of development and humanitarian aid' (Bundesminister der Verteidigung 1979: 27–28). Indeed, only briefly were developments in the Global South addressed explicitly and in security language inside the Federal Republic at the time. This was the case when conflicts in Angola and Ethiopia were actively debated and when concerns were voiced that these situations were proxy conflicts that could escalate into a global superpower war. Overall, however, such explicit security framings of the Global South were marginal in the FRG public policy debates. Concerns regarding economic relations and well-being, globalisation and the Global South became increasingly important in the 1980s, but they remained fairly poorly specified overall. As new and 'secondary' kinds of concerns, however, they nevertheless contributed to new conceptions of global interconnectedness and challenges. These new conceptions went beyond traditional concerns with East and West. They identified larger insecurity communities, and they also recognised non-state actors as viable sources of international danger (Bundestag 1980a).

Conclusion

The 'nature' of the 'Eastern threat' was not self-explanatory to West German politicians. On the contrary, whether the 'Eastern danger' emanated from a single source or multiple actors, whether all Eastern nations threatened West Germany similarly radically and who the 'Eastern threat' affected precisely – the North Atlantic community, Western Europe, West Germany alone or Europe in a continental sense, including countries such as Hungary, Romania, Czechoslovakia and Poland – were all subject to debate. Depending on how the 'Eastern danger' was construed, different conceptions of the organisation of international danger were projected abroad, and different foreign policy responses were enabled according to their own terms, be it a generalised countering of the East, a bivalent strategy of differentiated deterrence and dialogue, transatlantic cooperation, pan-European cooperation or autonomous defence. 'Pacifism' and anti-Americanism, too, were insecurity narratives that helped project abroad distinct conceptions of the international, as did 'secondary' notions of danger, such as terrorism, economic competition and globalisation. As was the case in France, these latter notions gradually shifted attention to the role of non-state actors (for a schematic overview, see Table 8.1). Also in neighbouring Switzerland, the next chapter shows, an international community of states would gradually be seen challenged by non-state actors. To do so, however, Swiss policymakers first had to articulate – and accept – an understanding according to which the Swiss Confederation was affected by the same challenges as others 'in reality'.

Table 8.1 West German constructions of international (in-)security in the late Cold War

		1970s	1980s
Eastern danger	Source		Individual Eastern nations[D] Entire Warsaw Pact[W]
	Target	North Atlantic nations[D]	North Atlantic nations[D] Europe[M] West Germany[M]
	Relation	Existential (USSR/GDR)[D] Challenge (Eastern Europe)[D] Challenge (GDR)[W] Existential (all actors)[W]	Existential (USSR/GDR)[D] Challenge (Eastern Europe)[D]
	World order description	Persistent challenge by USSR (and less so GDR and Eastern European countries) to North Atlantic community	Persistent challenge by USSR and GDR (less so Eastern European countries) to North Atlantic community, though potentially merely Europe and FRG
	Conditioning effects	Collective Western and European countering of the East, but also promotion of dialogue and bilateral contacts with Eastern European nations (esp. Poland, Czechoslovakia, Bulgaria, Hungary, Romania)	
	Policy enactment	Commitment to NATO (incl. 1979 *Doppelbeschluss*) and European institutions, but also Helsinki Process and bilateral improvement of relations with select partners in Eastern Europe	

continued

Table 8.1 Continued

		1970s	1980s
'Pacifism' – militarisation/ nuclear arms	Source	Militarisation of German states[M] Nuclear weaponry/overkill[M]	Militarisation of German states[W] Nuclear weaponry/overkill[W]
	Target	Everyone/German populations[W]	Everyone/German populations[W]
	Relation	Challenge[W] Existential[M]	Existential[W]
	World order description	Arms race and nuclear deterrence as lethal challenges to world in general and German states in particular	Arms race and nuclear deterrence as lethal challenges to world in general and German states in particular
	Conditioning effects	International arms control, national nuclear disarmament, rejection of 1979 *Doppelbeschluss*, withdrawal from military alliances (NATO)	International arms control, national nuclear disarmament, rejection of 1979 *Doppelbeschluss*, withdrawal from military alliances (NATO)
	Policy enactment	International arms control, Helsinki Process	International arms control, Helsinki Process
Anti-Americanism	Source	N/A	US nuclear weapons[M] US global interventions[M]
	Target	N/A	Everyone[M] German states[M]
	Relation	N/A	Existential[M]
	World order description	N/A	American unilateralism and focus on military conflict resolution as danger to world in general and German states in particular
	Conditioning effects	N/A	Rejection of US foreign and security policies
	Policy enactment	N/A	N/A

Terrorism	Source	Local criminals[D]
	Target	West German democracy[D]
	Relation	Challenge[W]
	World order description	Terrorism as criminal acts driven by local radicals
	Conditioning effects	Self-help strategy to counter a distinctively national challenge
	Policy enactment	National police responses
Global risks	Source	US (currency schemes, trade war)[W] OPEC/Conflicts in Middle East[W] Global economy[W] Non-state actors[M] Decolonisation struggles[M] Non-state actors[D] Interstate competition[D]
	Target	Everyone[W] Germany[M]
	Relation	Challenge[W]
	World order description	Emergent secondary challenges in the economic sector, associated with diffuse notions of interdependence and globalisation
	Conditioning effects	Unclear, sense of collective concerns/global risks
	Policy enactment	N/A

9 Switzerland embraces collective dangers

Towards collective insecurities in the 1990s

From the 1940s to the 1980s, the Swiss Confederation was not spared from security politics. As in other countries, political oppositions in world politics had been identified, and there was a conception of who threatened whom and how. Unlike other countries, however, Switzerland had seen no self-centric securitisation. Swiss policymakers identified strong antagonism between the two blocks – i.e. the Warsaw Pact and NATO – but they did not consider this conflict to directly affect their own country. This neutralist reading of world politics was little to debate in the Swiss political system. As a hegemonic reading of world politics, it disqualified 'political' types of cooperation with foreign partners – i.e. collaboration in security affairs. By the same token, it enabled a stringently isolationist kind of security politics, including substantial investments in military fortifications and a rigid focus on autonomous self-defence. In parallel, it also empowered a comprehensive agenda of humanitarianism, international arbitration and mediation. These latter efforts were seen as efforts to help others, motivated by solidarity. They were not justified using notions of a common challenge.

As Chapter 6 showed, this traditional conception of international security evolved slowly during the 1980s. At the time, there was a hesitant recognition of wider challenges beyond the military realm. The 1979 national security doctrine, for instance, rejected broader concepts of national security as standing 'outside security politics proper'. In spite of this relegation, however, it nevertheless also recognised issues such as global political stability and economic well-being as 'further' themes under the heading of 'comprehensive security'. Ideas of global interdependence emerged as well, to the point where global disarmament was vaguely posited as being beneficial to Switzerland as well as others. Within the Foreign Ministry, finally, a perspective consolidated according to which Swiss neutrality policy might gain further international recognition, if Switzerland was able to contribute 'solutions to the problems of the international community'. In arguing thus, the Foreign Ministry, too, was starting to point to collective concerns of sorts, even if their existence was underspecified and did not convince the Swiss electorate to accept UN membership in 1986.

This situation changed fairly rapidly after the fall of the Berlin Wall. Irrespective of the fact that the confrontation between the East and the West had not been held to affect Switzerland directly, the end of the Cold War rendered obsolete Swiss policymakers' established ways of systematising the international, and it forced a reconsideration of the categories by which world politics could be made intelligible. There are an unprecedentedly high number of security and foreign policy doctrines from the 1990s documenting this process. Indeed, a new national security doctrine set out a new reading of Switzerland's security context as early as 1990. Originally intended to legitimise the acquisition of new fighter aircraft, the *Bericht 90 zur schweizerischen Sicherheitspolitik* again advanced a military conception of security (Gabriel 1990). The government's emphasis on military forms of conflict was linked to two actors. On the one hand, the doctrine somewhat unexpectedly criticised Japan for its alleged militarisation of East Asian politics. On the other hand, the doctrine saw Europe as being in danger of military confrontation (Schweizerischer Bundesrat 1990: 4–5). There was an explicit fear that NATO might disintegrate and that a new continental insecurity system – i.e. a system in which each country confronted another militarily – might emerge in its place (De Dardel 1990). This meant that continental stability was identified as a common challenge to Europe at large, Switzerland included. The 1990 doctrine thus vaguely called for cooperative solutions in general and military confidence-building measures in particular.

Yet, despite its conceptual emphasis on military types of danger, the 1990 *Bericht* also addressed 'new threats'. 'Violence', it was argued, had become multidimensional, and following from this a broad range of new challenges, including HIV/AIDS, drug trafficking, organised crime, energy shortages, declining birth rates, overuse of environmental resources, natural disasters and food dependence, were identified (Schweizerischer Bundesrat 1990: 19ff). Although these dangers were still conceptually excluded from 'security politics proper', units of the armed forces, civilian protection and civilian service were dedicated to them. The new threats were also directly associated with international security cooperation, since solutions to them were deemed impossible without the support of other governments (Schweizerischer Bundesrat 1990: 4–6). The 1990 doctrine did not meet much criticism when it was discussed in parliament. Only the Greens challenged the military-centric focus of the doctrine. All other political parties rejected such criticism; some even repudiated it as an undue attack on the country's military institutions (Nationalrat 1991: 918/ Reimann). General Staff officers and security analysts endorsed the dedication of military units to new dangers, given that the effects of the latter 'often resembled those of armed conflict' (Kühner 1991: 252). The doctrine's broader suggestion, which was that the international security context had changed in ways that now required international security cooperation, was not turned into a subject of debate (Rickenbacher 1990). Just one parliamentarian explicitly addressed – and supported – the view that the current security environment was now 'putting Switzerland in a similar position as its neighbours' (Nationalrat 1991: 903–907).

Three years later, the 1993 *Bericht über die Aussenpolitik der Schweiz in den 90er Jahren* expanded on the foreign affairs implications of the new threat environment. Covering topics ranging from peace and security to human rights, democracy and rule of law, welfare and environmental sustainability, this comprehensive foreign policy report covered a wide terrain. In its discussion of national dangers, this *Bericht* again highlighted the threat of European disintegration. In the context of the enduring Balkan crises, rampant nationalism was seen as triggering conventional wars, which, it was suggested, then directly affected Switzerland (Schweizerischer Bundesrat 1993: 11–13). Furthermore, the foreign policy report emphasised the potential dangerousness of Russia, which was seen as highly militarised and utterly unstable, but it no longer presented Japan as a source of regional insecurity. Also, unlike the 1990 security doctrine, the foreign policy report finally abandoned the differentiation between 'real' and 'further' security themes. Whether the subject in question was migration, international organised crime, nationalism, underdevelopment, money laundering, drug trafficking, overpopulation, resource overuse, weapons proliferation, terrorism or social inequalities, military threats were no longer ranked higher than non-military types of dangers. Somewhat unexpectedly for a government that had been desirous to distance itself from foreign powers, the report also explicitly drew on NATO's 1991 *Strategic Concept* to justify its description of the international security context.

In terms of world ordering, these new threats were then consistently presented as collective challenges requiring collaborative responses. Indeed, the doctrine explicitly deplored Switzerland's absence from major multilateral security organisations such as NATO, the United Nations and the West European Union as a result of this view. A variety of rationales were used in support of this newfound internationalist perspective. In some instances, it was simply argued that the current security challenges were irresolvable without foreign aid. In others, international security cooperation was said to be requested or even demanded by the international community or it was presented as the most efficient means of countering contemporary dangers. Interdependence, too, was repeatedly posited as a reality that required cooperative foreign policymaking. As the Federal Government argued:

> Foreign policy increasingly becomes European domestic politics [...]. This is the logical consequence: The increasingly interdependent nature of international relations makes us share opportunities and risks, and security challenges in particular, with all other European states.
>
> (Schweizerischer Bundesrat 1993: 21)

Breaking fairly radically with earlier 'disentangled' readings of Switzerland's position in world politics, the 1993 report even concluded that Switzerland could not be secure if Europe was not (Schweizerischer Bundesrat 1993: 17).

Considering its novelty in Swiss security discussions, this distinct conceptualisation of the nation's international security context drew surprisingly wide and instant support. The military establishment explicitly endorsed the notion of interdependence and the need for multinational peacekeeping, though it also warned that the movement towards military peace operations must not impair national defence capabilities (Carell 1993). Leading politicians and parliamentarians, too, supported the view that the security environment was now also affecting Switzerland directly. Minister of Defence Kaspar Villiger, for instance, argued: 'Our problems are obtaining an international dimension [...]. Those who think that Switzerland is not affected by European events are subscribing to a dangerous illusion [...]. The global character of the new challenges requires more global answers than earlier' (Villiger 1995: 174, 178). A similar view was also expressed in the lower house's discussions of the 1993 *Bericht*:

> The North–South gap provides for dangerous tensions, which might result in violent conflict. Ecological problems are so grave that, seen from a global perspective, they may lead to virtual existential crises. The enormous and global migratory flows require us to live in multicultural societies. These questions are not questions that we can associate with the proverb *noli me tangere*. We are involved in these global processes.
>
> (Nationalrat 1994: 175/Mühlemann)

Eventually, this new perspective on world politics enabled some very concrete new foreign policy initiatives. One first such initiative was the creation of a 600-strong peacekeeping battalion, designed to assist in non-coercive UN and Organization for Security and Co-operation in Europe (OSCE) stabilisation missions. In public debates, the government and the great majority of the political parties of the time presented the peacekeeping battalion as compatible with neutrality policy (Loretan 1994). It was stylised as a continuation of traditional Swiss mediation efforts, even 'good offices in and by themselves' (Cotti 1994: 6). Military officers also supported this agenda, claiming that international operations would provide an excellent training ground for the armed forces (Mantovani 1994).

However, a small national-conservative party unexpectedly began to oppose this project after an extra-parliamentary interest group successfully forced a national referendum on the battalion. In their view, the creation of an international peacekeeping unit contradicted the populace's earlier rejection of UN membership. They argued that, instead of aiding mediation, it endangered neutrality policy and limited the space needed for good offices. Also, the battalion was deemed excessively costly and incompatible with the army's militia structure (Unser 1994). It was argued that Switzerland was better off supporting the humanitarian work of organisations such as the International Committee of the Red Cross. Switzerland was not to associate itself with the problems of others and thus needed to remain outside European and other international frameworks (Bachofner 1994). To the surprise of many, the federal law empowering the creation of the peacekeeping battalion was then rejected by 57 per cent of the electorate in the summer of 1994.

The 'breakdown' of the Swiss security policy consensus

Collective notions of danger, then, had been advanced gradually since the 1980s in the Swiss political system. Initially, international security contributions were derived from the international community's alleged demands for such efforts. Gradually, however, the justification for international security shifted towards an acknowledgment that Switzerland was located together with others in a common insecurity environment. Notions of globalisation and interdependence became a particularly popular aide in the 1980s and early 1990s. Even if these notions were rarely specified in a more meaningful way, they catered to an articulation of transnational insecurity. Further into the mid-1990s, international security cooperation was justified ever more directly by means of such 'self-interested' rationales, whereas solidarity with the problems of others became less often invoked as a justification (cf. Villiger 1995). Interestingly, however – and unlike the elaborate controversies on this issue witnessed in neighbouring France and West Germany earlier – the question of who exactly was held to be affected by the new collective insecurity environment was rarely specified or debated further. In some instances, it was argued that Switzerland shared similar positions to those of 'Europe'. In others, dangers were simply proclaimed to be global problems – i.e. challenges that everyone around the world was facing.

By contrast, during the period under observation it is possible to trace a certain evolution in the politics of determining the sources of the various identified dangers. In the immediate post-Cold War period, the issue that at first seemed most pressing was armed conflict between European states. With the rapid recognition of non-military types of threats, however, non-state actors were increasingly seen as responsible for both European and global insecurity. Whether the concerns centred on migration, weapons proliferation or food security, foreign governments – with the exception of Japan and Russia, who were intermittently pinpointed – were less and less often identified as sources of national insecurity by the Swiss Government and the major political parties in the mid-1990s (Gasteyger 1995). During this time, the projection of collective insecurities that were increasingly driven by non-state actors enabled a number of collaborative foreign policy initiatives, initiatives which were entered into with other foreign nations that appeared to be threatened in the same way. In 1995, 250 Yellow Berets were deployed to the OSCE mission in Bosnia. Following the conclusion of the Dayton Peace Accord in 1995, the Swiss government authorised the transfer of NATO arms and personnel through Switzerland. In 1996, Switzerland became a full member of the Conference on Disarmament (CD) and also acceded to NATO's Partnership for Peace (PfP) programme. In 1997, it joined the Euro-Atlantic Partnership Council (EAPC), and in 1999 it contributed a substantial number of troops to the multinational stabilisation force in Kosovo (Goetschel *et al.* 2005).

This internationalist foreign policy agenda differs remarkably from the country's earlier security and foreign affairs practices. Yet, as straightforward as the Swiss Confederation's new-found international agenda may have seemed, the unexpected outcome of the 1994 popular vote on the creation of an international peacekeeping battalion heralded a deep polarisation of Swiss foreign and security politics (Spillmann 1995). This polarisation no longer centred on the earlier controversy over the question of whether non-military dangers could or should be accepted into formal national security doctrines. Exceptions aside (e.g. Liener 1995), the securitisation of non-military dangers was by the mid-1990s widely accepted as valid by the major players in the Swiss political system. This means that instead of debating *which* themes were to be securitised and which not, a profound controversy emerged as to the question of *how* threats could be understood in practice. At the centre of this emergent controversy was the determination of who precisely was affected by the manifold new dangers of the time – i.e. the question of how they were organised 'in reality'.

Indeed, a powerful alternative reading of such organisation emerged in national-conservative quarters in the early 1990s. Their opposition to the novel discourse on 'common challenges' initially emerged in the economic sphere. Pushing for a rejection of Switzerland's planned membership of the European Economic Community (EEC), national-conservatives maintained that the country was not evolving in a common political space with others and should not be seen as such. They also maintained that it should *not* pursue international cooperation more actively as a consequence. Further into the mid-1990s, this syllogism was then transposed into security politics. According to national-conservative politicians, international security cooperation – such as through multinational peacekeeping – was both unnecessary and contrary to the popular will (Nationalrat 1994: 180/Frey). Rather than actively associating Switzerland with the challenges of others, these political forces argued that Switzerland should pursue national security autonomously. Indeed, they argued, instead of considering Switzerland as being implicated in common dangers together with others in the first place, the government should continue to provide solidarity contributions to the problems of others. As one influential National Councillor from that political camp argued in 1993, commenting on the government's foreign policy report described earlier in this chapter:

> The report lacks a clear commitment to armed neutrality. [...] Switzerland has, in front of world public opinion, committed itself to absolute neutrality. In opposition to ordinary neutrality, permanent neutrals have special rights and obligations. In particular, the permanent neutral has to abstain from all power politics. This is true peace policy! [...] One has to remain disentangled from the power politics clique. This is why we should develop our solidarity in the area of humanitarian aid, and on a global scale.
>
> (Nationalrat 1994: 180/Fehr)

By the mid-1990s, then, the traditional imagery of the home nation as an island of peace in a sea of problems – *problems of others* – returned in force to the national political arena. From this perspective, the country was surrounded by various kinds of confrontations and challenges, but neutrality ensured that it would not be directly affected by such problems. Towards the end of the decade, this return to dogmatic neutralism and neutrality was also aided by a prominent crisis in the financial industry. It was a time when the role of certain Swiss banks during World War II was being critically questioned. Some banks, it was soon proven, were not adequately cooperating in the restitution of financial assets that fascists had confiscated in the 1930s and 1940s, and others were even actively creating obstacles to such restitution. Following this discovery, the US Government put strong economic and political pressure on Swiss banks and the Swiss economy, demanding compensation for these dealings on behalf of the parties affected (Unabhängige Expertenkommission Schweiz – Zweiter Weltkrieg 2001). In the ensuing political debates, this American pressure was represented in particular ways. Politically, the banks became linked with 'Switzerland' as such, and criticism of the financial industry was presented as equalling criticism of Swiss wartime neutrality policy. American pressure on Switzerland was construed as a fairly pressing and exclusive challenge to the nation – it was seen as a deliberate attack on Switzerland, *but not others*. Given that no particular allies were indicated in this crisis, a very traditional, isolated and isolationist understanding of self-help politics re-emerged in force in the Swiss public debates.

By the late 1990s, then, Swiss security and foreign affairs was becoming ever more polarised. On one side stood the Federal Government and the great majority of political parties, advocating for international cooperation in what was seen to be a multidimensional, non-military and inherently collective security context. On the other side was the highly vocal – and increasingly powerful – national-conservative party advocating against common concerns and international cooperation. Surprisingly to many, this latter party soon succeeded in winning relevant national votes. Spectacularly, it managed to obtain rejection of Switzerland's association with the European Economic Community in 1992, and it also succeeded in denying the creation of a national peacekeeping battalion in 1994. Reacting to this deepening rift in Swiss foreign and security affairs, the Federal Council sought to re-establish a certain national security policy consensus later in the decade (Spillmann *et al.* 1999). Under the leadership of Edouard Brunner, a former high-ranking diplomat, the Ministry of Defence convened an independent study commission, with a view to developing a more sustainable national security perspective. The *Brunner Commission* included over 40 representatives from parliament, civil society and the public administration. Its concluding report had no formal governmental character. As will be demonstrated shortly, however, its findings had a very direct influence on the ensuing national security doctrine.

Published in 1998, the *Brunner Report* saw Switzerland as facing complex security challenges of all kinds, both military and non-military. These challenges, the report argued, were ever more pressing, and they were truly 'global' in nature. Conventional war was not seen as posing a danger to

Switzerland. Contrary to what other doctrines had argued earlier in the decade, large-scale military conflict in Europe was, indeed, held to be a non-issue for the entire post-Cold War period (Studienkommission für Strategische Fragen 1998: 1; Gabriel 1998). By the same token, earlier preoccupations with nationalism and European disintegration were reformulated into a non-state actor problem. In this view, it was not European governments that catered to a disintegration of the continent, but radicalised sub-national factions. Further, the *Brunner Report* strongly emphasised the security challenges caused by private actors. Nationalism, and also terrorism – in the late 1970s still associated with foreign states such as Iran – were directly attributed to such non-state actors, as were other contemporary dangers, such as illegal migration, organised crime, urban gang warfare, money laundering, cybercrime and trafficking in human beings (Studienkommission für Strategische Fragen 1998: 4ff.). Following from this description of the international security context, the *Brunner Commission* made a strong case for an expansion of international security frameworks: 'Guaranteeing our security no longer merely means to maintain a credible territorial military defence. It means especially to cooperate with our neighbours and the organisations and alliances surrounding our country' (Studienkommission für Strategische Fragen 1998: 5). Indeed, the lack of international cooperation in security affairs was presented as a source of national insecurity in its own right: 'If we do not succeed to participate in the European Union's cooperative security dispositif, the danger exists that our country turns into a gateway for illegal migration, transnational organised crime and international terrorism' (Studienkommission für Strategische Fragen 1998: 6).

In the parliamentary arena, this argumentation was met with overwhelming support. However, its findings were also harshly criticised by the national-conservative People's Party, whose leader, Christoph Blocher, publicly rejected the *Brunner Report*, although he himself had been a member of its study commission. Indeed, Blocher published an alternative position paper in response to the *Brunner Report* and distributed it to thousands of households across the country. In his view, it was Switzerland's choice whether or not it associated itself with the problem of others. International security cooperation, he argued, was an act of such voluntary political association, and it rendered the country *less* secure (Spillmann *et al.* 1999). With this open confrontation – highly unusual for the Swiss political system – two radically contending interpretations of world politics were positioned against each other. These views codified two very different – and, indeed, incommensurable – conceptions of the organisation of international danger, and they empowered very different kinds of foreign policy agendas. In the media and political arena, the two perspectives were then repeatedly brought into direct confrontation with each other. By the end of the millennium, this controversy had become so intense that scholars concluded there had been a veritable 'breakdown' of the national security consensus (Spillmann *et al.* 2001).

Fragile consolidation of collective insecurity

After this open breakdown of the debate, advocates of collective dangers and international cooperation can be seen to have consolidated their position in the early 2000s. This consolidation process was fragile, however, and it rested on an overt marginalisation of the epistemological opposition, although not the political opposition, since the Swiss People's Party was also a member of the government. Such confrontation was fairly unusual for Swiss public policymaking, which traditionally relied on lengthy processes of consensus-building. Yet the parliamentary majority – social democrats, Christian democrats, free democrats and greens – proceeded to advance and implement their own reading of world politics ever more forcefully, whereas national-conservatives showed little sign of compromise on their part, either. The 1999 national security and 2000 foreign policy doctrines bear witness to this process. Both documents straightforwardly promoted international cooperation – indeed, they even bore programmatic calls for 'security through cooperation' and 'cooperation in an interdependent world' in their titles. According to these two doctrines, cooperation in the security domain was required at all levels. The interconnectedness of the contemporary security environment required closer collaboration between local, cantonal and federal security actors and, in particular, more intimate cooperation with foreign governments and international organisations (Schweizerischer Bundesrat 1999). This strategy was necessary, given that 'violence and challenges' had become conceived as fundamentally transnational phenomena: 'The current threats are transnational. They affect our neighbours and partners as they do us. They can only be successfully solved through international cooperation, to which we are contributing our own strengths' (Schweizerischer Bundesrat 1999: 46).

> International challenges and opportunities do not stop at Swiss borders [...]. Globalisation does not only characterise economic and cultural activities. States' security problems are becoming increasingly global as well: Terrorism, organised crime and criminal sabotage of critical infrastructure, production and trade of narcotics are dangers that increasingly discomfort the international community. Also of concern are the financial gains that spring from such activities, as they enable corruption and fraud by criminal groups.
> (Schweizerischer Bundesrat 2000: 263, 277)

Indeed, the two government doctrines of 1999 and 2000 were pervaded by global conceptions of national insecurity. The financial markets, for instance, were attributed a global reach and a capacity to destabilise entire regions. Environmental catastrophes, migration and issues such as water shortage, soil erosion, climate change, pollution and toxic waste, too, were depicted as challenges for 'everyone'. Organised crime posed a particularly important security challenge in the view of Swiss authorities. It was considered global in organisation, and it was associated with a host of unwanted criminal activities ranging from money laundering to trafficking, blackmailing, weapons proliferation and political destabilisation. In light of this, the 1999 and 2000 doctrines focused strongly on shared insecurities, and they depicted an insecurity environment that was largely driven by non-state actors. International security cooperation was then derived from this 'reality', and Switzerland was asked to participate in those frameworks that managed current dangers most effectively. These frameworks included Schengen and Dublin, the United Nations, the OSCE, the Council of Europe and the Partnership for Peace programme. It excluded NATO membership as such, however, as the alliance's instruments were held to be inappropriate to counter the manifold non-military challenges of the day (Schweizerischer Bundesrat 1999: 48). Lastly, non-cooperation with such international frameworks was again presented as a source of national insecurity itself (Schweizerischer Bundesrat 2000: 298).

Hardly surprisingly, perhaps, national-conservatives opposed this description of world politics, despite the closing of ranks among its advocates. In the view of national-conservatives, neutrality was equated with international non-cooperation, and it was construed as a potent means for shielding the home nation from the problems of others. As one politician from that camp argued: 'Neutrality permits this country, this population, is not implicated in the conflicts of today, which are uncontrollable and whose effects are hard to delimit' (Nationalrat 1999/Schlüer). Yet all other major political parties, government officials and military officers forcefully defended the arguments made by the two doctrines. They hailed the doctrines' threat assessments as 'excellent', 'realistic' and, indeed, 'incontestable' (cf. Nationalrat 1999/Tschuppert, Borer or Cuche; Schweizerischer Ständerat 2000/Paupe), and they supported the foreign policy conclusion that was drawn from the security context described. Inversely, they also rejected alternative perspectives and solutions. As representatives from different national parties made clear: 'A passive stand is no longer possible in a world in which communication is global and economics globalised. Such a stand is not in our interest either. [...] International cooperation brings the best possible security to our country' (Nationalrat 1999/ Zapfel); 'Today, national security and independence can only be provided by international security cooperation' (Nationalrat 1999/Polla); 'Nations determine their own security policy, but not under the circumstances of their choosing. Whoever wants to pursue an autonomous, indeed an isolationist security policy has a solution, but this solution does not correspond to the problem' (Nationalrat 1999/Wiederkehr). In doing so, they were stressing a view according to which international cooperation derived from the very fact of the nation's self-interest. As the lead author of the 1999 security doctrine explained: 'Unlike what the security doctrine of 1973 suggested, the Swiss contributions to international security [...] are not expressions of solidarity, but of shared security interests' (Däniker 1999: 7).

In the early and mid-2000s, this majoritarian perspective was followed up with a number of internationalist security initiatives. In 2001, it led to a national vote on the armament of military specialists dispatched on missions abroad. Following the 1994 vote against a dedicated peacekeeping battalion, the few military personnel sent abroad – mainly small groups of military observers – were unarmed and, if necessary, physically protected by third parties. This was the case with the Swiss OSCE Yellow Berets in Bosnia and, in particular, Switzerland's detachment of a couple of hundred troops to Kosovo. In the latter case, Switzerland's most substantial military mission abroad thus far, troops were protected by Austrian armed forces, given the insufficient legal provisions for Swiss military self-defence abroad. Supporters suggested that armament of international deployments was necessary, given the need for multinational stabilisation missions in the contemporary security context (*Neue Zürcher Zeitung* [NZZ] 2001a). National-conservative and pacifist quarters, by contrast, opposed this perspective for different reasons, either based on different understandings of the contemporary security context or given a preference for non-military conflict resolution tools. In March 2001, the armament of military personnel abroad was accepted by a very narrow majority of 51 per cent of the electorate.

In 2002, the same agenda led to a second popular vote on UN membership. According to the Federal Government, which launched this campaign in 2000, the UN had become universal in membership, gained efficiency and was central to the handling of 'all major global problems' (NZZ 2000a: 13). Contrary to the 1986 vote, advocates of UN membership emphasised the self-interested nature of the project. It was argued, for instance, that the UN's efforts at post-conflict stabilisation were able to directly mitigate migratory pressure on Europe and Switzerland, and it was also presented as allowing for the repatriation of asylum seekers – a top concern in the Swiss public debates since the 1990s (NZZ 2001b). In the media and parliamentary debates of the time, supporters of UN membership can be seen mobilising established argumentations regarding collective dangers:

> Each and every instability has direct implications for Switzerland [...]. It is wrong to argue that we can refuge ourselves onto an island because world society is 'bad' [...]. This is stylised nationalist romanticism [...]. The question is not whether we associate with others' problems – we are implicated anyway. The question is how to deal with this implication [...]. It lies in our own interest to cooperate with others.
>
> (NZZ 2002: 13/Schlüer)

The terrorist attacks of September 2001 on American targets were compacted into this perspective as well. As one National Councillor argued: 'The horrible terrorist attacks in the US show how important cooperation is. Terrorism is a global crime, which no country can handle by itself' (Nationalrat 2001/Gysin). Again, this argument was decidedly rejected by national-conservatives. In their view, UN membership implied an association with the organisation's failures and problems, be it its unsuccessful interventions in places such as Yugoslavia and Somalia (Nationalrat 2001/Wenger) or the crude and egotistical power politics of the Security Council's permanent members. Addressing the 2001 attacks of Al-Qaeda on US targets, they also suggested that Switzerland was associating itself with the problems of the US Government if it defined terrorism as a common challenge (NZZ 2002/Mörgeli). In March 2002, UN membership was accepted by a modest majority of 54.6 per cent of the electorate.

Also in 2005, the same epistemological and argumentative confrontation resurfaced, this time in the context of Schengen/Dublin. The Schengen and Dublin Accords addressed asylum and migration issues at the European level, yet did not directly form part of the European Union, of which Switzerland was not a member. Whereas the government and the majority of political parties endorsed these two treaty frameworks, the Swiss People's Party again successfully forced a national referendum on their signature. In their view, the two treaties opened up the borders to the uncontrolled flow of persons and a wave of organised crime, thus making Switzerland more insecure (NZZ 2005a). Advocates, in contrast, argued that current dangers were transnational in nature already – i.e. that the agreements would respond to those challenges, *not* create them (NZZ 2005b). Indeed, access to the Schengen Information System was deemed a particularly powerful means for countering transnational crime. In the summer of 2005, association with both the Schengen and Dublin Accords was approved by – again – a small majority of 54.6 per cent of the national electorate.

In the first decade of the new millennium, then, the 'appropriate' interpretation of international politics was far from settled in the Swiss political system. On the contrary, two contending perspectives were portrayed in ways that were outright incommensurable with each other. The political system, too, was strongly divided. The majority in government and parliament felt that Switzerland shared numerous challenges with other nations. From their perspective, the international state system of the early 2000s was collectively challenged by non-state actor challenges in particular. The securitisation of 'new themes' – ranging from terrorism to migration, organised crime, environmental change, resource scarcity and social inequality – turned a great number of foreign governments into 'fellows' of Switzerland. Placed in similar positions in the international security context as Switzerland, they were identified and seized on as viable cooperation partners in the pursuit of national and international security. A comprehensive survey of Swiss politicians, professionals and specialised academics illustrates the remarkable depth of this perspective. In 2009, 75 per cent of surveyed actors felt that current insecurities were caused by non-state actors, and most of the remainder thought that foreign governments caused danger only inadvertently, if at all. Ninety-eight per cent considered the current challenges affected all of Europe; 70 per cent thought of them as truly global problems (Hagmann 2010). Not a single respondent argued that a current danger targeted Switzerland alone.

Interestingly, the great majority of actors surveyed in this study also felt that colleagues abroad – in Europe especially, but to lesser degrees also in North America – shared this description of the international security context. Indeed, respondents felt much more confident that their colleagues abroad shared such views than representatives of the Swiss political system did. This result is instructive. It shows the degree to which local knowledge of world politics is projected abroad, while also testifying to the particular epistemological polarisation of Swiss security politics of the time. In the late 2000s, the vocal national-conservative parliamentary minority continued to radically challenge the dominant reading of world politics. Invoking direct democracy instruments, this minority punctually succeeded in reversing the cooperative foreign policy agenda advanced by the country's political majority. In many cases, it also managed to make popular decisions extremely tight, such as in the cases of the armament of military personnel abroad, UN membership and Schengen/Dublin. Taken together, cooperative foreign policymaking *was* Switzerland's preferred strategy in the 1990s and 2000s, but its implementation was, and remained, a hard fight. The 2007 foreign policy and 2010 national security policy doctrines testify to this process. In the discussions of either document, the established lines of argumentation were reproduced again. The 2010 doctrine, drafted by the Ministry of Defence, which had come under control of a hard-line representative of the Swiss People's Party, even sought to shift attention away from international cooperation and towards national cooperation – a politically unsustainable agenda that was promptly discredited by the political majority, as well as by cantonal authorities, who feared the intervention of the Federal Council in their competencies.

Conclusion

Swiss security debates of the 1990s and 2000s moved away from military conceptions of national security and towards widespread recognition of dangers sponsored by non-state actors. More importantly, a great majority of the Swiss political system began arguing that international insecurity had become globalised – i.e. that dangers now affected the international community of states as a whole, the Swiss Confederation included. This self-insertion of Switzerland into collective insecurity created a new sense of place for Switzerland, and it was met with heavy political opposition. This controversy – the question of *how* current dangers threatened Switzerland, and no longer the question of *what* could be held to threaten the Confederation – is important in explaining Swiss foreign policymaking during the period in focus, given that different answers to this question enabled different foreign policy strategies (for a schematic overview, see Table 9.1). From one perspective, danger affected others, but *not* the home nation, and as a consequence, Switzerland was merely to provide humanitarian aid to the problems of others. From another perspective, collaborative foreign policy projects, such as membership of the Partnership for Peace programme, the deployment of armed military personnel abroad, adherence to the United Nations and membership of the Schengen/Dublin frameworks, were seen necessary. As shown in the next two chapters, the Swiss polity was hence chiefly occupied with a different dimension of international ordering than its neighbouring countries.

Table 9.1 Swiss constructions of international (in-)security in the 1990s and 2000s

		1990s	*2000s*
Continental disintegration	Source	Nationalism (of sub-state actors)[D] Nationalism (of governments)[W]	N/A
	Target	Europe (incl. Switzerland)[D] Europe (excl. Switzerland)[W]	N/A
	Relation	Existential[W]	N/A
	World order description	Fear of continental disintegration – driven by governments or radicalised sub-state actors – return to generalised military confrontation between all European states	N/A
	Conditioning effects	Generalised collective continental stability challenge, driven by governments or sub-state actors, also affecting Switzerland	
	Policy enactment	General support to international security, Yellow Berets to Bosnia, Partnership for Peace membership	N/A
Japan/Russia	Source	Militaristic policies[W]	N/A
	Target	East Asia[W] Europe[W]	N/A
	Relation	Existential[W]	N/A
	World order description	Japan and Russia as unpredictable regional dangers	N/A
	Conditioning effects	N/A (short-lived discourse)	
	Policy enactment	N/A (short-lived discourse)	

continued

Table 9.1 Continued

		1990s	2000s
New threats: Organised crime, terrorism, migration, environmental catastrophes etc.	Source	Non-state actors[W] Foreign governments[W]	Non-state actors[D] Foreign governments[M]
	Target		Europe (incl. Switzerland)[D] International community[W] Europe (excl. Switzerland)[W]
	Relation		Challenge[W]
	World order description	Basket of new and largely non-military dangers as transnational problems for Europe and/or world, affecting Switzerland in a similar way to other nations	
	Conditioning effects	International security cooperation on common themes	
	Policy enactment	Yellow Berets, Partnership for Peace, international peacekeeping, UN membership, Schengen/Dublin	

10 France and the reconstruction of European insecurities

State-sponsored insecurities in the 1990s

Chapter 7 showed how French policymakers advanced fairly differentiated conceptions of international insecurity between the mid-1950s and the late 1980s. These conceptions centred particularly strongly on West Germany, the USSR and the United States, and in each case different factions in France argued for or against the presentation of these countries as sources of international insecurity. However, a central element of debate was also the question of *how* these actors could be held, precisely, to pose a threat – who they targeted and whom they did not, together with the Fifth Republic or without it. Indeed, this latter question was particularly controversially debated in France between the 1950s and the late 1980s, as the epistemological confrontation between Gaullists, Atlanticists, nationalists, communists and others has shown. Different conceptions of how these various dangers threatened France and others 'in reality' then conditioned France's foreign policymaking on their own terms. The idea that the US was no longer threatened by the USSR, for instance, had a considerable influence on French foreign affairs, as did the emergent conceptualisation of the superpowers as forming a global directorate. As the dominant local conception of the international security context, it helps explain France's rejection of NATO, the initiatives it took in respect to European integration, its rapprochement with Moscow and its costly efforts at autonomous nuclear defence.

In the 1980s, Gaullist interpretations of world politics still provided the key parameters of international systematisation in Paris, despite the fact that a socialist President had come to power and that new themes such as southern instabilities, energy security, terrorism and migration had been endangered. In 1989/1990, the fall of the Berlin Wall then radically challenged these established ways of world ordering (Yost 1990; Grant 1990). Unlike in neighbouring Switzerland, however, the ensuing French perspectives did not shift so paradigmatically to notions of global, non-state actor-driven insecurities. Instead, French analysts and policymakers focused predominantly on Germany and Russia in the early 1990s. Indeed, the sudden and intense preoccupation with Germany is striking. As shown earlier, there had been a prolonged period of normalisation between the two countries. Although Germany continued for a long time to be viewed sceptically in France, hardly any French politician still declared their neighbouring country a source of national insecurity by the 1980s. Indeed, rather than presenting Bonn in such terms, French politicians had by that decade actively extended cooperation with the FRG. Based on notions of shared insecurity with West Germany, they developed the Elysée Treaty further and established new transnational military structures, such as Eurocorps.

The rapid unification of the two German states took the French political establishment by surprise, however. Arguably, the German unification process unfolded rapidly – too rapidly perhaps – and thus the creation of a single, large and powerful German state caused much distress among French policymakers (Musitelli and Védrine 1991). However, a careful analysis shows that a unified Germany was not securitised in a straightforward manner as a present and direct danger. Rather, it was its future international behaviour that became an object of anxiety and intense speculation. Would Germany's foreign policy stances change following unification, and if so, then in what direction? In the view of French commentators, Germany had two options from which to choose and with which to position itself vis-à-vis France and other European nations:

> Either unified Germany integrates itself without hesitation into a political and economic European union [...], or it plays for time in order to re-establish its power independently. In this second case, having achieved its reunification, Germany will become more powerful and less tempted to base her economy in the European framework. Her security context will become increasingly distinct. She'll be looking egoistically towards the East.
>
> (Giraud 1990: 516)

This specific interpretation of possible German danger is instructive, because its syllogism is based on both future action and Central Europe. This is to say that Germany was mainly considered a potential danger to Eastern Europe, and this situation was then seen as threatening European stability more generally in return. Indeed, the idea that Central Europe would be particularly strongly exposed to 'German ambitions (Moïsi 1995) had arguably already motivated President Mitterrand to refrain from supporting Mikhail Gorbachev's reform programmes in the 1980s. Seemingly, a weakening of the USSR would have helped Germany's resurgence, for it would have left Central and Eastern Europe vulnerable to German foreign policy. Of course, such reasoning concealed – rather poorly – an analogy to fascist Germany's earlier quest for *Lebensraum*. And, indeed, after the fall of the Berlin Wall, a small number of French politicians also predicted a European 'reversal of alliances' similar to that witnessed in the 1930s. It was speculated that a resurgent Germany would once again enter into a strategic coalition with a weakened Russia. Forming an unholy alliance, the two governments would thus be able to divide up Central and Eastern Europe between themselves (Brenner 1990).

Some French politicians pushed this syllogism even further. In their view, Moscow might not even be able to defend its 'own share' of Eastern Europe in the event of such a division, given its recent loss of power. French analysts even argued that Moscow might want to rely on the US, in order to control the new 'German *Reich*': 'Certain Soviet declarations let us think that their authors prefer a Germany under the influence of the United States or bound by its European allies rather than a grand *Reich* too independent' (Valentin 1990: 537). Indeed, French journalists and academics suggested that the US, too, was concerned with Eastern Europe's ability to thwart Germany's alleged new-found ambitions (LeM 1991). The superpower agreement, whereby the former Eastern Germany was not allowed to become a NATO operations theatre, served, they claimed, as much to reassure Moscow against NATO expansion as it helped to protect Europe against Germany (Musitelli and Védrine 1991).

In 1991 and 1992, unified Germany's quick recognition of Slovenia and Croatia as independent states lent weight to these French fears, as did the argument made by German politicians that the Atlantic Alliance had become obsolete after the disintegration of the Soviet Union (Scharping 1994). The 'correct' interpretation of the new entity of Germany, then, figured prominently in the French debates after the fall of the Berlin Wall, yet it was also undetermined (Bozo 1991; Heisbourg 1994). There was much speculation – but not yet conviction – that France's neighbour might turn into a danger to Eastern Europe and consequently to Europe as a whole. As a result, one finds politicians during that time who put significant emphasis on the relevance of France's nuclear weaponry. And, indeed, concerns over a unified Germany arguably also motivated France's fairly aggressive nuclear arms tests of the early 1990s (LeM 1995a). Going further, some politicians also launched the idea of a pre-emptive counter-German alliance with Russia. Even President Mitterrand seems to have briefly supported this idea, although he then rejected it again as unwarranted (Touraine 1993; Hoffmann 2000).

Besides Germany, Russia also figured prominently in France's security debates of the early 1990s. Pointing to Russia's military arsenal, observers stressed that in military terms, Moscow was still the capital of a global superpower (Gnesotto 1990). Advocating against a lowering of Western defences, Foreign Minister Pierre Joxe, for example, stressed the fact that Russia was still producing 1,800 tanks per year, and that this was more than the total number of tanks that France possessed (Assemblée 1991: 2841). Whereas the concern with Germany gradually dissolved again by the mid-1990s, the presentation of Russia as an important danger to European security endured considerably longer. It was explicitly reproduced in the French *Livre Blanc* of 1994 (Gouvernement Français 1994: 12) – i.e. France's official defence doctrine of the 1990s. It was also sustained by French assessments of Russian operations in Chechnya, as well as Russian economic boycotts of the Baltic states (Robin 1995). French observers feared, moreover, that ultra-nationalists such as Vladimir Zhirinovsky might come to power in Moscow, making unpredictable use of Russia's awe-inspiring military arsenal. There was thus a fair amount of anxiety regarding the possibility of a nationalist counter-revolution in Russia (Maresca 1995; Froment-Meurice 2000). This syllogism was developed further over time. By the late 1990s, Russia's military leadership was deemed ready to stage a coup in Moscow, given its alleged quest to reposition Russia as a global superpower (Facon 1999). All told, Russia was hence portrayed in somewhat less existentialist terms in the France of the 1990s compared to the 1980s. Yet it was still considered a highly significant and, indeed, persistent danger to France and Europe at large.

Preoccupations with Germany and Russia had a great deal of influence on the French conceptualisation of the international, and thus they affected French foreign policymaking in a very direct way. Most importantly, concerns regarding Germany and Russia facilitated a comprehensive agenda for European stabilisation. This agenda featured two components. On the one hand, the French Government sought to prevent a general return to unilateralism in Europe. This agenda was mainly aimed at Germany, whose future foreign policies were to be directed to cooperative measures (Hoffmann 2000). But it also targeted the United States, whose withdrawal of forces from Europe and contradictory stance on Yugoslavia were also viewed sceptically in Paris (Bertram 1995). In the early and mid-1990s, French politicians were highly overt in their search for new 'common threats' that would help sustain both multilateralism and the Atlantic Alliance. There was a strong sense that in the absence of a common agenda, the Atlantic Alliance would be incapable of keeping a unified Germany integrated in a multinational framework, and that it would then quickly disintegrate. On the other hand, the French Government also sought to assist democratic transitions in the post-Soviet space (Asmus 2002). There was a sense that instability in Eastern Europe posed a problem to Europe as a whole, and that, consequently, the European Union should become an active institution-builder in that region. However, opinions diverged in France as to what precisely caused this Eastern European instability and whom it affected most directly. In the view of some, Eastern Europe posed an essentially 'European' problem, and solutions therefore had to be found on the continent itself. In the view of others, the stability of Eastern Europe was intimately linked to the security threats posed by Russia and Germany, and so it was better for NATO and the United States to be involved (Gnesotto 1997).

This ambivalent perspective gave way to a two-track strategy at the operational level, a foreign policy strategy whose elements were advanced in the 1990s with uneven forcefulness. First, the French Government pursued a strategy of revitalising European security structures and capabilities (Gautier 1999). As shown earlier, this strategy had already been relaunched in the late 1980s. At that time, the West European Union was being revived as a forum for European security discussions, with the exclusion of the United States and Canada. This was also when Eurocorps was founded, initially with Germany. It was later expanded to Spain, Belgium, the Netherlands, Luxembourg and – in the decade after 2010 – Poland. These European frameworks for swift and targeted multilateral military intervention evolved considerably faster than those developed by NATO. In 1992 already, the West European Union adopted the *Petersberg*

Tasks, directing its defence apparatuses towards international peacekeeping, humanitarian aid and other kinds of international stabilisation missions. Also in 1992, the Maastricht Treaty integrated these tasks into the European Union's Common Foreign and Defence Policy framework, thus creating the nucleus for what later would be developed further into the European Defence and Security Policy (Quermonne 1992). As shown in Chapter 7, this European security agenda was originally driven by a presentation of the continent as threatened by the 'superpower condominium'. In the 1990s, however, it was increasingly widely based on the understanding that the contemporary challenges affected Europe much more directly than the North Atlantic community (LeM 1995a).

Second, the focus on European stabilisation also empowered reinvigoration of the Atlantic Alliance. Immediately in 1990–1991, numerous French analysts felt that this alliance had lost its *raison d'être* following the implosion of the Warsaw Pact (LeM 1995b). This assessment seemed reminiscent of traditional Gaullist perspectives on Atlantic defence. Gaullists had in the past been in favour of the disintegration of NATO and the Warsaw Pact (cf. Gouvernement Français 1972). Towards the mid-1990s, however, this perspective had changed. Instead of working towards the dissolution of the Western alliance, French government officials endorsed the new security agenda set out in the alliance's new *Strategic Concept*. Instead of putting more distance between themselves and the alliance, French officials sought *closer* relations with NATO, and different justifications were advanced in this regard. On one hand, it was argued that France's return to NATO would increase its ability to influence Germany's future foreign and defence policies, and that this was necessary given the lingering transatlantic challenge posed by both Germany and Russia (Brenner 1990). On the other, rapprochement with NATO was driven by newer concerns with 'regional instabilities' outside alliance territory. As shown in more detail later in this chapter, in the 1990s French policymakers started to identify such instabilities as key challenges to international security. Having pushed military transformation with particular rapidity, the French Government felt that it was capable of promoting and leading this international stabilisation agenda in NATO as well (Sauder 1996; Howorth 2002). In 1996, however, French rapprochement with NATO came to a sudden halt after the US Government blocked the transfer of NATO's Southern Command to France (Menon 2000). Arguably, the US Government had invested the alliance with its own – much more global – mandate by that time, thus seeking to direct NATO operations more forcefully to such ends (Andréani 1998; Asmus 2002).

During the 1990s, then, the balance between 'European' and 'North Atlantic' responses to the perceived international security context of the time remained a delicate one. While in the 1980s an antagonist rendering of the US had been a key reason to be against transatlantic and in favour of European solutions, in the 1990s the two approaches started to be portrayed in more compatible terms following the end of the 'superpower condominium' and the perceived resurgence of Germany and Russia. They did not become fully complementary, however. The question of whether a return to NATO would limit the effectiveness of

European frameworks, for instance, was a recurrent point of debate in France. Also, it remained unclear which nations were affected most directly by the challenges of the time. This is to say that in the 1990s, the type of insecurity community that France was seen as being located in, together with others, was not always clearly delimited. Although Europe was clearly identified as the core of that community, its precise external boundaries were not unanimously accepted. And, indeed, throughout the 1990s it is possible to find a fair number of contending articulations in this regard, with majority views shifting back and forth from one to another. In the Paris of the early 1980s, for instance, conceptions of continental insecurity were forcefully advanced, while in the mid-1990s, a more transatlantic perspective prevailed among the ruling parties. By the end of the decade, however, as the 1998 French-British summit in St. Malo shows, the tendency was once again to defend more 'European' perspectives on international insecurity (LeM 1998). This ambivalent securitisation process continued into the 2000s, and it has not yet been fully settled today, although a more European perspective appears to have become dominant again in recent years, as the national defence and the foreign policy doctrines of the late 2000s suggest (Gouvernement Français 2008a, 2008b).

New threats: constructing the 'European periphery'

As the discussion on Germany and Russia shows, dangers caused by foreign states remained central to French security thinking in the 1990s and early 2000s. This does not mean, however, that no new dangers centred on non-state actors were recognised in France in addition to the above concerns. However, unlike in Switzerland, where a large number of non-military dangers were now identified as guiding rationales, the French articulation of 'new threats' in the 1990s was more restricted. Indeed, governmental statements, parliamentary debates, academic studies and media articles at the time focused strongly on the more select insecurity themes of 'regional instability', migration, organised crime and weapons proliferation. In particular instances, these new threats were intertwined with each other in the local debates. In part, they were also associated more or less directly with the 'classic' state-centric danger narratives set out above – such as in the case of 'regional instability', which emerged as a distinct focal point for the security debates of the 1990s, but which in part also alluded to conceptualisations of Central and Eastern Europe and thus to the challenges of Germany and Russia. Unlike in Switzerland, then, France's new threat agenda was not as neatly differentiated from further concerns with 'classic', statist threats.

This being said, concerns over 'regional instabilities' in the 1990s also developed outside these categories. Indeed, the focus on this danger initially emerged from older notions of violent turmoil in the Global South. In the 1970s and 1980s, French politicians had begun to consider these conflicts as challenges to international security in general. In doing so, however, they often linked violent conflicts in the Global South to the superpowers. In the 1990s, there was a reinterpretation of the deeper causes of 'regional instabilities', broadly defined.

According to an increasingly popular view, violent confrontations abroad now had to be explained by cultural factors (David 1999). Deep-rooted nationalist hatreds, not governmental actors, were responsible for ethnic cleansing and civil wars in places such as the Balkans, Moldova, Georgia or Armenia and Azerbaijan (Assemblée 1994a: 690–691/Richard Cazenave) – and consequently, French foreign policymaking had to be directed against those actors, not foreign governments. As these latter examples suggest, regional turmoil was thus also connected ever more directly to Europe with its re-articulation. Compared to what had been the case earlier, regional conflicts were now seen as taking place in Europe proper or along its borders. Where they were located further away, it was argued that accelerated and globalised 'transmission mechanisms' were turning them into direct and immediate challenges to Europe. The Gulf War of 1991 is a prominent example of this latter reasoning being advanced in France. In this instance, French policymakers stated that the motivation for French support for UN actions against Iraq was based on the unwarranted and instant repercussions that Iraqi politics allegedly had throughout Europe (Assemblée 1991; Gouvernement Français 1994: 13).

Concerns with regional turmoil, broadly defined, thus became highly popular in the 1990s, when they were linked more directly to Europe. Indeed, many regional conflicts were identified along what became termed the 'European periphery' – i.e. the southern and eastern borders of the continent (Delpech 1999). It was argued that instabilities there challenged France and, subsequently, Europe as a whole. They were *not* construed as problems affecting others beyond Europe, although the identified regional dynamics were adjacent to further, non-European nations and regions. Portrayed as European problems, regional instabilities then contributed directly to the multinational peacekeeping agenda (Andréani 1998). For example, the notion of an insecure European periphery creating security implications for all European nations was invoked widely during the Yugoslav crises, when French leaders mobilised that conception to justify military contributions to the United Nations Protection Force (UNPROFOR) (Assemblée 1992: 1727/Defence Minister Pierre Joxe, 1993: 2695ff./ Foreign Minister Alain Juppé). Remarkably, the framing of regional instabilities as collective challenges that were increasingly driven by non-state actors was little debated in France in the 1990s. There were some ongoing discussions around the question of whether the new challenges had transatlantic implications beyond their European configuration, but in general, criticism focused more strongly on technical aspects, such as the transformation of the conscript army into an organisation capable of multinational cooperation and rapid international deployment.

Migration was also turned into an ever more pressing transnational security concern in the 1990s (Bigo 1996). During the 1980s, immigration had started to be approached through an increasingly narrow policing perspective. After the economic recession of the 1970s, French immigration policy had become more restrictive, shifting towards tighter government control (Weil 1994). Chapter 7 showed how, in the 1980s, national-conservative politicians such as Jean-Marie Le Pen and

Bruno Mégret had begun linking immigration to notions of terrorism and crime. In the 1990s, such linkages were also endorsed by more centrist politicians, and they were developed further in conceptual terms. Notably, migration was now linked to regional conflicts and instabilities, with the latter becoming seen as particularly powerful generators of large-scale population movements. Importantly, migration was also associated with demographic developments along the Mediterranean southern rim, where, it was argued, high unemployment and birth rates created enormous migratory pressure. Given the material affluence and political liberty found in Europe, that pressure was seen as naturally directed against the European continent, whose market and social fabric it was claimed to threaten (Papademetriou 1994; Froment-Meurice 2000). Indeed, migratory pressure from North Africa in particular was considered so intense that no physical or political barrier could stop it from affecting or reaching the continent. As one parliamentarian argued rather dramatically in the early 1990s: 'No frontiers and no oceans impede the exchange of populations. The Maghreb is our neighbour today as much as Belgium or Italy. The global exchange of populations is becoming the law of the 21st century' (Assemblée 1991: 2847/Jean-Michel Boucheron).

Eventually, this demographic and economic pressure from North Africa became linked to other European nations' concerns with immigration – notably, anxieties over immigration from the post-Soviet space (Loescher 1994). Conceptually, this linkage again assisted in the construction of the European periphery as a larger, threatening entity or problem space. Migration became portrayed as a collective danger to Europe as a whole, precisely because it was seen to emanate from a geopolitical space that enveloped the entire continent – an unstable and problematic space stretching from Casablanca to Cairo, Istanbul and Tallinn (LeM 2002). Towards the end of the decade, this distinct conceptualisation of migration was also interwoven with further types of insecurity. It became associated ever more closely with the notion of organised crime, and it was also intertwined with the challenges posed by weapons proliferation. With this linkage, the latter danger was itself reinterpreted in the 1990s. During the Cold War, weapons proliferation had been attributed to the superpowers, but in the 1990s it was mainly reframed as a problem driven by warlords, private traders and other transnational criminal gangs (Dunn 1995; LeM 1998). Lastly, select French politicians also drew on notions of Islamist fundamentalism in North Africa – and thus on the spectre of the terrorist bombings witnessed in the 1980s – when defining migration as a pressing contemporary danger (Assemblée 1994b: 2127/Defence Committee President Jacques Boyon).

'New threats', then, were not only recognised in the French political system of the 1990s. They were also crafted in fairly specific ways. On the one hand, the securitisation of new threats contributed to a conception of world politics that was ever more strongly structured by problems relating to non-state actors. The dangers caused by 'regional instability', for instance, were linked more closely to the activities of such actors. Also the challenge of weapons proliferation was reinvigorated in the 1990s and transposed into a non-state actor problem. On the other hand, the focus on new dangers also helped describe a world of shared insecurities.

There was a general understanding that given their 'location' in the European periphery, the new dangers affected Europe as a whole, including France. Some argued that these same new dangers also affected the entire North Atlantic region as such or that they represented global problems affecting 'everyone'. In terms of foreign policymaking, this collectivist and predominantly 'Eurocentric' securitisation was particularly conducive to the pursuit of pan-European responses. In the 1990s, it enabled pan-European collaboration on international peacekeeping, and it also provided the epistemological basis for an expansion of continental police and immigration frameworks, such as Schengen, Dublin and Frontex.

Terrorism and US interventions

Finally, in the early 2000s, it was the danger of terrorism and the securitisation of US global interventions that provided the key elements in French systematisations of international insecurity. Terrorism, as Chapter 7 showed, had already been endangered earlier in the French political system. Following a series of international hijacking attempts, but in particular after several bloody attacks in Paris, terrorism became a salient topic in France in the mid-1980s. Although by this time terrorism was recognised as an important security challenge, its origins had yet to be clearly defined: as has been shown, some politicians attributed terrorist activities to states such as Iran, Libya, the United States or the USSR. Others refrained from identifying actors and tied the problem to North Africa, which they portrayed as a larger 'problem region'. A third group of politicians linked the problem of terrorism to international crime and migration. The threat of terrorism thus constituted an important topic in the Paris of the mid-1980s. After that, however, it quickly lost much of its salience. Indeed, a closer look at the security debates of the 1990s shows that no sizable political grouping continued to present terrorism as a serious challenge to national and international security during that period (Bureau 2002).

This situation changed again after Al-Qaeda's attacks on US targets in 2001. At that time, the danger of terrorism was very quickly revived in the French polity. Compared to the 1980s, however, terrorism was construed in new terms. In 2001, terrorism was framed both as a major transnational security challenge and as a threat that was generated by hard-to-control non-state actors. As one Christian-democrat parliamentarian argued in the immediate aftermath of the September 11 attacks:

> Since 9/11 the world is no longer as it was before. We find ourselves in a new kind of violence, and we must establish the conditions for a new kind of peace [...]. No longer are we in the logic of confrontations of blocs, and neither are we any more in the logic of confrontations of states, controllable by fear or reason. Here, there is no longer fear, and there is no longer reason. International terrorism is composed by non-state actors, unpredictable and uncontrollable.
>
> (Assemblée 2001b: 27–28/Philippe de Villiers)

Conceptually, this rendering of the danger termed 'terrorism' caused France and other states to associate closely with the United States, which had been the physical target of Al-Qaeda's attacks. Indeed, going further, it gave way to an impressively globalist representation of terrorism. In this view, it was not just the West that was challenged by terrorism. Instead, all democracies worldwide were deemed to be threatened by terrorism – and maybe all other nations as well. In France, this distinct conception of international insecurity provided the epistemological basis for extensive anti-terrorist collaboration with various other states, given that these were seen to be developing similar positions vis-à-vis the danger of terrorism as France. As Prime Minister Lionel Jospin argued in 2001:

> Our ambition must be to give a universal character to the anti-terrorist union. This union will not dissolve all tensions of the world. It does not aim at imposing a monolithic identity to peoples. But it would be wrong to invoke critical appreciations of US responsibilities in recent history to argue that that 'this fight is not ours'. The fight against terrorism is an imperative common to all democracies, and it must become an imperative to all nations. This is not the war of some other into which we are being implicated, it is a necessary action to which we are freely contributing our efforts.
>
> (Assemblée 2001a: 2)

The conceptual self-positioning of France in a broader insecurity community (composed of mainly democratic nations) thus had fairly direct consequences in the realm of foreign policymaking. Most important perhaps, it justified French support for the first-ever invocation of Article 5 of the Washington Treaty. According to this central treaty clause, an attack on one member state of the Atlantic Alliance must be construed as an attack on all member states, and it must then also be countered collectively. France vigorously supported the invocation of this article, and it also supported related proposals for global counterterrorist responses generated by the United Nations, whether this meant the authorisation of US military operations in Afghanistan or the expansion of international counterterrorism frameworks in the realms of finance or travel control. Subsequently, however, the challenge of terrorism was gradually reinterpreted. By 2002, the American 'Global War on Terrorism', in particular, came to be viewed sceptically in France (Howorth 2002). French observers considered this agenda highly unilateralist and excessively global. Moreover, it was considered to be connected to issues and actors that did not originally form part of the post-9/11 securitisation of terrorism as French politicians had endorsed it. As one analyst argued:

> [T]he war against terror has been extended to terrorist networks that have no global reach whatsoever, but also to states which are giving cover to such groups. With the discourse on the 'axis of evil' of 29 January 2002, the war has then been stretched to those states which are in possession of weapons of mass destruction and susceptible to transfer these to terrorist groupings.
>
> (Tertrais 2004: 534–535)

Fairly quickly, then, terrorism started to be approached as a danger on which multiple perspectives existed. In the view of many in France, terrorism as it was securitised by the Atlantic Alliance in 2001 was a different issue to that into which it was made and acted upon by Washington in 2002 and 2003. Indeed, the US Government became increasingly widely seen as advancing its own perspective on world politics, promoting a view that was deemed to differ fairly significantly from France's and Europe's own securitisation of terrorism (Makki 2004). On the one hand, the American compartmentalisation of world politics into 'good' and 'evil' was deemed excessively crude and totalising (Assemblée 2002: 15/Jean-Marc Ayrault). On the other hand, the US Government's existentialist pitching of the first such entity against the latter was considered an overstatement of the 'actual' dangerousness of terrorism. Taken together, then – and from a perspective not all that dissimilar from the ways in which US foreign policymaking had been construed by Gaullists during the Cold War – the 'American' rendering of terrorism was gradually seen as propagating and projecting abroad an unrealistically simplistic notion of threatened community, and as counter-positioning this community in untenable existentialist terms against an equally simplistic idea of threatening actor.

As if these differences of interpretation were not enough, French politicians also felt that their US counterparts were trying very hard to impose this distinct view onto others. Once again, the US Government was accused of trying to enforce its own world ordering. As the rhetoric on 'good' and 'evil' evolved, American framings of terrorism and 9/11 became ever more widely seen as a hegemonic and rather crude attempt to arrange the international relations of others in an authoritative fashion (Charillon 2002; Tertrais 2004). By the mid-2000s, the majority of French politicians put a critical distance between themselves and this alleged American agenda. As the 2008 *Livre Blanc* made clear, they considered that France and Europe construed terrorism in a more differential and fine-graded manner (Gouvernement Français 2008a; Makki 2004). As Prime Minister Jean-Pierre Raffarin argued in 2003, referring to European governments' perspectives on terrorism, as well as their relations with Washington:

> A different vision unifies us, the vision of a multi-polar world [...]. We see and wish a diversified world which does not accept a single voice, and which nourishes dialogue between its different poles without the endeavouring to align them.
>
> (Assemblée 2003: 23/Prime Minister Jean-Pierre Raffarin)

While the French Foreign Ministry strongly supported the common counterterrorism agenda set out in 2001, by the mid-2000s it was positioning itself at a more critical distance from the US. Such action was *not* motivated by a de-securitisation of terrorism. Prime Minister Raffarin, for instance, explicitly endorsed the presentation of terrorism as an international challenge. As he argued: 'Whether it is about terrorism, the proliferation of weapons of mass destruction or the fight against organised crime: The fight against the new plagues must be collective' (Assemblée 2003: 2).

French policymaking hence began to rest on an understanding that terrorism was a collective challenge, but that it also posed less of a totalising danger than what was suggested – i.e. that it was better presented as an important nuisance, rather than an existentially threatening 'evil'. As time progressed, the view also emerged that US policymaking itself was responsible for creating the danger of terrorism, at least in part. This antagonistic rendering of the US was articulated with the US invasion of Iraq. Here, too, French leaders did *not* claim that the threat posed by Iraq was harmless. As Foreign Minister Dominique de Villepin succinctly argued in 2002: 'Today the menace exists in Iraq. We can discuss its degrees but not its reality' (Assemblée 2002: 28). Prime Minister Raffarin also made it clear that Iraq posed a particular kind of problem to the world, given its past actions. As he argued in parliament:

> To be sure, Iraq is not the only country in which questions of weapons of nuclear, chemical and biological mass destruction are being raised, but it is the one country upon which the international community had imposed, by reason of Iraq's past actions especially during the Gulf War, the most stringent obligations.
>
> (Assemblée 2002: 10)

Whether Iraq posed a superior danger to France, however, was a question of debate in the French polity, and in the view of many, a military invasion of Iraq was to be avoided. The association of Iraq with global terrorism was considered particularly doubtful in Paris, as was the evidence that American and British intelligence services presented regarding Iraq's alleged weapons of mass destruction (WMD) programme. When the US and Britain occupied Iraq, their invasion then became construed as a source of international insecurity in its own right. The invasion itself was endangered, since it was seen as stimulating further acts of terrorism and destabilising the Middle East at large (Assemblée 2003). Iraq, then, was endangered as a problem of sorts in France. The challenge that this dictatorship presented, however, was not immediately seen as affecting France or Europe directly – instead, it was construed rather as a problem for the Gulf region. Via the detour of the US/UK invasion of Iraq, however, the notion turned into a signifier for US unilateralism. Once that invasion transformed into an ongoing occupation, it was then reinterpreted into a source of international – and not just regional – insecurity in its own right.

Eventually, then, America's responses to the terrorist attacks of 9/11 became securitised as collective dangers to international security, France included. As a result, international terrorism was increasingly presented as more of an 'American problem'. Although it was still considered a global challenge by many in France, such terrorism was increasingly interpreted as

more likely to target the US than other countries and as being partly stimulated by US foreign policy itself. In the 2000s, this view generated some
fairly major diplomatic quarrels between Paris and Washington. While select
minority factions in France also supported the US agenda, the now dominant
French reading of terrorism and US foreign policy had a fairly strong influence on French foreign policymaking. In the 2000s, after a period of strong
support for the US reactions to 9/11, this reading eventually led to criticism
of French military deployments to Afghanistan, rejection of the US/British
invasion of Iraq and opposition to a possible Iraqi mission by NATO. Assert-
ing a more Eurocentric insecurity agenda instead, French policymakers
advocated more strongly for collective security operations in Europe or along
its southern and eastern external borders (LeM 2004, 2008).

Conclusion

Unlike their counterparts in Switzerland, French policymakers remained more
strongly concerned with state-sponsored dangers overall after 1990. However,
non-state actor-driven threats were eventually recognised in the French political system as well and challenges of either category were recurrently transposed into each other. International terrorism, for example, had been
construed as a state-driven challenge in the 1980s; it was reinterpreted into a
non-state actor problem after 9/11; and it was sometimes associated with US
foreign policymaking in the 2000s. At the same time, identified dangers were
consistently rendered as collective challenges. Germany and Russia were held
to challenge the entire continent and potentially also the North Atlantic
region, and 'new threats' emanating from the European periphery were argued
to threaten France and other countries together. Terrorism, too, was collectivised, even if it was reconstructed, by some, from a global challenge into a
more pressing problem for the US than Europe. Such evolving understandings
of the organisation of international insecurity facilitated different kinds of
foreign policy agendas under their own terms (see Table 10.1 for an overview). A continuing focus on Europe as a community united by common
dangers, for instance, legitimised proposals for West European institution-
building in Eastern Europe, the creation of proper European stabilisation and
rapid reaction forces, diplomatic attempts to direct NATO instruments toward
regional stabilisation in Europe, as well as initiatives for pan-European policing and migration frameworks. In the 2000s, the framing of terrorism as a
global challenge initially empowered French support for an international anti-
terrorism agenda – and inversely, as the quote from Prime Minister Lionel
Jospin suggests, it also disqualified French abstention from global counterterrorism. The eventual reformulation of terrorism into an 'American problem'
disempowered French support for the US/UK invasion of Iraq. Also the
security debates of unified Germany evolved to such conclusions, the following chapter shows, even if they started from different premises after the fall
of the Berlin Wall.

Table 10.1 French constructions of international (in-)security in the 1990s and 2000s

		1990s	2000s
Unified Germany	Source	Unilateralist opportunity[D] Uncertainty, re: future policymaking[D]	N/A
	Target	Eastern Europe[D] Europe at large[D]	N/A
	Relation	Serious challenge[D]	N/A
	World order description	Fear of unilateralist German policymaking and alleged quest for *Lebensraum*, anxiety with disintegration of multilateralism	N/A
	Conditioning effects	Direct danger to Eastern Europe, but also to continental stability and multilateralism	N/A
	Policy enactment	Renewal of multilateralism, proposal for French–Russian alliance, reinvigoration of European defence, return to NATO, emphasis on autonomous nuclear defence	N/A
Russia	Source		Militarism/ultra-nationalism[D] Defence of superpower status[D]
	Target		Europe[D] North Atlantic region[D]
	Relation		Serious challenge[D]
	World order description		Fear of Russian military arsenal, political radicalisation and alleged attempt to restore superpower influence over Eastern Europe, continent at large if not entire world
	Conditioning effects		Collective countering of alleged Russian ambitions by European and transatlantic responses
	Policy enactment		Extension of European defence capabilities, maintenance of NATO, return to NATO

'New threats': Regional instability, migration, organised crime, weapons proliferation	Source		European periphery (South/South East/East)[D] Various non-state actors[D] Some non-state actor complicity[W]
	Target		Europe[D] Entire world[W] Europe[D]
	Relation		Serious challenge[D]
	World order description		Unstable European periphery as multidimensional danger to Europe at large, its economy and social fabric in particular, and challenges largely (though not solely) driven by non-state actors
	Conditioning effects		Collective European security agendas on regional stabilisation along continental borders, coordination of European policing, migration and asylum regimes
	Policy enactment		Promotion of European rapid reaction forces, European institution-building abroad, *Petersberg Tasks*, support to NATO out-of-area operations, Schengen/Dublin
Terrorism/US interventions	Source	N/A	Non-state actors (Al-Qaeda, etc.)[D] US foreign policy[W]
	Target	N/A	All democracies worldwide[D] United States only[W] Entire world[W]
	Relation	N/A	Problematic[D] Existential[W]
	World order description	N/A	Terrorism revived as important global security challenge, though eventually characterised as more of an 'American problem' (as target and source)
	Conditioning effects	N/A	Global cooperation against terrorism, but eventually rejection of US global interventions
	Policy enactment	N/A	UNSC resolution on Afghanistan, support to global counterterrorism regimes (on financing, travel restrictions, etc.), eventually rejection of US counterterrorism policy

11 Unified Germany in the post-Cold War era

German unification and 'complacency'

In the FRG of the 1970s and 1980s, Chapter 8 showed, the USSR was held to pose a supreme threat to West Germany and the Western world as a whole. In Bonn, this perspective continued into the late 1980s. The USSR's unpredictable succession process was at that time a matter of much concern to many West German politicians. Gorbachev's initiatives concerning national transparency and European dialogue were seen sceptically, too, with many considering them a ruse. Also, the USSR was seen as having overstretched itself. Its operations in Afghanistan and Ethiopia were deemed unsustainable in Bonn, and its influence over allies and protectorates in Eastern Europe was seen as diminishing. Given this, the USSR was expected to sooner or later seek to reassert its influence along and beyond its periphery, and it was thought likely to do so by military means. In the late 1980s, there was thus a more or less consensual reading of the international security context in Bonn. There was a fairly uncontested understanding of what the home nation's position was in terms of world politics, whom it opposed together with whom else and how foreign policymaking had thus to be devised. And, indeed, based on its continuing securitisation of the USSR as a superior and collective danger, the West German Government helped reinvigorate the West European Union, assisted in the expansion of the Elysée Treaty and contributed loyally to NATO (Enders und Siebenmorgen 1988; Zinner 1988).

This situation changed drastically with the political events of 1989, the dynamics of which seemingly also surprised West German politicians. The changes inside East Germany were, indeed, dramatic at the time. In the late 1980s, East Germans had protested virulently against the regime of the *Sozialistische Einheitspartei* (SED), which for its take responded with massive repression. Pressure for emigration from the GDR was high, and once Hungary and Czechoslovakia opened their own borders to Austria, thousands of East German citizens took this opportunity to move via this route to the FRG. In November 1989, East Germany then opened its own borders to the West for what was meant to become controlled emigration. But the authorities quickly lost control of the process, and the regime disintegrated. As early as December, the SED regime was removed from power, and in March 1990, free elections instituted a transitory CDU/SPD grand coalition government. In September 1990, the World War II Allies relinquished their supervision powers over Germany in the Two-plus-Four Treaty. In October of the same year, the *Einigungsvertrag* settled the unification of the two German states – or, more precisely, East Germany's accession to the FRG, for the former factually joined the latter as new *Bundesländer*.

As these dates suggest, German unification was, indeed, a speedy process. However, it was also a laborious one, given that innumerable political, legal and economic regulations had to be negotiated and harmonised in the years to come. With this tremendous task at hand – but also given the historical importance of German unification as such, after 40 years of militarised and ideological confrontation – virtually all public policy debates of the time related to the unification process (Fassbender 1991). Starting in 1989, countless debates were held in the old (West German) and the new (unified) *Bundestag* on all kinds of aspects of German unification; hundreds of declarations were made emphasising the historical meaning of the event; and emotional controversies were aired with a view to settling the question of which political party could be credited for the end of Germany's partition (cf. Bundestag 1990a, 1990b). Given this focus, German debates on international security were almost non-existent in the immediate post-Cold War years. In the early 1990s, the protocols of the time show, members of the *Bundestag* were largely absorbed by inner-German affairs. They did not actively advance concepts of national insecurity.

This being said, foreign affairs were addressed on a few occasions. Regarding the future of NATO, for instance, politicians from many camps felt that given the new lack of military danger to Germany and the West, this organisation was no longer required. Also, based on the same reading of world politics, left-wing politicians in particular demanded major cuts in defence spending (Bundestag 1990b: 18869/Ehmke SPD). But NATO was not abandoned by the unified Germany, which had finally become sovereign after decades of foreign tutelage. Even if most felt that NATO's founding premises had become obsolete in the post-Cold War era, many policymakers nevertheless sought to maintain membership. In the early 1990s, this foreign policy strategy was justified by NATO's alleged representation of Western values (cf. Bundestag 1991: 4365/Chancellor Kohl CDU). However, what these were, what was to be done with them and what they had to be enforced or protected against was left unclear in these statements; in the early 1990s, German continuation of NATO membership was justified only very vaguely in terms of democratic peace and cooperation (Weidenfeld 1995). A similar situation existed with regard to the frequent, new and fairly insistent demands that Germany play a greater role in world politics (Hellmann 2004). What such a role would be, and against what alternative interests it might be directed, was not explained at the time. In 1995, Foreign Minister Klaus Kinkel, for instance, can be found demanding such a role, without yet being able to specify its content and ambit in any meaningful way (Bundestag 1995: 3956–3959).

In the view of politicians and commentators from other countries – particularly from societies that identified common European, transatlantic or global dangers – this stance of Germany towards world politics was often criticised as contemplative in the early 1990s – i.e. as a failure to engage with the 'true' challenges of the time (Nerlich 1993). However, the non-recognition of such dangers was an epistemological reality in the German political system of the time. In a way similar to the traditional Swiss perspective on the international described earlier in this book, it represented an understanding according to which world politics mainly consisted of the problems *of others*. In a unified Germany, this interpretation was articulated repeatedly in the early 1990s. Iraq's invasion of Kuwait in 1991, for instance, was recognised as posing a challenge to the immediate Gulf region. However, it was not considered a danger to Germany or Europe as such, and as a consequence the government did not feel compelled to contribute more than financial means to the UN campaign against Iraq (Gutjahr 1994). The Yugoslav Wars of Secession were also construed in similar such terms in the *Bundestag*. Most of its members viewed these conflicts as creating tremendous human suffering. Yet, according to the political majority of the time – though not everyone (cf. Bundestag 1995: 3965/Schäuble CDU) – these conflicts also posed no danger to Germany itself (Bundestag 1994b: 46/Chancellor Kohl CDU).

Eastern challenges: the return to national insecurity

In the early 1990s, these examples suggest, a large part of the German political arena did hence not identify any meaningful threat to the home nation. Established methods of systematising the international had largely vanished from the German polity with the fall of the Berlin Wall, and new ones had not yet been articulated. Eventually, however, notions of international insecurity did return to German politics, and Eastern Europe became the first object of such world ordering. This is particularly instructive, insofar as around 1990, Eastern Europe – and countries such as Poland, Czechoslovakia, Hungary and Romania in particular – were conceived in very positive terms. Following their post-communist revolutions, the citizens of these countries were praised in the highest terms by German policymakers. Chancellor Kohl, for instance, 'warmly welcomed' these states 'to Europe', which he conceived as a community of states that lacked any hostile relations among its members (Bundestag 1990a: 17439ff.).

Eventually, however, different factions of the *Bundestag* endangered Eastern Europe. According to a small group of nationalists, German unification was only complete if former German territories in contemporary Poland and Czechoslovakia were integrated as well. This view framed Germany's eastern neighbours as conditional members of Europe and implicitly also as potential opponents of Germany. They were welcomed into the 'European democratic community' only on the condition that they allowed the reattachment of Germany's former eastern territories (Gutjahr 1994; earlier Bundestag 1988: 8196/Lintner CDU). Most policymakers did not support this post-fascist rendering of the East, however, and it was also rejected as unfounded by the 1992 German–Polish Border Treaty.

A second, and much more widely accepted, endangering of Eastern Europe focused on the perceived re-nationalisation of security politics in the East. For sceptics, the regional security cooperation arrangements promoted by and amongst Eastern European countries catered to the establishment of yet another exclusionary military block on the European continent (Broer and Diehl 1991). Finally, a third epistemological group advanced the most salient reading of Eastern Europe of the post-Cold War era. In their view, the challenges of economic, political and social transformation in the post-Soviet space created social unrest and nationalist backlashes, they fostered a return to irredentist policymaking in the East. Importantly, and as was the case with the fear of a new political block in Europe, this latter situation was also consistently presented as a collective challenge to (Western) Europe at large (Freudenstein 1998; Bundestag 1999b).

Following from this distinct rendering of danger in Eastern Europe – and the dismissal of the nationalists' view of Eastern Europe, which claimed that such danger exclusively targeted Germany – collective stabilisation of the East turned into a key policymaking theme in Germany by the mid-1990s (Schmidt 1996). However, German policymakers tended to disagree on the ways in which such stabilisation should be pursued. Some thought Germany was morally disqualified from sending peacekeepers to the region, given its own fascist past and history of military violence in Eastern Europe. Others believed the Chancellor lacked the necessary legal means to deploy military personnel on missions other than those involving collective self-defence (Bundestag 1993; Sager 1996). More importantly perhaps, German leaders also disagreed on the ways in which such a stabilisation agenda related to Russia. In the view of a sizable group, European and transatlantic policies towards Eastern Europe could be expected to antagonise Moscow and thus themselves to stimulate hostile relations with Russia. Other political camps rejected this alleged boomerang effect of Western policies in Eastern Europe, and a few even suggested that Russia was itself partly the cause of the 'Eastern European problem', if only for historical reasons.

Russia thus became the object of yet another insecurity narrative in post-Cold War Germany. As had been the case with Eastern Europe, however, this representation was slow to be articulated. Indeed, after the fall of the Berlin Wall, the end of the USSR and the termination of the Warsaw Pact, Russia was no longer considered a threat to Germany, Europe and others. Although individuals still pointed to Russia's military arsenal, most politicians were either positive about, or indifferent to, Russia's role in world politics in the early 1990s (Martin 1992; Bundesminister der Verteidigung 1994). In addition, public figures such as Manfred Wörner, NATO Secretary-General and former Minister of Defence, and Dieter Senghaas, a noted peace researcher, forcefully campaigned for 'non-discrimination' against Russia. Such figureheads presented Eastern Europe as a shared security space for Germany and Russia alike and argued that, consequently, strategies towards its stabilisation should necessarily be developed by these two nations together, *not* unilaterally by Germany and/or its allies (Senghaas 1995; Sager 1996). All in all, German politicians in the 1990s thus advanced a fairly non-antagonist view of Russia. At the same time, the government also made considerable efforts to facilitate Russia's military withdrawal from the GDR. As the *Weissbuch* of 1994 argued, it was a national objective to have Russian soldiers leave Eastern Germany 'with a good impression of the Germans' and to maintain good relations with Russia thereafter (Bundesminister der Verteidigung 1994: 14).

This perspective gradually shifted after the 1993 constitutional turmoil in Russia. There were major concerns regarding the strong showing by the nationalists in the Russian elections. Zhirinovsky's movement, for instance, was explicitly qualified as an international danger by the leading political parties (Bundestag 1994a). Later, concerns were also voiced with regard to Russia's operations in Chechnya (Kinkel 1995; DZ 1996). Compared to neighbouring France, however, this latter view was more ambivalent in Germany. Former Chancellor Helmut Schmidt and Egon Bahr (another key architect of *Ostpolitik*), for instance, actively opposed an antagonistic framing of Russia (DZ 1995). There was, however, a subtle but not univocal trend towards a more antagonistic interpretation of Russia in the late 1990s. Moscow was not framed in existential terms during that time, but the period did see the consolidation of an understanding that Russia nonetheless posed a certain security challenge to Europe, that Eastern European stability was crucial to the entire continent and that the latter might have to be pursued against Russian preferences. Consequently, German foreign policy supported continued membership in NATO and began to support its eastward enlargement more forcefully. In 1999, Germany's incoming centre-left government even provided military contributions to NATO's military operation against Russia's ally Serbia, based on the explicit argument that the Kosovo conflict posed a problem to the whole of Europe (Bundestag 1999a: 2673/Chancellor Schröder SPD). Still, the 'problematic' rendering of Russia was not advanced consistently during this period, and it was also partially linked to proxy actors. The Russian mafia, for example, was often attributed an important role in the creation of Eastern European instabilities in the 1990s – much more explicitly so than the Russian Government (Schelter 1997).

New threats and the 'arch of instability and insecurity'

This latter focus on mafia operations suggests that new concerns with the East were not the only new insecurity narratives articulated in the unified Germany. As in neighbouring France and Switzerland, German policymakers also began to securitise a broad set of 'new threats' further into the mid-1990s – topics ranging from migration and organised crime to environmental degradation, energy security and weapons proliferation (Kaiser 1995; Herzog 1995). Also, as in neighbouring countries, the precise modes of articulation and contestation of these different insecurity narratives are somewhat difficult to disentangle at the empirical level. More often than not, the various new security topics were simply amalgamated in public discussions. Unlike during the Cold War period, when a limited number of danger narratives circulated in West Germany, providing relatively clearly discernible objects of differential interpretation and debate, the 'new threats' basket of the 1990s cannot be easily ascribed to clearly demarcated political camps.

However, it is still possible to trace the securitisation of some of the new threats, and to give indications as to their world ordering dimensions. The securitisation of migration, for instance, evolved as a long some political process. Migration first became an object of government declarations in the 1980s. At that time, it was presented as a fairly standard policy challenge – namely, in terms of difficulties and best practices for cultural integration in public schools (Bundestag 1980a). During the same decade, refugee flows, too, were recognised as national challenges of sorts. As shown in Chapter 8, however, this concern was subordinated to the danger of proxy wars back then. It was their potential escalation into generalised war between East and West that posed an overriding concern to policymakers in the FRG in these discussions, not the displacement of people per se. Only by the early 1990s – after the influx of migrants from the GDR and other Eastern European nations – was migration constructed as a veritable national security challenge in Germany (cf. Bundestag 1989: 11836ff./ Penner SPD, 1994b: 39/Chancellor Kohl CDU). It was not until the 1990s, then, that migration became endangered (Gasteyger 1996). After that, however, it became actively enmeshed with further danger narratives, such as organised crime (DZ 1993) and, later, international terrorism (DZ 2001).

But migration was not merely argued to be a threat. It was also claimed to threaten in a fairly *distinct* manner. This is to say an idea was created that migration was a challenge driven mainly by non-state actors – whether by violent minorities or the very personal desire of individuals for better economic and political prospects – and that it was a danger that affected all of Europe. This latter rendering of migration, in particular, was sometimes advanced in fairly instrumental ways. For instance, the argument was made by some that the acceptance by German politicians of French concerns with the Mediterranean region would have to be reciprocated politically and epistemologically by France (Kolboom 1989). Policymakers in Bonn also argued that Germany's support for Portugal's and Spain's accession to the European institutions would stimulate French policymakers' interest in acknowledging Eastern Europe – the influx of migrants from that space, as well as its stability – as a collective European security agenda (Jacobs and Masala 1999). President Roman Herzog set out this collectivising construction process in 1995 in a discussion focusing on Eastern European immigration:

> We need to stabilise the East. Also our French friends start to understand that only through this, Europe can be stabilised in return. The French understand this challenge because they have come to struggle with similar issues along their southern borders [...]. Europe's security is indivisible. Instability in Eastern European threatens also France; instability in the Mediterranean region also threatens Germany [...]. In times of globalisation of risks, geography is rapidly losing any relevance.
>
> (Herzog 1995: 7)

The collective securitisation of migration is analytically important, because this political systematisation – and not merely its basic endangering or securitisation in the Copenhagen sense of the term – is of great help in explaining German foreign policy practice. Indeed, German politicians used this collective conception of the 'migration' danger as the key justification for German participation in pan-European asylum, policing and migration regimes during the 1990s and after (Werthebach 2004). It was on the basis of the construction of migration as a regional challenge to a multiplicity of Western states that these cooperative security arrangements could be devised, since this *distinct* systematisation allowed German policymakers to recognise other states as fellows in the insecurity context that migration arguably created. The German push for transnational policing and migration policies, then, rested on a highly specific and locally valid understanding of the organisation of international danger – an understanding of international insecurity that had fairly little to do with the disciplinary notion of international anarchy as generalised insecurity between states.

Migration was not the only new threat identified by German politicians in the 1990s, however. Other topics were constructed in similar terms. Organised crime, for instance, was claimed to be a major national security challenge during the same period. It was argued that it was driven by non-state actors such as the Russian mafia, and it was soon also posited to affect the entire European continent – i.e. all the other European nations, as well as Germany (Schelter 1997). Environmental degradation, too, was collectivised. Having become a political theme in the 1980s, it was framed as a veritable security challenge in the early 1990s, premised on the 'environmental crimes' committed by the GDR (Broer and Diehl 1991: 367). By the mid-1990s, it had been reinterpreted as a problem caused by the pollution practices of communist regimes in general (Noack 1996), and by the turn of the millennium, it was argued that it was a truly global security challenge caused by industry and other private polluters (DZ 2007). Energy insecurity, too, was presented as a collective issue, and it was gradually transposed from state to non-state actor responsibility. In the 1970s, Chapter 8 demonstrated, it was claimed that the economic policies of the Organization of the Petroleum Exporting Countries (OPEC) had caused the challenge of energy security; in the 1990s, it was argued that it was caused by the deliberate market behaviour of private companies; and in the 2000s, it was derived from disruptions to global supply lines caused by terrorism and piracy (Umbach 2004). Finally, weapons proliferation was subjected to a similar (re-)construction process. Between the 1970s and early 1990s, this threat had been associated fairly exclusively with states such as India, Iraq, South Africa and North Korea (DZ 1974b; DZ 1994). By the mid-1990s, however, it increasingly often referred to the activities of non-state actors, such as, again, the Russian mafia, which was caught smuggling weapons-grade plutonium by the German police (Schmidbauer 1995). In the 2000s, it was also directly linked to international terrorism (Bundesminister der Verteidigung 2003; Bundestag 2004b: 12785/Schmidbauer CDU).

Of course, a more detailed analysis would show that the various world ordering dimensions of these individual danger narratives sometimes evolved in less linear terms than this. Still, this abridged presentation suffices to show how distinct ways of interpreting national danger emerged in the polity and time period that are the focus of this chapter and how these affected foreign policy practice, given that they associated individual danger narratives with broader, and distinct, conceptions of world order. And, indeed, German foreign policies were consistently motivated by the epistemological world ordering thus created. The rendering of nuclear proliferation as a global problem, whether state-driven or caused by non-state actors, for instance, justified German support for arms control arrangements, such as the Non-Proliferation Treaty (Bundestag 1996), or, later, international counterterrorist frameworks; 'continental' conceptions of organised crime and immigration were drawn on as motivation for pan-European policing and migration agreements (Schelter 1997; Werthebach 2004); and the new-found global idea of the danger posed by climate change provided the political imaginary of world politics necessary for Germany's support for international environmental protection schemes, such as the Kyoto Protocol (DZ 2007). Foreign policymaking in the security realm, these examples suggest, consequently rested on particular interpretations of how a threat 'operated' in practice – i.e. the larger question of who caused it, whom it affected and how.

Generally speaking, the securitisation of new threats witnessed in the 1990s thus projected abroad a specific – and surprisingly convergent – understanding of the international insecurity context in the case of Germany. In this view, insecurity was multidimensional and encompassed a variety of challenges, from migration to energy shortages and climate change. It was also highly globalised, with each of these dangers affecting various other societies together with the home nation. In stark contrast to the asecure self-positioning seen during the unification years – i.e. Germany's temporary practice of *not* characterising world politics and their own position therein by means of threat narratives – many contemporary dangers were seen as challenging Germany and others in similar ways 'in reality' from the mid-1990s onwards. As part of this process, the new dangers were often also conceived as challenges produced by non-state actors, and this interpretation facilitated the political projection of the international community of states as a homogenous insecurity community. Globalisation – 'not of economics but of insecurity', as the defence doctrine of 1994 argued (Bundesminister der Verteidigung 1994: 32) – became the guiding rationale for the German security and foreign policy agenda, both on epistemological and operational levels.

Documents of the time indicate that this 'global' construction of current insecurity was, indeed, commonplace in the German polity during this period. At times, however, contemporary dangers were also collectivised to a more restrained set of actors – namely, the European continent. In such cases, identified insecurities were argued to emanate particularly often from what was described as the 'arch of instability and insecurity' surrounding Europe (Rühe 1995; Gasteyger 1996). Similar to the notion of the 'European periphery' advanced in Paris, this concept suggested that a great number of current insecurities affected Europe as a whole, as the result of geographical logic – i.e. from both across the Mediterranean and from the post-Soviet space. Still, this 'arch of instability and insecurity' was not referred to consistently in the political discussions of the 1990s. More often, the new threats were simply posited as continental or global dangers. Unlike in France, where the 'European periphery' was a highly popular concept, German policymakers thus tended to project abroad a more global notion of contemporary insecurities than their French counterparts, although based on the same security topics.

Terrorism and Germany's defence 'at the Hindu Kush'

Once the federal political establishment moved to Berlin, these 'new threat' narratives were continued into the 2000s. Often, the various new dangers were presented in amalgamated forms as sets of highly interconnected challenges. They were also continuously presented as global dangers, and more often than not it was suggested that they pitched non-state actors against the international community of states. In the early 2000s, this enduring narrative was then joined by a new anxiety concerning international terrorism. As shown earlier in this book, terrorism was not a novel concern to the German polity. In the 1970s, the Red Army Faction's activities were qualified as acts of terrorism. Back then, however, the securitisation of terrorism evolved in distinct ways. Instead of being integrated into the national security doctrine, the Red Army Faction was qualified as a national group committing ordinary crimes in Germany and against German authorities. Seen in this way, terrorism was a challenge to the FRG as a democratic society at large, but it was not construed as a transnational phenomenon. In the 1980s, concerns over terrorism then vanished from the public policy debates. By the early 1990s, though, one finds a cursory suggestion in the *Weissbuch* of 1994 that home-grown extremists to the right of the political spectrum might pose a new terrorist challenge to Germany.

Seen in this way, terrorism was securitised 'anew' in the autumn of 2001. The focus now, however, was on Al-Qaeda's attacks on American targets, and terrorism was now construed in different terms than it had been earlier. According to Chancellor Schröder, for instance, terrorism now presented a superior danger, as well as a threat that affected 'the entire civilisation' (Bundestag 2001a: 18303/Schröder). Journalists, too, argued that terrorism posed a threat to 'the entire world' (DZ 2005). In 2001, this transnational rendering of the challenge provided the necessary epistemological basis for Germany's invocation of NATO's alliance clause – i.e. Article 5 of the Washington Treaty (Bundestag 2001a, 2001b). Germany's counterterrorism policy, a quote from Joschka Fischer shows, derived directly from the prevailing collective presentation of terrorist danger. As the Foreign Minister succinctly argued: 'Germany takes part in the global anti-terror coalition. It assumes its responsibilities in international solidarity, and in own interest, because international terrorism threatens us very directly' (Bundestag 2002a: 532).

Eventually, the same presentation of terrorism also helped justify German military contributions – and maintenance thereof – to the multinational security operation in Afghanistan. Two quotes from the Minister of Defence make clear to what extent this strategy rested on an epistemological construction of common insecurity, and how this construction must not necessarily derive from an experience of material damage in the home nation proper. As Peter Struck argued:

> Even if German territory had thus far been spared from attacks, the threat is real for us. International terrorism also concerns our country, our way of life and the fundament on which our political culture is resting. Thus we continue our military deployments to Afghanistan.
>
> (Bundestag 2002c: 379)

> Our security will be defended, though not exclusively, at the Hindu Kush, where threats against us – such as international terrorism – are forming.
>
> (Bundestag 2004a: 8601)

In the aftermath of 9/11, the conservative opposition parties also endorsed this existential and collective rendering of terrorism (cf. Bundestag 2001a: 18305/ Merz CDU). Soon, however, interpretations of terrorism in the German polity started to diverge over the question of how pressing this danger truly was. According to the evolving interpretation of the ruling parties, terrorism posed a collective problem, but was not necessarily a more pressing one than other security challenges, such as organised crime or climate change. Also, the same parties began to put increasingly strong emphasis on civil peacebuilding and conflict resolution instruments, and consequently they also felt that European institutions – and not necessarily the NATO military alliance – were the most useful counterterrorism tools. Unlike in neighbouring France, then, the German variant of a more 'critical' interpretation of terrorism did not suggest that it was 'more of an American problem'. Multilateral operations in Afghanistan, for instance, were still supported by social democrats and greens, based on the view that terrorism was a common concern. However, the coalition government questioned the existential nature of the threat that terrorism was argued to have by some (Bundestag 2004b: 12783/Minister of Defence Struck SPD). This meant that conflicting views on terrorism emerged in the *Bundestag*, given that conservatives and liberals advanced a much more existentialist reading of terrorism, preferring military and NATO solutions to it. As one representative of this latter camp maintained, opposing government positions:

> The threat of international terrorism continues to be high for Germany! We do not have concrete indications for attacks. But Madrid, Casablanca, Djerba and Istanbul show that there are global autonomous cells of Islamist terrorism, which can strike at any moment's notice.
>
> (Bundestag 2004b: 12784/Schmidbauer CDU)

Conflicting interpretations of international danger also emerged with US and British preparations for war against Iraq. In this case, too, the ruling social democrats and greens rejected the proposed existential rendering of Saddam

Hussein's dictatorship. In their view, Iraq posed a challenge to the Gulf region, and as such weapons inspectors were seen as useful instruments. This understanding of the Iraqi threat was not supported by conservatives, however. Conservative leader Wolfgang Schäuble, for instance, harshly criticised the government for failing to recognise that Iraq presented a direct danger to Germany 'in reality'. Depicting Iraq as a 'pressing Western security problem', he dismissed the government's foreign policy as irresponsible (Bundestag 2002a: 536–538, 2004a: 8605–8607). Following that argument, Michael Glos, deputy faction leader of the CDU, also described the government's failure to recognise Iraq as a common challenge to the West as 'selling out the Atlantic Alliance' (Bundestag 2002b: 873). This argument was readily rejected by Chancellor Schröder and his political allies, who claimed for their part that the conservatives had failed to advance a 'sober analysis' of the Iraqi danger (Bundestag 2002b: 876–877). As this example suggests, the nature of the Iraqi danger – whom it affected and how dangerous it could legitimately be held to be – was also an object of political struggle and interpretation, and one that had fairly immediate foreign policy consequences. Only after the US-led invasion of Iraq actually unfolded did the political ranks close again in the *Bundestag*. It was not that the threat assessments of the major parties were harmonised at this time, but the different factions began to agree that in the absence of a UN Security Council Resolution, military intervention in Iraq was strictly illegal and illegitimate (Bundestag 2003).

The major political powers in Germany, then, competed with each other in the early 2000s over the appropriate interpretation of both terrorist and Iraqi danger. Apart from these two controversies, however, their perspectives on international insecurity tended to converge surprisingly strongly during this period overall. There was an impressively widespread understanding that the bulk of the twenty-first century's new challenges had to be construed as global dangers requiring collaborative foreign policy responses. For instance, addressing the contemporary security context, the 2003 *Verteidigungspolitische Richtlinien* – de facto the centre-left coalition government's new White Book – claimed:

> The international security context of Germany is today completely different than ten years ago. There is growing interdependence between the countries of this world [...]. No state can guarantee peace, security and welfare for itself by itself under the current circumstances. The shaping of the international context, the management of the complex challenges, the mitigation of risks and threats and the protection of Germany from them are not possible through self-help. Shared efforts are necessary.
>
> (Bundesminister der Verteidigung 2003: 6, 21)

Based on this reading of international insecurity, the *Richtlinien* demanded reorganisation of the national security apparatus. The tasks of the *Bundeswehr*, for instance, were argued to include: (1) the safeguarding of independence in foreign policymaking; (2) contributions to European and global stability; (3) protection of national and allies' security; and (4) the promotion of international cooperation and integration (Bundesminister der Verteidigung 2003: 27). These are highly cooperative tasks to set out for a national army, yet they all followed directly from the collective insecurity context described in the doctrine's early pages. In parliament, there was also little contestation of this general policy orientation and underlying threat assessment. Opposition politicians merely challenged the proposed process of military transformation as such – for liberals, the reduction of the defence budget was not substantial enough, whereas conservatives felt that too much emphasis had been put on rapid deployment units too quickly (Bundestag 2004a). But the social democrat and green coalition government defended its perspective against such criticism. As key members of the ruling parties argued, once again stressing that the 'nature' of contemporary insecurity required a transformation of this kind:

> The *Bundeswehr* must and will transform itself, given that threats have become multi-dimensional and unpredictable. More actors are threatening our security than before. Next to state actors, transnational forces have appeared. Thanks to developments in communication technology, the latter are capable of playing destructive roles across the entire planet.
>
> (Bundestag 2004a: 8607/Arnold SPD)

A few years later, the incoming grand coalition government's *Weissbuch* repeated to the letter this distinct perspective on world politics. Again, a poorly differentiated basket of new threats ranging from terrorism to weapons proliferation, failed states, migration, pandemics, energy security and resources scarcity were listed as the key security challenges of the time (Bundesminister der Verteidigung 2006: 20–22). And again, this basket of dangers was not merely securitised, but also systematised in specific ways – namely, as distinctly global problems, created by non-state actors and confronting an international community of states. The pervasiveness of this distinct view on international insecurity is truly instructive and thus worth quoting at length:

> With globalisation, new opportunities open up for Germany. At the same time, the profound changes of the international security context also entail new risks and threats. These do not merely have destabilising effects on Germany's close environment, but also on the security of the entire international community. Germany's security is indivisibly linked with the political development of Europe and the world [...]. Many of the new risks and security threats that come in hand with globalisation are transnational, are being caused by non-state actors and affect our security also over great distance. Poverty, underdevelopment, education deficits, resource scarcity, natural catastrophe, environmental destruction, pandemics, inequalities and human right violations constitute, next to other factors, a fertile soil for illegal immigration and secular and religious extremism. As such, they can become causes for instability and – in their most radical form – precursors

for international terrorism. In an increasingly interdependent world these threats do not only affect their proximate context, but affect in many different ways the security of the entire international community.

(Bundesminister der Verteidigung 2006: 8, 19)

By the mid- to late 2000s, then, the German political system advanced a highly globalised conception of international insecurity, a *distinct* rendering of the international whose ordering dimensions were surprisingly rarely debated. Indeed, in the parliamentary debates following the 2006 *Weissbuch*, no party questioned the world ordering presentation of any of the manifold new proclaimed dangers (Bundestag 2006). Opposition only emerged in regard to the selection of instruments with which the government sought to react to the insecurity context thus described, such as when the Greens and post-communists (i.e. *Die Linke*) criticised German foreign policy as being too reliant overall on military means of stabilisation (Bundestag 2006). In the late 2000s, only the newspaper *Die Zeit* can be found to explicitly question the political establishment's practice of presenting contemporary issues – such as the stabilisation of Afghanistan – as a global challenge (DZ 2008, 2009).

Conclusion

In the 1990s and 2000s, German security concerns moved from an existentialist preoccupation with the Soviet Union to temporary non-securitisation, new concerns with Eastern Europe, the endorsement of a large basket of highly diverse 'new threats' and issues such as global terrorism and Iraq. The ways in which these dangers were construed in Bonn and Berlin – who were seen to cause them, who was seen to be affected by them besides the home nation and how – were consequential to foreign politics, since they provided the epistemological material of world politics with which policymakers had to deal when crafting foreign policy responses (see Table 11.1 for an overview). In the 1990s and 2000s, German policymakers' consequent collectivisation of insecurity to Europe and the 'world' strikes as particularly impressive. It is based on this distinct construction process – of migration, environmental degradation, terrorism and other threats – that collaborative security strategies could be pursued by Germany, since they put the home nation in a position similar to other states. Compared with grand IR theory's explanation of international politics, this practice of subject-positioning is particularly instructive. Contrary to what such theory suggests, German policymakers did *not* make sense of world politics in the ways that the disciplinary anarchy narrative suggests. In Germany, foreign states were decreasingly identified as sources of national insecurity in the decades after World War II. States were not considered to oppose each other in a generalised way, and insecurity was almost never construed in an exclusively self-centric fashion. Instead, threats were almost always construed in ways that identified fellows in a broader, shared insecurity context, and this widespread practice of projecting abroad larger insecurity communities is highly important in explaining the foreign policy strategies adopted by Germany.

Table 11.1 German constructions of international (in-)security in the 1990s and 2000s

		Mid-1990s	2000s
Eastern Europe	Source	Instability, nationalism, irredentism[D] Exclusionary military block[W] Obstacle to German unification[M]	N/A
	Target	Europe at large[D] Germany alone[M]	N/A
	Relation	Serious challenge[D]	N/A
	World order description	Concern with regional instability, militarised violence and transborder conflicts in the Eastern European space, processes that also affect Western Europe	N/A
	Conditioning effects	Collaborative – not unilateral – stabilisation of Eastern Europe, with or against Russia	N/A
	Policy enactment	Eastward expansion of NATO, eastward expansion of European institutions, civilian and military peacekeeping deployments (e.g. to Kosovo)	N/A

continued

Table 11.1 Continued

		Mid-1990s	2000s
Russia	Source		Obstacle to stabilisation of Eastern Europe^D Politically instable country^W Ultra-nationalism^W
	Target		Eastern Europe^D Europe at large^W
	Relation		Potential challenge^D
	World order description	Russia as an unproblematic nation, but also as highly armed and potentially unstable, as a country potentially coming under ultra-nationalist control, as an obstacle to regional stability in Eastern Europe (which itself is important to pan-European security)	
	Conditioning effects	Fostering of positive bilateral relations, but also continuing subtle countering of Russia through NATO and selective disregard of Russian preferences over Eastern Europe	
	Policy enactment	Continuation of NATO membership, enlargement of NATO and European institutions	
'New threats': **Migration, organised crime, weapons proliferation etc.**	Source	Various non-state actors^D	Various non-state actors^D
	Target	'Arch of instability and insecurity'^{W} Entire world^D Europe^W	Entire world^D
	Relation		Serious challenge^D
	World order description	Multi-thematic insecurity context as a danger to the entire international community of states, at times emanating more directly from Europe's border regions (in such instances targeting Europe more directly than others)	
	Conditioning effects	Collective international – and especially European – security agendas against migration, climate change, weapons proliferation, organised crime, etc.. cooperation with foreign states, not against them	
	Policy enactment	Promotion of rapid reaction forces, European institution-building abroad, pan-European policing agreements, Schengen/Dublin, Kyoto Protocol, etc.	

Terrorism and Iraq			
Source	N/A	Non-state actors (Al-Qaeda, etc.)[D] Iraqi Government[W]
Target	N/A	Entire 'civilisation'[D] Entire world[D] Gulf region only[W]
Relation	N/A	Existential[D] Problematic[D]
World order description	N/A	Terrorism as an existential – or merely pressing – global security challenge, Iraq as regional or global security concern
Conditioning effects	N/A	Global cooperation against terrorism, eventually also multinational collaboration over Iraq
Policy enactment	N/A	International cooperation against terrorism (invocation of Washington Treaty Article 5, military deployments to Afghanistan, etc.), partial collaboration with US/UK on stabilisation of Iraq

Part III

(In-)security and the production of international relations

12 Conclusion

Constructions of international insecurity

West European societies have advanced a considerable number of insecurity narratives since 1945. The political systems of France, West Germany and Switzerland *endangered* the international on a regular basis and by means of various themes, and in doing so they set out problem situations requiring some sort of reaction. Threats were not merely recognised to exist, however. Throughout the six decades covered by this book, threats were also consistently associated with broader understandings of who caused them, whom they affected and how. With this, articulations of national insecurity *ordered* the international. The presentation of communism, migration, terrorism and other themes as security challenges did not merely haul these into the security domain. It also served to systematise world politics epistemologically and create a sense of place for the home nation in international politics as thus recognised. Indeed, local insecurity narratives always came with larger conceptions of who or what threatened whom and how, as the empirical case studies have shown. These ideas were directly complicit in structuring the international in specific ways and in relating the home nation both to sources of danger and other possible co-victims of a given threat.

The substantive patterns of such epistemological systematisation are instructive, not least since they differ so significantly from traditional accounts of international politics. As regards the identification of sources of insecurity (*who or what threatens?*), the case studies initially point to a dominance of state-centric narratives. Between 1945 and the early 1980s, it was foreign governments and alliances that were most often held responsible for contemporary insecurities overall. However, the preoccupation with other states was not 'totalising' during that period. French, West German and Swiss politicians did not consider all foreign governments to be actual or potential sources of national insecurity. On the contrary, the genealogies show that state-centric threat narratives were fairly selective. As a rule, only a very few – and often highly specific – foreign states were held to cause insecurity. Geographical logic did not play a particularly compelling role in this selection. Even if policymakers did sometimes classify neighbouring countries as sources of national insecurity, a 'natural' concern with proximate states is difficult to identify. Also, in cases where neighbouring states were identified as sources of national security, it was usually one specific such state – and not all adjacent countries – that was construed in such antagonistic terms.

State-centrism in the identification of sources of insecurity was thus predominant in the early stages of the Cold War, but it was not 'totalising'. And, indeed, it was not fully consistent either. French readings of the international in the late 1940s and early 1950s, for example, focused strongly on Germany and the USSR, and thus they were fairly state-centric in orientation. But they were not exclusively portrayed in such terms. The securitisation of capitalism, for instance, which was also advanced in Paris at that time, focused on a wider notion of threatening actors, including the US Government, a political thought system and industrial leaders. Similarly, West Germany's first post-war security debates were notably concerned with 'Germanness' proper – i.e. the German populace's seeming vulnerability to militarism and totalitarian ideology – rather than with other states. Furthermore, in the 1970s and 1980s, policymakers from all three polities recurrently associated emergent insecurities with non-state actors, whether regarding environmental degradation, southern instabilities, energy insecurity, terrorism or migration. During the Cold War, foreign governments were hence often and selectively attributed responsibilities for the creation of national insecurity, but no more than that.

Importantly, in the wider historical perspective, this focus on other states gradually diminished. Certainly, the French and German case studies of the 1990s and 2000s show that there was no perfect paradigm change in this regard, since some state-centric insecurity narratives continued to be articulated. However, by that time, non-state actors were clearly being attributed more prominent roles. From the mid-1990s at least, the majority of contemporary dangers were regularly being ascribed to the activities of such entities and thus not to foreign governments. This wider shift in world ordering is also reflected in the very designation of these new insecurities. Whereas in the past government officials, parliamentarians, experts and doctrines discussed the 'German problem', the 'Soviet threat' or the 'confrontation between NATO and the Warsaw Pact', by the 1990s they began talking about issues such as 'energy insecurity', 'migration' or 'terrorism' – i.e. threat concepts that lacked direct references to state agents. A certain historical shift in world ordering – an empirical practice, not an inevitable or irreversible trend – can thus be observed in Europe following World War II. Foreign governments became less often depicted as sources of national insecurity in this process, and by the mid-1990s, threat narratives predominantly focused on actors other than states.

Practices of world ordering are also interesting with regard to the determination of the targets of various threats (*who is threatened?*). On a few occasions, dangers were claimed to exclusively challenge the home nation. In the immediate post-war period, for instance, many French policymakers felt that Germany was a specific danger to France, because it was a hereditary and eternal danger. West Germany's *Sonderbedrohungsdebatte* of the 1980s suggested that the FRG had become the sole target of 'Eastern danger' following the deployment of intermediate-range missiles. Swiss politicians in the 1990s also claimed that the Confederation was confronting international insecurity by itself, given foreign governments' focus on the activities of the national financial industry. Surprisingly, perhaps, such articulations of threats as facing no one other than the home nation were, however, truly exceptional. Indeed, the genealogies show that policymakers almost always collectivised insecurity beyond their home nation. The securitisation of the Soviet Union as a challenge to the entire North Atlantic region, the rendering of bloc politics as a common threat to Europe, the framing of migration as a danger to high-income countries and the presentation of terrorism as a threat to democracies worldwide are all cases in which the 'reach' of insecurity was attributed to larger groups of nations. Such renderings consistently projected larger insecurity communities on to world politics, and they put a number of other societies in positions similar to the home nation.

The exact determination of these other societies – who was included and who was not – differed considerably in practice. The French post-war construction of Germany as a threat to Western Europe, for instance, largely ignored other possible co-victims of German aggression to the east and south. The Gaullist securitisation of superpower politics, by contrast, delimited that threat to Europe at large, foregoing explicit identification of other possible subjects of the identified tutelage, whether in Asia, Africa or Latin America. The widespread securitisation of migration, finally, positioned that challenge as a threat to Europe and did not generally address the ways in which other regions of the world might be affected by it. In many instances, then, the securitisation practices described in this book constructed 'club problems' of different Western variations. Only by the 1990s were 'new threats' defined in more global terms, as challenges to 'everyone', 'the world' or 'civilisation'. However, this trend towards constructions of ever larger insecurity communities is not irreversible. Interpretations of Eastern European instability and post-9/11 terrorism, for instance, were recurrently argued to pose challenges to democratic regimes, the North Atlantic space, Europe or the US alone and thus *not* to the entire world. Even if the collectivisation of insecurity is a standard practice and the ever more 'global' extension of such collectivisation a dominant trend, such practices of world ordering must hence be construed as evolving social realities, *not* as an inevitable transhistorical development.

Interestingly, however, the epistemological collectivisation of insecurity did not always align the home nation with others. Sometimes, the determination of who was threatened also helped to construct radically 'disentangled' conceptions of the international, such as when danger was argued to exist *among others*. This type of world ordering differed markedly from the much more widespread practice of positioning the home nation in larger insecurity communities *together* with others. Still, the projection of 'problems of others' was a recurrent systematisation practice. It is particularly important in explaining Switzerland's foreign policy behaviour during the Cold War, as well as its more recent foreign policy polarisation. However, it was also observed in Germany in the early 1990s, when problems such as instability in South Eastern Europe were framed as being a concern of others, and in France in the 2000s, when some politicians argued that terrorism was more of an 'American problem'.

Lastly, empirical practices of world ordering are also instructive when considering the analytical dimension of intensity (*how is something/someone threatened?*). Certainly, the assessment of antagonisms in world politics is difficult to operationalise, and this book has merely used some simple qualitative markers in gauging the degree of antagonism, or hostility, with which different danger narratives were invested. However, these qualitative rankings suffice to show that threats were not always posited in existentialist terms. On the contrary, the question of how pressing a given danger was 'in reality', and thus also of whether a danger was truly fundamental or not, was often subject to sophisticated political elaboration. In post-war France, for instance, the presentation of Germany as a lesser threat than the USSR was a hard-fought political process. Similarly, the FRG's ruling parties' presentation of Eastern Europe as less of an existential danger than Moscow was highly controversial during *Ostpolitik*, and the emergent characterisation of terrorism as a less important danger compared to organised crime and climate change was also contested in the early 2000s.

Seemingly, assessments of antagonism were often subject to debate precisely because they helped to articulate *overlapping* world order imageries. In the French polity of the early 1950s, the framing of the USSR as a more pressing danger than Germany allowed the former, more transatlantic world ordering to dominate over the latter, more continental one, while not yet denying its general validity. Also in the FRG, assessments of antagonisms placed *different* international systematisations into a hierarchy. The characterisation of Eastern Europe as a lesser type of danger allowed for punctual cooperation with such nations, whereas the greater threat posed by Moscow was still being countered forcefully. However, a graded conception of antagonisms does not merely allow the ranking of coexistent threat narratives. It also permits addressing the question of whether general levels of antagonist framing evolved over time. Did the three European societies described in this book come to consider themselves less strongly threatened overall in the 2000s, compared to the 1940s or early 1950s? The European focus on secondary 'new threats' and non-military means of security policy, which can be observed since the 1990s, points in such a direction. Still, a more refined conceptualisation and sophisticated measure of antagonisms are necessary to substantiate this claim. Also, in case such a shift can be validated more thoroughly, it must still be considered an evolving social practice. The seeming shift towards constructions of lesser dangers is not an irreversible development, as the more existentialist characterisation of post-9/11 terrorism makes clear.

Towards a political sociology of insecurity politics

Patterns of constructing international insecurity are highly instructive in terms of the specific orders that they articulate and the wider historical evolution to which they are subject. However, the securitisation practices described in this book are also interesting on a procedural level. This is to say that in terms of *contestation*, the genealogies describe different national dynamics of articulating and engaging with insecurity narratives. Among these, original ways of articulating insecurity – endangering or 'securitisation' in the basic sense of the term – were surprisingly rare overall. Of course, topics such as Germanness, Eastern instability, the 'European periphery' and terrorism all had to be hauled into the basic logics of insecurity at a certain point in time. Over the six decades analysed here, however, only a dozen or two themes were actually endangered. At times, such original endangering met with *fundamental* opposition. In the Fifth Republic, for example, local communists virulently rejected the endangering of the USSR, and in a similarly radical way, Atlanticists disqualified any endangering of the United States.

More often, however, politicians were preoccupied with differences in world ordering, rather than the yes-or-no of basic endangering as such. Whether weapons proliferation was caused by state or non-state actors, communism was a transatlantic or a European challenge and terrorism an existential threat or a lesser nuisance, for example, were all controversial questions. Indeed, ways of systematising the international were particularly contested in cases where parallel threat narratives defined *contradictory* subject-positions. Whether the 'Soviet threat' was more important than the 'German danger', for instance, was highly controversial in the Fourth Republic, partly because it implied a fundamental determination of whether France was evolving in a similar security context as the North Atlantic nations and Germany or whether instead it opposed Germany together with other European nations. Whether Switzerland's position was determined by the East–West conflict, a 'problem of others', or emergent 'new threats', global insecurities that affected Switzerland as much as they affected others, was a similarly controversial question, and one that by the 1990s led to a pronounced polarisation of the Swiss polity.

Then again, concepts of international insecurity were not always contested. At times, they were also reproduced in fairly consensual terms. Such periods existed in all three polities. In Switzerland, neutralism did not meet with any meaningful opposition for decades, despite the country's sophisticated instruments of direct democracy and political pluralism. In West Germany, a singular notion of anti-communism was hegemonic in the late 1950s, while in France, post-Cold War 'new threat' narratives were little discussed. Practices of world ordering were hence fairly variable on both the *substantive* and *procedural* side. Yet, while there was a more general trend towards non-state dangers, collective insecurities and lower levels of threats on the *substantive* side, developments on the *procedural* side were considerably less steady. In Switzerland, there was no epistemological security policy controversy between 1945 and the 1980s and thereafter ever deeper polarisation. French discussions were particularly controversial in the 1950s, after which there was continuing confrontation between multiple minor and one hegemonic perspective. In the 1990s, French security debates became more consensual, a situation that changed again with the arrival of differentiated views on terrorism and Iraq. In (West) Germany, a multiplicity of varied security perspectives had been articulated after World War II, but this plurality of interpretations was drastically reduced to a single concept of anti-communism in the 1950s. In the *Ostpolitik* years, two interpretations of anti-communism were pitched against each other; in the 1990s, elaborations of the international insecurity context were more consensual; and in the 2000s, new rifts emerged over the questions of Afghanistan and Iraq.

As this suggests, patterns of political engagement varied fairly significantly across time and space, irrespective of the three polities' larger cultural, political, economic and geographical similarities. Sometimes, international ordering was consensual, but more often it was subject to some form of critique, and distinct patterns of debate also stabilised themselves across longer periods of time. This observation is instructive, since it supports the argument that international construction is a politically laden process. The 'correct' description of the international, it shows, is one that is considered relevant by policymakers, and a process that is often worth competing over. Security politics is known and practised as ideational competition or an epistemological kind of power politics. By the same token, the observed patterns of political debate are also instructive, insofar as they raise further questions about the determination of insecurity politics, such as: why are certain definitions of international insecurity fought over, while others are not? Who contests a given insecurity narrative? What explains sequences and forms of political debate? And, most importantly perhaps, why are insecurity narratives specified (*ordered*) in the particular ways that they are? The patterns of insecurity politics described here open the door to a veritable political sociology of insecurity politics, of which this book – which is more narrowly interested in the substantive ways in which insecurity is ordered and how such ordering affects foreign policymaking in return – can only provide some preliminary indications.

For instance, the empirical chapters showed that formal rules of political conduct are important. The institutionalisation of the Federal Republic in 1949, for example, coincided with one of the most drastic rearrangements of local security debates. The definition of the *Bundestag* as the primary site of national politics, the allocation and distribution of political powers by virtue of elections, the regulation of areas of competence and the definition of national decision-making processes significantly reshaped the West German political arena. Other interventions at this level – notably, the expulsion of the *Reichspartei* and the German Communist Party from the *Bundestag* in the 1950s – affected the local dynamics of international sense-making as well, because they altered the ways and places in which certain readings of world politics could be articulated. In France, a similar situation applied in relation to the instauration of the Fifth Republic. Also this change of formal political rules found a fairly direct echo in the national security debates. The ability of the ruling party to articulate and implement its reading of world order was strengthened considerably by this constitutional reform.

Still, formal rules of political conduct are only part of a comprehensive political sociology of insecurity politics. Already, national governance structures only regulate a certain kind of political space. Even if security politics and foreign affairs are highly statist issues, and thus largely negotiated in statist frameworks such as ministries and parliaments, statist frameworks are not equally expansive everywhere, and groups outside such arenas recurrently have significant influence over the ways in which international insecurity is defined in society. In West Germany, the peace movement and new environmental groupings had by the 1980s become powerful forces in this regard. In Switzerland, extra-parliamentary interest groups were seen as important to the maintenance of a specific understanding of national security, as, for example, when private business groups lent their weight to Swiss neutralism during the final Cold War years. Outside the realm of formal politics, then, a variety of other actors, resources and systems of rule contribute to the generation and shaping of knowledge about international danger, and these actors and arenas of knowledge politics and production are often subject to their own organising logics.

The media, for instance, may be complicit in the propagation and selection of insecurity concepts, yet it is itself affected by the political, economic and professional penchants of editors, investors and the journalistic field at large. The orientation and impact of specific media channels differ, with some reaching larger and more relevant audiences than others. Swiss politician Christopher Blocher, for instance, was an affluent opinion-maker capable of communicating his national-conservative positions to households across the country, whether by means of leaflets, the newspapers under his control or through his personal TV channel – a communication capability unmatched by other actors in Switzerland. Local cultures of journalism, too, are conducive to directing security debates towards some configurations, but not others. In France, newspapers have taken fairly independent stands on national politics overall. The daily newspaper *Le Monde*, for example, regularly published and discussed contending assessments of French foreign and security politics. This was not the case with the leading newspaper in Switzerland, the *Neue Zürcher Zeitung*, which until the 1990s merely reprinted government statements. Since it presented governmental doctrines in a matter-of-fact way and without further discussion, this latter culture of media reporting was less conducive to fostering public debate.

A similar situation applies to academia, which develops some of the most influential analytical frameworks with which to make sense of world politics, but whose contributions are also the products of distinct professional dispositions and developments. Archive research shows that scholarship published in the West German flagship journal *Europa-Archiv* between the 1950s and 1980s was strongly geared towards legal analyses and structural theorising. Such scholarship left little space for agency in foreign and security affairs, and it set out a fairly predetermined and non-negotiable course of action for national leaders. In France, articles written in *Politique Étrangère* tended for decades to be fairly close to the ruling parties' positions, and in Switzerland, the foreign and security policy debates held in the *Allgemeine Schweizerische Militärzeitschrift* are today still characterised by a heavy-handed focus on neutrality, military concepts of security and militia expertise. However, it was not only by virtue of its distinct and evolving analytical gazes that academia affected insecurity politics. Scientific work also concerned the latter by virtue of its empirical findings. In Switzerland, for instance, new insights from the medical sciences that the transmission of HIV/AIDS depended on controllable human behaviours – i.e. that it was not an unavoidable global pandemic – was taken up by politicians as a reason to, again, remove that challenge from the national security agenda.

In linking different formal and informal fields of knowledge production, a comprehensive political sociology of insecurity politics also has to address the relative attribution of authority to *different* actors and professions. Are presidents and ministers better placed to define national security politics than academics and journalists? How and why do attributions of expertise differ across time, political systems and even between individuals? The case studies suggest that the privilege to authoritatively articulate national insecurity evolved over time and differently in different places. In West Germany, for instance, peace researchers and the Green Party had by the 1980s emerged as new authorities of national security policy. In Switzerland, military officers only became meaningfully challenged by civilian security experts in the 1990s and traditional parties by new ones in the 2000s. In all three countries, the ability to articulate national insecurity authoritatively on behalf of society seems in recent times to have moved to actors of homeland security, as well as to private interests. In addition, foreign authorities such as the UN Secretary-General, European Commissioners, transnational NGOs, global elite universities, think tanks and news networks have recurrently gained a certain degree of political authority at home, even if their perspectives are often only imported when they support already existing opinions there.

If these were not enough elements to work with, a comprehensive sociology of insecurity politics also has to address larger local, cultural and historical limitations to debates in national security affairs. In other words, security discourses are often bounded in their substantive dimension. In Switzerland, for example, non-military conceptions of national security were unthinkable during some decades, harshly disciplined as idealism or treason in others, yet perfectly acceptable during other periods. Criticism of neutrality, too, was for a long time barely possible and is still difficult to articulate today. Similarly, arguments made by extremist parties on either side of the political spectrum were deemed unacceptable in post-war West Germany. They were – and still are – actively marginalised by centrists, who discredited such arguments in the newspapers, boycotted and shouted them down in parliament and endeavoured to eject extremists from the *Bundestag* altogether. Such ideational and cultural limits to what can or cannot be legitimately thought and said about the international are important to insecurity politics. As bounded knowledge systems – or policed discourses – they are themselves contingent on the distinct historical narratives, preferred values, cultural practices, religious beliefs and material configurations of a given society, and a comprehensive sociology of insecurity politics thus necessarily also has to investigate the configuration and roles of these factors in different places and at different points in time.

(In-)security and the production of international relations

Answers to the questions of why recognised dangers are ordered in some ways but not others, who contests such orderings, why and when thus call for a substantial research programme. This book can only provide some initial indications of that programme – for example, by pointing to different sites and rules of knowledge generation, dissemination and competition. It cannot – and it does not seek to – contribute a comprehensive sociology of insecurity politics itself. However, this book has provided systematic evidence regarding the interplay between knowledge of insecurity and national foreign policy strategising – its core research objective. In this regard, the chapters have shown repeatedly how foreign policymaking relies on the distinct knowledge of international insecurity held to be truthful within a given society. Securitisation has been seen to *condition* the foreign policy behaviour of states. The recognition of insecurity projected distinct kinds of symbolic orders onto the international, and in doing so it made some but not other foreign policy options possible on its own terms. Securitisation created and arranged frameworks of reality with which local policymakers had to deal when designing foreign policy responses.

Examples of this linkage abound in the empirical chapters, and thus a few shorthand illustrations suffice to recapitulate this linkage here. In the 1950s, for instance, the West German rendering of the Soviet Union as a danger to the West empowered military cooperation with a select set of Western nations, which were placed in similar positions as West Germany itself, even if they were in geographical locations that could not be touched by Soviet military might. At the same time, this distinct securitisation of the 'Eastern danger' worked against closer security cooperation with nations in Latin America or Africa, since these were not usually identified as further co-victims of that same danger, and it also disqualified national opposition to other neighbouring countries of West Germany, such as Denmark, Sweden, Austria or France, which were constructed as fellows of sorts. In the 1960s, to give another illustration, Gaullists' simultaneous endangering of the US and the USSR created an understanding of Europe as being threatened by both superpowers at the same time, even if with uneven intensity. With time, this notion of a 'threatened Europe' was expanded to the East, and with this it did as much to enable an ever more continental quest for European integration as it disqualified closer association with either Moscow or Washington.

In the 1970s, then, Swiss politicians' conception of world politics defined the home nation as a proverbial island of peace in a sea of conflict. The Swiss political establishment identified neither a need to counter direct danger, nor possible fellows that could be drawn on in such a process. Based on this local truth about world politics, a self-help strategy in the most ideal-typical sense of the term was then adopted in Bern, justifying a highly autonomous and non-cooperative defence and foreign policy strategy. In the 1980s and 1990s, finally, a very distinct rendering of organised crime and migration as caused by non-state actors and targeting the entire European community of states provided the knowledge necessary to craft and expand continental policing, migration and asylum schemes within France, Germany and Switzerland. At the same time, this conception of the organisation of danger disqualified foreign policy strategies that confronted European states in the management of organised crime and migration, since such states were not seen as responsible for creating these challenges.

In these and many more instances, specific ways of defining danger thus had an important impact on foreign policymaking. Securitisation mattered in latter arena, precisely because it was attended by broader, often controversial, claims about threatening and threatened actors in world politics, as well as by ideas regarding the nature of relations between these actors and the home nation. The articulation of national (in-)security was directly complicit in constructing differentiated local knowledge of the organisation of the international security context, and in doing so it directed state behaviour to some outcomes but not others. *How* something was securitised in France, (West) Germany and Switzerland, not just *whether* something was securitised, was seen to be of fundamental policy relevance. The relational/positional conceptualisation of securitisation proposed by this book is directly helpful in addressing this dimension and thus in linking the politics of articulating insecurity with foreign affairs strategising.

A relational/positional conception of securitisation imparts new analytical, theoretical and political perspectives to the study of international security. On the *analytical level*, it provides a framework of analysis that contextualises insecurity politics more thoroughly across time and space – i.e. a framework capable of producing fairly complex accounts of international insecurity politics. In the cases covered by this book, these accounts challenge popular imageries of Cold War politics. They show that such politics was considerably more dynamic and varied than what is often claimed, since the determination of what threatened whom and how was far from unmistakably clear in Paris, Bonn and Bern. At the same time, the genealogies show that security politics *after* 1990 was much less contested, confused and unclear than has often been argued. Certainly, the implosion of the USSR withdrew the basis of a major threat narrative, but the turn towards 'new threats' witnessed in the 1990s was highly comprehensive and widely accepted. Indeed, the construction of 'new threats' as global and non-state actor-driven challenges was so consistent that it has to be asked whether post-1990 insecurity politics should not actually be considered *more* stable than Cold War insecurity politics. In terms of sense-making, the post-Cold War period appears more settled than the former, and this insight overturns popular imageries of the Cold War as representing stability and the post-Cold War period as uncertainty.

Indeed, a multi-dimensional notion of securitisation questions established ways of categorising international history. If insecurity politics is a complex ordering practice, then what use is there in categorising history using markers such as the post-war, Cold War, post-Cold War and 9/11? The latter periodisation relies on specific conceptions of turning points, experiences of armed violence in particular and it also refers to orderings of the international that were often distinctly Western in orientation. A relational/positional notion of insecurity politics proposes alternatives to such a way of sequencing history. For instance, it shows that practices of locating the home nation in larger insecurity communities became 'normal' after 1945, and that around the mid-1980s they evolved from continental to global collectivisation. Patterns of identifying sources of insecurity then evolved in the mid-1990s from state-centric narratives to constructions of insecurity contexts populated by non-state actors. Assessments of antagonisms in world politics became seemingly less existential by the 1990s, and by the end of that same decade European societies' wider world order narratives appeared to be converging ever more comprehensively. If categorised by such analytical dimensions, then *other* histories of international relations can be told. These are oriented towards different political fault lines and temporal turning points than conventional markers such as 1945, 1949, 1989 or 2001. Indeed, such alternative methods of temporal categorisation recurrently appear more appropriate than conventional ones, such as in the Swiss case, which was much more directly structured by the question of whether or not the Confederation was part of a larger insecurity context than by superpower bloc politics or 9/11.

With its ability to contextualise political practices, this book's analytical framework also allows questioning the externalist accounts to which *individual* polities are so often exposed. French foreign affairs strategising in the 1950s and 1960s, for instance, can be shown to have derived from fairly differentiated, and locally truthful, elaborations of the international. As a consequence, it is probably better not explained as a petty quest for *grandeur*, or envy of superpower, as the literature so often does (e.g. Posner 1991). West German foreign politics, too, was rooted in specifically local knowledge of the international; knowledge that was actively constructed and politically negotiated. Foreign policymaking was neither 'imprinted' on West German society by the winning coalition of World War II, nor was it predetermined by constitutional arrangements, even if these factors did have a certain amount of influence on local practices of sense-making. West German policymaking was not decided in 1945, and it was not a mere mechanistic response to the 'international system' or 'the Cold War logic', as scholars so often proclaim (e.g. Haftendorn 1983). At the same time, *Ostpolitik* did not rest on an understanding that Eastern Europe suddenly seized to pose danger, and thus de-securitisation in a practical sense, but on a differentiated new rendering of this danger. Swiss foreign policymaking during the Cold War, finally, is shown to have relied on a distinct substantive and procedural construction of the international, a social practice that was itself sustained by the Swiss polity's distinct political sociology of insecurity politics. This Swiss construction of the international was pursued and enacted very actively and at the expense of alternative orientations. This means costly self-help policymaking without international cooperation was yet another product of local knowledge politics. It did not simply constitute 'natural' state behaviour for a small state, as is recurrently maintained (e.g. NZZ 2002).

Lastly, the framework developed in this book allows to identify how meanings of past events are redefined retrospectively *within* polities proper – i.e.

how societies construe and use their own history differently in later stages. The Brussels Treaty, for instance, is today hailed on NATO's website as that alliance's founding document. In France, however, the conclusion of that specific agreement was motivated by a very specific construction of the 'German threat', *not* by anti-communism. Similarly, the Elysée Treaty has recently been celebrated as the point at which Franco-German amity was reached, yet the empirical genealogies show that antagonistic framings of the FRG persisted in Paris long after the conclusion of the treaty, and that they also returned in force in the early 1990s. European integration, finally, is often portrayed as the result of efforts to prevent another generalised interstate war in Europe today, yet the case studies suggest that initiatives for continental cooperation were based much more prominently on *current* assessments of international insecurity. More often than not, European integration was motivated in a straightforward manner by contemporary and forward-looking ideas of world politics – i.e. concerns with the present and future of international affairs, not by elaborations of what had been in the past. All in all, then, the notion of securitisation as a practice of world ordering helps to generate immanent accounts of insecurity politics, and these are instructive for national and international historiography alike.

The international is what societies make of it

However, this book's relational/positional reading of securitisation also contributes a distinct *theoretical* contribution to International Relations – namely, an alternative explanation of state behaviour and international cooperation. This explanation rests on the theorisation of (in-)security as a politically consequential systematisation device. Instead of conceiving 'security' as a thematically 'broad' or 'deep' concept, and instead of approaching its construction in terms of extraordinary politics, this theorisation posits insecurity politics as a variable practice of international sense-making and enactment. This means that securitisation is reconceptualised as an interlinked argument concerning the construction, shaping and enactment of national security knowledge or 'interests'. This argument holds that states' international behaviour depends on the knowledge of the organisation of international insecurity that is available and prevalent inside their society, whereas security cooperation between states depends, first, on the conceptualisation of transnational insecurity communities and, second, on the interlocking projection and enacting of mutually implicated conceptions of this kind by different societies.

This is a differential, reflexive and insecurity-based explanation of state behaviour and international cooperation – one that contrasts, to varying degrees, with other security theories. Unlike *securitisation theory* in its original variant (Waever 1995; Buzan *et al.* 1998), for instance, this book's framework is interested in the construction of larger insecurity environments and less in the effects of the security label on national methods of elaboration. It emphasises the question of *how* insecurity is articulated, and it associates a less existentialist and predetermined view to such an articulation. In other words, rather than claiming that insecurity narratives are necessarily existential and anti-democratic, or that they 'in themselves' mechanistically guide policymaking, they are posited as conditioning factors of variable configurations. Imageries of international insecurity may, but do not need to be, about existential relations; they are both actively constructed and appropriated; and their specifications are often overtly debated and thus not a matter of cabinet politics.

Unlike the Copenhagen School's tentative idea of *security constellations* (Buzan and Waever 2009), the articulation of insecurity is not necessarily self-centric. Self-centrism is possible, but not analytically legislated by the perspective of this book, since danger can also be construed as applying to larger collectives of states or even to other nations, but *not* the home nation. Similarly, unlike *regional security complex theory* (e.g. Buzan and Waever 2003), more emphasis is given to the construction of variable world order imageries. These are shown to evolve and often be contested locally, which means that polities can rarely be characterised by singular local ideas of the international. World ordering through insecurity, then, is more complex in the present framework. It is not as much guided by material and geographical logics as regional security complex theory would suggest, and it does not necessarily pitch states against each other, since other sources of insecurity can be recognised. Indeed, the empirical chapters suggest that an exclusive focus on the construction of 'other states' as threats misses some important practices of insecurity politics, and that it perpetuates a highly selective, statist account of international politics.

As already suggested, the epistemological and practical 'production' of international relations theorised in this book also differs somewhat from the Minnesota School and/or post-structuralist security studies more broadly defined (e.g. Doty 1993; Weldes *et al.* 1999; Hansen 2006). Unlike these works, the present framework is more concerned with practices of international systematisation in general and not with the attribution of distinct qualities – being 'democratic', 'uncivilised', 'aggressive' and so on – to foreign actors. By the same token, international systematisation is argued to be more complex than it is held to be by many post-structuralists. Instead of requiring an existential pitching of a singular Other against a singular Self, the social theory underpinning this book here includes the possibilities of coexistent, varied and differently antagonistic frameworks of the international. These frameworks may project abroad larger concepts of insecure communities, and it is not claimed that these equal identity formation in a sociological sense of the term. The securitisation of terrorism as a global danger, for instance, locates countries as diverse as the United Kingdom, Liechtenstein, Angola and Kyrgyzstan in a common insecurity community – but it does not foster the convergence of cultural, linguistic, social and other practices on a larger scale, and thus identity formation in a conventional sense of the term, among such nations.

The present framework also provides a reflexive input to *democratic peace theory* (e.g. Russett 1993). It may well be that democracies tend to not fight each other or tend to engage more rarely in military conflict in general, because, among other things, their political designs distribute the costs of such actions more widely. Yet, the empirical chapters suggest that on the epistemological level, democracies can hardly be qualified as conflict-averse in general. Irrespective of the democratic instruments available in France, (West) Germany and Switzerland, these polities were found to articulate notions of insecurity on a regular basis. Democratic structures as such have a fairly limited influence over the ways in which societies make sense of world politics and the ways in which such knowledge is then enacted. In some cases, democracies have been seen to advance fairly existentialist readings of international danger, while in others, democracies did not give rise to any debates on international sense-making whatsoever, despite their sophisticated instruments for adversarial politics. This insight is of interest to the democratic peace debate, for it suggests that even if democracies are more peaceful on the military side, they might not actually be less hostile on the epistemological level.

The focus on insecurity politics also poses questions regarding the idea of *security communities*. Security community theory (e.g. Adler and Barnett 1998) argues that dependable expectations of peaceful change can emerge through interaction, which brings about a sense of 'we-ness', and that international security cooperation or 'mutual aid' may then derive from routine action or trust. In the perspective of this book, this latter argument seems incomplete, for it lacks an effective reason for the very activation of international cooperation. A sense of 'we-ness' does not equal convergent projections of common insecurity – the trend of getting to know each other better does not yet explain how transnational concepts of shared insecurity emerge, and yet it is such concepts of collective insecurity that set out actual needs for security cooperation. Routine interaction does not necessarily create convergent knowledge of world politics on the epistemological level, and thus it remains unclear why 'mutual aid' should emerge in the first place, beyond expectations for peaceful conflict resolution. Without a theory of the construction of common danger, security community theory may explain the absence of war between nations, but not the emergence of security cooperation.

Most importantly, perhaps, unlike *grand IR theory*, the focus on insecurity politics emphasises empirical enquiry, rather than material (e.g. Morgenthau 1962) or systemic (e.g. Waltz 1979) logics, in order to assess actually existing concepts of international insecurity. In doing so, it challenges the argument that interstate anarchy is the 'naturally true', supreme or sole possible interpretation of world politics. Indeed, this book suggests that interstate cooperation may not have to be explained by the discipline *despite* or *under* interstate anarchy, given that such anarchy is often *not* an accepted conception of world politics. Grand IR theory is right to argue that no governmental type of supranational authority regulates the conduct of states, but this insight does not necessarily translate into a political recognition of generalised interstate insecurity in societies, and thus it is not a secure starting point for international theorising. In the polities analysed by this book, international insecurity is defined in much less generalised, state-centric, egoistic and existentialist terms than those suggested by grand IR theory, and this raises the fundamental question of whether anarchy is the proper point of departure for international theorising.

In the last instance, this implies that *systemic constructivism*, too, is problematised by the notion of insecurity politics. Anarchy may well be what states make of it (e.g. Wendt 1992, 1999), but anarchy in the ideal-typical disciplinary sense of the term seems not to be a social reality in many instances. Societies do not merely construct responses to the international. They also actively systematise the international in the first place. Societies construct world politics and enact such constructions at the very same time; they both create the international and make something out of it. These political processes are anything but straightforward, since both the interpretation and enactment of imageries of the international are subject to geographically and historically distinct variants of local politics. The construction of the international itself, then, has to be engaged with in more varied and pluralistic terms than those proposed by systemic constructivism. Indeed, the ever more widespread focus on non-state actor challenges described in the empirical chapters, as well as their construction as common challenges for an international community of states, shows that actual imageries of the international are quite different from the very distinct disciplinary understanding of the international that is propagated by, and that provides the foundation for, systemic IR theory, whether rationalist or constructivist.

Towards an ethics of international ordering

Last but not least, the conceptualisation of insecurity politics as an epistemological and practical production of international relations also contributes to the discipline at a *political level*. By moving IR from systemic theorising to a theory of systematisation, this book's framework attributes agency to world ordering practices. It posits world ordering as a man-made and thus modifiable practice, and with this it allows political actors to be held responsible for defining threats in certain terms but not others. As international (in-)security orders are shown to be constructed, arranged and enacted through securitisation, insecurity politics can thus be contrasted with normative standards of choice. Insecurity politics can be made the object of emancipatory action – not by virtue of a thematic redirecting of its attention to more civilian or human needs (Booth 1991) or calls against securitisation *tout court* (Waever 1999), but on the basis of the reflected re-articulations of those orders that securitisation helps to portray.

Might some patterns of international ordering through insecurity be more or less warranted than others, relatively speaking? A relational/positional conceptualisation of securitisation allows to raise this challenging question and to envisage political strategies aimed at transforming distinct delineations of international orders. Such political strategies might be informed by various interconnected kinds of ethical standards. An ethics of numbers, for example, might call for more inclusive articulations of insecurity – i.e. expansions of those transnational orders of shared interest, or 'fate', into which societies are projected and by virtue of which international cooperation between nations is expanded. By contrast, an ethics of decentring might cater to the moving of insecurity politics away from macro-level container concepts such as 'foreign governments' and 'nations' in the identification of sources of danger, thus shifting security affairs away from a generalised countering of other nations and human beings. Alternatively, an ethics of *Entfeindung* might focus on an attenuation of those antagonistic relations by which subjects are related to each other and the home nation.

Certainly, the advantages and pitfalls of such normative guidelines are exceedingly difficult to ponder. They are difficult to specify, challenging to compare with each other and hard to relate to further effects of insecurity politics beyond the world ordering framework. However, instead of positing insecurity contexts as immutable givens, as traditional IR does, and instead of disqualifying insecurity articulations as altogether unwarranted, as much of critical security studies has come to do in recent years (Nunes 2012; Hynek and Chandler 2013), a relational/positional conceptualisation of securitisation *does* allow re-engaging with the interplay between security and emancipation. It allows for an assessment of the political ordering effects of security talk in 'spatial' terms, and in doing so it posits practices of international ordering as new objects of emancipatory debate and action. As a variable concept of international systematisation, insecurity politics is again positioned as a 'transformative analytics' (Marcus 1999: vii) – the outcomes of securitisation themselves rely on social practices, and this is why they may be steered to directions of choice. Considering the powerful ordering effects of insecurity narratives on state behaviour and international relations described in this book, such a reflexive and critical engagement with securitisation seems to be highly warranted. On different levels, it presents a formidable challenge to both theorists and practitioners of international relations.

Bibliography

Abelein M (1963) Frankreichs Vertrag mit der Bundesrepublik – Vorgeschichte und Bedeutung. *Europa-Archiv* 18(4): 125–134.

Abrahamsen R (2004) A breeding ground for terrorists? Africa & Britain's war on terrorism. *Review of African Political Economy* 102(31): 677–684.

Adler E and Barnett M (1998) *Security Communities*. Cambridge: Cambridge University Press.

Adrets A (1984) Les relations franco-allemandes et le fait nucléaire dans une Europe divisée. *Politique Étrangère* 49(3): 649–664.

Allen RV (1964) Die sowjetischen Bemühungen um eine 'Détente'. *Europa-Archiv* 19(7): 245–254.

Althusser L (1971) *Lenin and Philosophy and Other Essays*. London: New Left Books.

Anderson B (1991) *Imagined Communities*. London: Verso.

Andréani G (1998) La France et l'OTAN après la Guerre Froide. *Politique Étrangère* 63(1): 77–92.

Apel H (1984) Deutschland-Politik: Möglichkeiten und Grenzen. *Europa-Archiv* 39(20): 609–616.

Aradau C (2004) Security and the democratic scene: Desecuritization and emancipation. *Journal of International Relations and Development* 7(4): 388–413.

Aradau C and Van Munster R (2007) Governing terrorism through risk: Taking precautions, (un)knowing the future. *European Journal of International Relations* 13(1): 89–115.

Archer MS (1985) Structuration versus morphogenesis. In: Eisenstadt SN and Helle HJ (eds) *Macro-Sociological Theory: Perspectives on Sociological Theory*. London: Sage Publications, 58–88.

Archer MS (1990) Human agency and social structure: A critique of Giddens. In: Clark J, Modgil C and Modgil S (eds) *Anthony Giddens: Consensus and Controversy*. London: Falmer Press, 73–84.

Archer MS (1995) *Realist Social Theory: The Morphogenetic Approach*. Cambridge: Cambridge University Press.

Archer MS (2000) *Being Human: The Problem of Agency*. Cambridge: Cambridge University Press.

Aristotle (1991) *The Art of Rhetoric*, Lawson-Tancred H (trans). London: Penguin.

Aristotle (1998) *Metaphysics*. Harmondsworth: Penguin Books.

Armengaud A (1960) Les Européens contre l'Europe? *Politique Étrangère* 25(2): 122–151.

Aron R (1949) Les chances d'un règlement européen. *Politique Étrangère* 14(3): 249–262.

Aron R (1986) La Communauté Atlantique: 1949–1982. *Politique Étrangère* 51(1): 229–239.

Ashley RG (1987) The geopolitics of geopolitical space: Toward a critical social theory of international politics. *Alternatives* 12(4): 403–434.

Asmus RD (2002) L'élargissement de l'OTAN: Passé, présent, future. *Politique Étrangère* 67(2): 353–376.

Assemblée Nationale (1951) Annexe no. 1373. *Documents Parlementaires*, séance du 6 novembre: 2711–2712.

Assemblée Nationale (1952) Accession de la Grèce et de la Turquie au Traité de l'Atlantique Nord. *Procès-Verbaux des Séances*, séance du 24 janvier: 326–338.

Assemblée Nationale (1953) Politique européenne. *Procès-Verbaux des Séances*, 3e séance du 17 novembre: 5221–5230.

Assemblée Nationale (1954a) Communication du gouvernement sur les négociations internationals. *Procès-Verbaux des Séances*, séance du 7 octobre: 4569–4585.

Assemblée Nationale (1954b) Annexe no. 9432. *Documents Parlementaires*, séance du 9 novembre: 2387–2388.

Assemblée Nationale (1954c) Annexe no. 9703. *Documents Parlementaires*, séance du 11 décembre: 2782–2388.

Assemblée Nationale (1954d) Annexe no. 9763. *Documents Parlementaires*, séance du 18 décembre: 2701–2796.

Assemblée Nationale (1954e) Accords de Paris. *Procès-Verbaux des Séances*, 1re séance du 27 décembre: 6872–6886.

Assemblée Nationale (1954f) Annexe no. 2283. *Documents Parlementaires*, séance du 29 décembre: 3595–3596.

Assemblée Nationale (1954g) Rapports entre les nations européennes, réduction et contrôle des armements. *Procès-Verbaux des Séances*, 3e séance du 30 décembre: 7008–7010.

Assemblée Nationale (1959a) Déclaration du gouvernement sur la politique étrangère. *Procès-Verbaux des Séances*, 2e séance du 28 avril: 319–323.

Assemblée Nationale (1959b) Politique étrangère. *Procès-Verbaux des Séances*, séance du 29 avril: 379–388.

Assemblée Nationale (1959c) Politique étrangère: Déclaration du gouvernement. *Procès-Verbaux des Séances*, 1re séance du 27 octobre: 1962–1964.

Assemblée Nationale (1959d) Politique éxtérieure: Communication du gouvernement. *Procès-Verbaux des Séances*, 1re séance du 28 décembre: 3668–3686.

Assemblée Nationale (1960) Annexe 662. *Documents Parlementaires*, séance du 1er juin: 201–203.

Assemblée Nationale (1962) Politique générale. *Procès-Verbaux des Séances*, 1re séance du 13 décembre: 41–65.

Assemblée Nationale (1963) Annexe no. 299. *Documents Parlementaires*, séance du 31 mai: 486–487.

Assemblée Nationale (1964a) Politique étrangère. *Procès-Verbaux des Séances*, 1re séance du 28 avril: 965–988.

Assemblée Nationale (1964b) Politique étrangère. *Procès-Verbaux des Séances*, séance du 29 avril: 1010–1028.

Assemblée Nationale (1966a) Politique générale. *Procès-Verbaux des Séances*, 1re séance du 13 avril: 621–692.

Assemblée Nationale (1966b) Discussion sur une motion de censure. *Procès-Verbaux des Séances*, séance du 19 avril: 765–786.

Assemblée Nationale (1966c) Annexe no. 2233. *Documents Parlementaires*, séance du 8 décembre: 1084–1090.

Assemblée Nationale (1967) Politique générale du gouvernement: Déclaration du gouvernement et débat sur cette declaration. *Procès-Verbaux des Séances*, séance du 18 avril: 665–678.

Assemblée Nationale (1968) Politique militaire: Déclaration du gouvernement et débat sur cette déclaration, *Procès-Verbaux des Séances*, 1re séance du 5 decembre: 5128–5141.

Assemblée Nationale (1973) Politique étrangère: Déclaration du M. le Ministre des Affaires étrangères et débat sur cette declaration. *Procès-Verbaux des Séances*, 1re séance du 19 juin: 2258–2271.

Assemblée Nationale (1975) Politique étrangère: Déclaration du gouvernement et débat sur cette declaration. *Procès-Verbaux des Séances*, 2e séance du 27 juin: 4923–4943.

Assemblée Nationale (1976) Politique étrangère: Déclaration du Ministre des Affaires Etrangères et débat sur cette declaration. *Procès-Verbaux des Séances*, 1re séance du 6 mai: 2695–2707.

Assemblée Nationale (1978) Politique étrangère: Déclaration du gouvernement et débat sur cette declaration. *Procès-Verbaux des Séances*, 1re séance du 8 juin: 2668–2686.

Assemblée Nationale (1980) Politique étrangère: Déclaration du gouvernement et débat sur cette declaration. *Procès-Verbaux des Séances*, 1re séance du 17 avril: 475–486.

Assemblée Nationale (1982) Déclaration du gouvernement sur sa politique étrangère. *Documents Parlementaires*, séance du 6 juillet: no. 1014.

Assemblée Nationale (1983) Politique étrangère: Déclaration du gouvernement et débat sur cette declaration. *Procès-Verbaux des Séances*, 1re séance du 6 octobre: 3819–3845.

Assemblée Nationale (1986a) Déclaration du gouvernement sur la lutte contre le terrorisme. *Documents Parlementaires*, séance du 8 octobre: no. 373.

Assemblée Nationale (1986b) Lutte contre le terrorisme: Déclaration du gouvernement et débat sur cette declaration. *Procès-Verbaux des Séances*, 1re séance du 8 octobre: 4443–4454.

Assemblée Nationale (1986c) Rapport d'Information au nom des Délégués de l'Assemblée Nationale à l'Assemblée de l'Union Européenne Orientale sur l'activité de cette Assemblée au cours de ses 31e et 32e sessions ordinaires (1985–1986). *Documents Parlementaires*, séance du 18 décembre 1986: no. 596.

Assemblée Nationale (1991) Orientations de la politique de défense: Déclaration du gouvernement et débat sur cette declaration. *Procès-Verbaux des Séances*, 1re séance du 6 juin: 2840–2861.

Assemblée Nationale (1992) Création du corps de défense franco-allemand. *Procès-Verbaux des Séances*, séance du 27 mai: 1727–1728.

Assemblée Nationale (1993) Communication hebdomadaire du gouvernement. *Procès-Verbaux des Séances*, 3e séance du 29 juin: 2695–2705.

Assemblée Nationale (1994a) Ex-Yougoslavie et prévention des conflits en Europe. *Procès-Verbaux des Séances*, séance du 12 avril: 681–704.

Assemblée Nationale (1994b) Programmation militaire pour les années 1995 à 2000. *Procès-Verbaux des Séances*, 2e séance du 24 mai: 2121–2160.

Assemblée Nationale (1999) Rapport d'information sur les négociations relatives au concept stratégique de l'OTAN et leurs conséquences sur la politique de défense et de sécurité. *Documents Parlementaires*, séance du 24 mars: no. 1495.

Assemblée Nationale (2001a) Déclaration du gouvernement relative à la situation consécutive aux attentats perpétrés le 11 septembre 2001 aux Etats-Unis d'Amérique. *Documents Parlementaires*, séance du 3 octobre: no. 3297.

Assemblée Nationale (2001b) Débat sur la déclaration du gouvernement relative à la situation consécutive aux attentats perpétrés le 11 septembre 2001 aux Etats-Unis d'Amérique. *Compte-Rendu Analytique Officiel,* 1re séance du 3 octobre: 2–36.

Assemblée Nationale (2002) Déclaration du gouvernement sur la question de l'Irak et débat sur cette declaration. *Compte-Rendu Analytique Officiel,* 2e séance du 8 octobre: 10–30.

Assemblée Nationale (2003) Déclaration du gouvernement sur la question de l'Irak et débat sur cette declaration. *Compte-Rendu Analytique Officiel,* 1re séance du mercredi 26 février: 1–24.

Austin JL ([1955] 1962) *How to Do Things with Words?* Oxford: Clarendon Press.

Bachofner H (1994) Die Blauhelmvorlage im Kreuzfeuer der Argumente. *Allgemeine Schweizerische Militärzeitschrift* 159(5): 8–10.

Bahr E (1991) *Sicherheit für und vor Deutschland.* München: Hanser.

Baillot L (1983) Une défense pour l'Europe. *Politique Étrangère* 48(2): 381–384.

Baldwin DA (1997) The concept of security. *Review of International Studies* 23(1): 5–26.

Balzacq T (2005) The three faces of securitization: Political agency, audience and context. *European Journal of International Relations* 11(2): 171–201.

Barandon P (1952) Deutschland im System der Sicherheitspakte. *Europa-Archiv* 7(12): 4975–4980.

Barnett J (1997) Reclaiming security. *Peace Review* 9(3): 405–410.

Bartsch G (1965) Neue Konzeption im westeuropäischen Kommunismus. *Europa-Archiv* 20(3): 69–76.

Bates SR (2006) Making time for change: On temporal conceptualizations within (critical realist) approaches to the relationship between structure and agency. *Sociology* 40(1): 143–161.

Bauer MW and Gaskell G (1999) Towards a paradigm for research on social representations. *Journal for the Theory of Social Behaviour* 29(2): 163–186.

Beaufre A (1962) Les armements et la paix. *Politique Étrangère* 27(4): 321–331.

Beltran J (2000) Sécurité européenne et sécurité des états baltes: Les vertus de l'ambiguïté stratégique. *Politique Étrangère* 65(1): 33–46.

Berger PL and Luckmann T (1966) *The Social Construction of Reality: A Treatise in the Sociology of Knowledge.* Middlesex: Penguin Books.

Bernstein S, Lewbow R, Stein J and Weber J (2000) God gave physics the easy problems: Adapting social science to an unpredictable world. *European Journal of International Relations* 6(1): 43–76.

Bertram C (1979) La sécurité européenne et le problème allemand. *Politique Étrangère* 44(1): 21–31.

Bertram C (1995) Quel avenir pour l'OTAN? *Politique Étrangère* 60(1): 147–158.

Bhaskar R (1978) *A Realist Theory of Social Science.* Brighton: Harvester Press.

Bhaskar R (1979) *The Possibility of Naturalism.* Hemel Hempstead: Harvester Wheatsheaf.

Bhaskar R (1989) *Reclaiming Reality: A Critical Introduction to Contemporary Philosophy.* London: Verso.

Bhaskar R (1993) *Dialectic: The Pulse of Freedom.* London: Verso.

Bialer S (1983) Die Sowjetunion und der Westen in den achziger Jahren. *Europa-Archiv* 38(18): 539–550.

Bieler A and Morton AD (2001) The Gordian knot of agency-structure in International Relations: A neo-Gramscian perspective. *European Journal of International Relations* 7(1): 5–35.

Bigo D (1996) Circuler, refouler, enfermer, éloigner: Zones d'attente et centre de rétentions aux frontières des démocraties Occidentales. *Cultures & Conflits* 23: 3–5.

Bigo D (2005) La mondialisation de l'(in)sécurité? Réflexions sur le champ des professionnels de la gestion des inquiétudes et analytique de la transnationalisation des processus d'(in)sécurisation. *Cultures & Conflits* 58: 53–100.

Bigo D and Tsoukala A (2008) *Terror, Insecurity and Liberty: Illiberal Practices of Liberal Regimes after 9/11.* London: Routledge.

Booth K (1991) Security and emancipation. *Review of International Studies* 17(4): 313–326.

Boyer Y (1985) Images et réalités de la menace militaire soviétique. *Politique Étrangère* 52(3): 683–696.

Boyer Y and Palmer DR (1989) L'Alliance Atlantique et la coopération européenne en matière de sécurité. *Politique Étrangère* 54(1): 107–118.

Bozo F (1991) La France, l'OTAN et l'avenir de la dissuasion en Europe. *Politique Étrangère* 56(2): 513–527.

Bozo F (1995) La France et l'Alliance: Les limites du rapprochement. *Politique Étrangère* 60(4): 865–877.

Brandt W (1964) Gemeinschaftsideale und nationale Interessen in der deutschen Aussenpolitik. *Europa-Archiv* 19(12): 419–426.

Brandt W (1971) Aktuelle Fragen der deutschen Aussenpolitik. *Europa-Archiv* 26(13): 437–442.

Brenner M (1990) Une nouvelle optique sur la sécurité européenne. *Politique Étrangère* 55(3): 543–557.

Brock L (1968) Die Renaissance nationalstaatlicher Interessenpolitik in den internationalen Beziehungen. *Europa-Archiv* 23(20): 727–734.

Broer M and Diehl O (1991) Die Sicherheit der neuen Demokratien in Europa und die NATO. *Europa-Archiv* 46(12): 367–376.

Brunner D (1976) Die militärische Lage Europas. *Allgemeine Schweizerische Militärzeitschrift* 142(12): 457–459.

Brunner D (1980) Die strategische Lage Europas um die Jahrzehntwende 70er/80er Jahre. *Allgemeine Schweizerische Militärzeitschrift* 146(2): 63–67.

Büger C and Villumsen T (2007) Beyond the gap: Relevance, fields of practice and the securitizing consequences of (democratic peace) research. *Journal of International Relations and Development* 10(4): 417–448.

Bundesminister der Verteidigung (1969) *Weissbuch 1969 zur Verteidigungspolitik der Bundesregierung.* Bonn: Presse- und Informationsamt der Bundesregierung.

Bundesminister der Verteidigung (1970) *Weissbuch 1970 zur Sicherheit der Bundesrepublik Deutschland und zur Entwicklung der Bundeswehr.* Bonn: Presse- und Informationsamt der Bundesregierung.

Bundesminister der Verteidigung (1976) *Weissbuch 1975/1976 zur Sicherheit der Bundesrepublik Deutschland und zur Entwicklung der Bundeswehr.* Bonn: Presse- und Informationsamt der Bundesregierung.

Bundesminister der Verteidigung (1979) *Weissbuch 1979 zur Sicherheit der Bundesrepublik Deutschland und zur Entwicklung der Bundeswehr.* Bonn: Presse- und Informationsamt der Bundesregierung.

Bundesminister der Verteidigung (1983) *Weissbuch 1983 zur Sicherheit der Bundesrepublik Deutschland.* Bonn: Presse- und Informationsamt der Bundesregierung.

Bundesminister der Verteidigung (1985) *Weissbuch 1985 zur Entwicklung der Bundeswehr.* Bonn: Presse- und Informationsamt der Bundesregierung.

Bundesminister der Verteidigung (1994) *Weissbuch 1994: Weissbuch zur Sicherheit der Bundesrepublik Deutschland und zur Lage und Zukunft der Bundeswehr*. Bonn: Presse- und Informationsamt der Bundesregierung.

Bundesminister der Verteidigung (2003) *Verteidigungspolitische Richtlinien für den Geschäftsbereich des Bundesministers der Verteidigung*. Berlin: Bundesministerium der Verteidigung.

Bundesminister der Verteidigung (2006) *Weissbuch 2006 zur Sicherheitspolitik Deutschlands und zur Zukunft der Bundeswehr*. Berlin: Bundesministerium der Verteidigung.

Bureau JF (2002) L'étranger dans le champ de vision des Français. *Politique Étrangère* 67(4): 899–914.

Buzan B (1991) *People, States and Fear*. Boulder, CO: Lynne Rienner Publishers.

Buzan B (1997) Rethinking security after the Cold War. *Cooperation and Conflict* 32(1): 5–28.

Buzan B (2006) Will the 'global war on terrorism' be the new Cold War? *International Affairs* 82(6): 1101–1118.

Buzan B and Hansen L (2009) *The Evolution of International Security Studies*. Cambridge: Cambridge University Press.

Buzan B and Waever O (2003) *Regions and Powers: The Structure of International Security*. Cambridge: Cambridge University Press.

Buzan B and Waever O (2009) Macrosecuritization and security constellations: Reconsidering scale in securitization theory. *Review of International Studies* 35(2): 253–276.

Buzan B, Waever O and De Wilde J (1998) *Security: A New Framework for Analysis*. Boulder, CO: Lynne Rienner.

Campbell D (1992) *Writing Security: United States Foreign Policy and the Politics of Identity*. Minneapolis, MN: University of Minnesota Press.

Carell LF (1993) Die Friedensförderung im Spannungsfeld Schweizerischer Sicherheitspolitik. *Allgemeine Schweizerische Militärzeitschrift* 159(2): 55–59.

Carlsnaes W (1992) The agency-structure problem in foreign policy analysis. *International Studies Quarterly* 36(3): 245–270.

Carlsnaes W (2002) Foreign policy. In: Carlsnaes W, Risse T and Simmons B (eds) *Handbook of International Relations*. London: Sage Publications, 331–349.

Cartwright N (2004) Causation: One word, many things. *Philosophy of Science* 71(5): 805–819.

C.A.S.E. Collective (2006) Critical approaches to security in Europe: A networked manifesto. *Security Dialogue* 37(4): 443–487.

Centre d'Etudes de Politique Etrangère (1953) Rapport du comité d'études de l'Organisation Atlantique. L'O.T.A.N. et le réarmement de l'occident. *Politique Étrangère* 18(5): 401–412.

Centre d'Etudes de Politique Etrangère (1959) Problèmes et perspectives de l'Alliance Atlantique. *Politique Étrangère* 24(2): 128–178.

Centre d'Etudes de Politique Etrangère (1967) Modèles de sécurité européenne. *Politique Étrangère* 32(6): 519–541.

Chandler D (2012) Resilience and human security: The post-interventionist paradigm. *Security Dialogue* 43(3): 213–229.

Charillon F (2002) Peut-il encore y avoir une politique étrangère de la France? *Politique Étrangère* 67(4): 915–929.

Ciuta F (2010) Conceptual notes on energy security: Total or banal security? *Security Dialogue* 41(2): 123–144.

Cohen S (1989) La politique étrangère entre l'Elysée et Matignon. *Politique Étrangère* 54(3): 487–503.

Collier A (1994) *Critical Realism: An Introduction to Roy Bhaskar's Philosophy.* New York, NY: Verso.

Cornides W (1963) Die Bundesrepublik vor der Ratifizierung des deutsch-französischen Vertrages. *Europa-Archiv* 18(7): 237–240.

Cornides W and Volle H (1950) Die Diskussion über den deutschen Verteidigungsbeitrag: Die Interpretationen der New Yorker Beschlüsse durch die Hohen Kommissare. *Europa-Archiv* 5(24): 3576–3593.

Cornides W and Volle H (1952) Atlantikpakt und Europäische Verteidigungsgemeinschaft: Die Einbeziehung der Bundesrepublik in die Europäische Verteidigungsgemeinschaft. *Europa-Archiv* 7(13/14): 5020–5040.

Cotti F (1994) Mehr Gute Dienste dank Blauhelmen. *Allgemeine Schweizerische Militärzeitschrift* 159(6): 5–8.

Coudenhove-Kalergi RN (1939) La paix de demain. *Politique Étrangère* 4(4): 377–386.

Cox R and Sinclair T (1996) *Approaches to World Order.* Cambridge: Cambridge University Press.

Cramer D (1970) Die DDR und die Bonner Ostpolitik. *Europa-Archiv* 25(5): 167–172.

Croft S (2012) Constructing ontological insecurity: The insecuritization of Britain's Muslims. *Contemporary Security Policy* 33(2): 219–235.

Czempiel EO (1984) Diagnose der Atlantischen Gemeinschaft: Stabile Strukturen, aber unterschiedliche Konfliktbilder. *Europa-Archiv* 39(2): 53–62.

Däniker G (1973) Die Armee im Rahmen der neuen Sicherheitspolitik. *Allgemeine Schweizerische Militärzeitschrift* 139(12): 56–57.

Däniker G (1999) Sicherheit durch Kooperation: Zum Konzept der neuen Sicherheitspolitik. *Allgemeine Schweizerische Militärzeitschrift* 1999(1): 7–9.

David CP (1999) Visions constructivistes et réalistes de la consolidation de la paix en Bosnie – ou – Quand Alice au pays des merveilles rencontre le monstre de Frankenstein. *Revue Française de Science Politique* 49(4): 545–572.

Davies B and Harré R (1990) Positioning: The discursive production of selves. *Journal of the Theory of Social Behaviour* 20(1): 43–65.

De Bavière C (1968) Réflexions sur une politique de défense pour l'Europe. *Politique Étrangère* 33(6): 561–574.

De Chambrun G (1949) Y a-t-il une alternative à la politique étrangère de la France? *Politique Étrangère* 14(4): 355–364.

De Clermont-Tonnerre T (1954) L'armée européenne. *Politique Étrangère* 19(2): 169–194.

De Dardel JJ (1990) New challenges facing Swiss foreign policy. In: Milivojevic M and Maurer P (eds) *Swiss Neutrality and Security: Armed Forces, National Defence and Foreign Policy.* New York, NY: St. Martin's Press, 122–136.

De la Gorce PM (1981) Bilan d'un septennat la politique extérieure française. *Politique Étrangère* 46(1): 89–104.

De la Serre F (1982) La politique européenne de la France New Look ou New Deal. *Politique Étrangère* 47(1): 125–137.

De Maupeou J (1956) OTAN et sécurité collective. *Politique Étrangère* 21(2): 143–164.

De Rosé F (1980) La sécurité de l'Europe dans un monde multipolaire. *Politique Étrangère* 45(4): 967–974.

De Weck H and Maurer P (1990) Swiss national defence policy revisited. In: Milivojevic M and Maurer P (eds) *Swiss Neutrality and Security: Armed Forces, National Defence and Foreign Policy.* New York, NY: St. Martin's Press, 65–80.

Debré M (1953) Contre l'armée européenne. *Politique Étrangère* 18(5): 367–400.

Delpech T (1999) Pour un retour de la stratégie envers les dictatures. *Politique Étrangère* 64(2): 257–268.

Dessler D (1989) What's at stake in the agent-structure debate? *International Organization* 43(3): 441–70.

Deudney D (1990) The case against linking environmental degradation and national security. *Millennium: Journal of International Studies* 19(3): 461–476.

Deutscher Bundestag (1949a) Verhandlungen des Deutschen Bundestages, 17. Sitzung. *Stenographische Berichte* 1. Wahlperiode (15. November): 397–448.

Deutscher Bundestag (1949b) Verhandlungen des Deutschen Bundestages, 24. Sitzung. *Stenographische Berichte* 1. Wahlperiode (16. Dezember): 733–743.

Deutscher Bundestag (1950) Verhandlungen des Deutschen Bundestages, 68. Sitzung. *Stenographische Berichte* 1. Wahlperiode (13. Juni): 2490–2502.

Deutscher Bundestag (1951) Verhandlungen des Deutschen Bundestages, 113. Sitzung. *Stenographische Berichte* 1. Wahlperiode (24. Januar): 4261–4267.

Deutscher Bundestag (1954a) Verhandlungen des Deutschen Bundestages, 61. Sitzung. *Stenographische Berichte* 2. Wahlperiode (15. Dezember): 3114–3154.

Deutscher Bundestag (1954b) Verhandlungen des Deutschen Bundestages, 62. Sitzung. *Stenographische Berichte* 2. Wahlperiode (16. Dezember): 3177–3213.

Deutscher Bundestag (1955) Verhandlungen des Deutschen Bundestages, 115. Sitzung. *Stenographische Berichte* 2. Wahlperiode (2. Dezember): 6155–6188.

Deutscher Bundestag (1963) Verhandlungen des Deutschen Bundestages, 73. Sitzung. *Stenographische Berichte* 4. Wahlperiode (25. April): 3417–3429.

Deutscher Bundestag (1969) Verhandlungen des Deutschen Bundestages, 244. Sitzung. *Stenographische Berichte* 5. Wahlperiode (27. Juni): 13603–13605.

Deutscher Bundestag (1970) Verhandlungen des Deutschen Bundestages, 54. Sitzung. *Stenographische Berichte* 6. Wahlperiode (2. Juni): 2750–2773.

Deutscher Bundestag (1971a) Denkschrift. *Drucksachen des Deutschen Bundestages* VI (3157).

Deutscher Bundestag (1971b) Verhandlungen des Deutschen Bundestages, 93. Sitzung. *Stenographische Berichte* 6. Wahlperiode (28. Januar): 5043–5105.

Deutscher Bundestag (1971c) Verhandlungen des Deutschen Bundestages, 94. Sitzung. *Stenographische Berichte* 6. Wahlperiode (29. Januar): 5127–5146.

Deutscher Bundestag (1971d) Verhandlungen des Deutschen Bundestages, 196. Sitzung. *Stenographische Berichte* 6. Wahlperiode (23. Juni): 11489–11507.

Deutscher Bundestag (1972a) Verhandlungen des Deutschen Bundestages, 171. Sitzung. *Stenographische Berichte* 6. Wahlperiode (23. Februar): 9769–9825.

Deutscher Bundestag (1972b) Verhandlungen des Deutschen Bundestages, 172. Sitzung. *Stenographische Berichte* 6. Wahlperiode (24. Februar): 9833–9873.

Deutscher Bundestag (1972c) Verhandlungen des Deutschen Bundestages, 173. Sitzung. *Stenographische Berichte* 6. Wahlperiode (25. Februar): 9941–10009.

Deutscher Bundestag (1973a) Verhandlungen des Deutschen Bundestages, 7. Sitzung. *Stenographische Berichte* 7. Wahlperiode (18. Januar): 121–148.

Deutscher Bundestag (1973b) Verhandlungen des Deutschen Bundestages, 8. Sitzung. *Stenographische Berichte* 7. Wahlperiode (18. Januar): 157–173.

Deutscher Bundestag (1973c) Verhandlungen des Deutschen Bundestages, 14. Sitzung. *Stenographische Berichte* 7. Wahlperiode (15. Februar): 534–579.

Deutscher Bundestag (1973d) Verhandlungen des Deutschen Bundestages, 29. Sitzung. *Stenographische Berichte* 7. Wahlperiode (9. Mai): 1427–1542.

Deutscher Bundestag (1973e) Verhandlungen des Deutschen Bundestages, 48. Sitzung. *Stenographische Berichte* 7. Wahlperiode (13. September): 2741–2746.

Deutscher Bundestag (1974) Verhandlungen des Deutschen Bundestages, 90. Sitzung. *Stenographische Berichte* 7. Wahlperiode (27. März): 5906–5933.

Deutscher Bundestag (1976a) Verhandlungen des Deutschen Bundestages, 254. Sitzung. *Stenographische Berichte* 7. Wahlperiode (25.. Juni): 18102–18145.

Deutscher Bundestag (1976b) Verhandlungen des Deutschen Bundestages, 6. Sitzung. *Stenographische Berichte* 8. Wahlperiode (17. Dezember): 55–123.

Deutscher Bundestag (1977a) Verhandlungen des Deutschen Bundestages, 14. Sitzung. *Stenographische Berichte* 8. Wahlperiode (10. Februar): 609–719.

Deutscher Bundestag (1977b) Verhandlungen des Deutschen Bundestages, 39. Sitzung. *Stenographische Berichte* 8. Wahlperiode (8. September): 2987–3074.

Deutscher Bundestag (1977c) Verhandlungen des Deutschen Bundestages, 42. Sitzung. *Stenographische Berichte* 8. Wahlperiode (15. September): 3164–3268.

Deutscher Bundestag (1977d) Antwort der Bundesregierung. *Drucksachen des Deutschen Bundestages* 8 (464).

Deutscher Bundestag (1978) Verhandlungen des Deutschen Bundestages, 65. Sitzung. *Stenographische Berichte* 8. Wahlperiode (19. Januar): 4959–5047.

Deutscher Bundestag (1980a) Verhandlungen des Deutschen Bundestages, 5. Sitzung. *Stenographische Berichte* 9. Wahlperiode (24. November): 25–42.

Deutscher Bundestag (1980b) Verhandlungen des Deutschen Bundestages, 6. Sitzung. *Stenographische Berichte* 9. Wahlperiode (26. November): 45–127.

Deutscher Bundestag (1981) Verhandlungen des Deutschen Bundestages, 31. Sitzung. *Stenographische Berichte* 9. Wahlperiode (9. April): 1541–1639.

Deutscher Bundestag (1982a) Antrag: Militärisches potential der DDR. *Drucksachen des Deutschen Bundestages* 9 (1884).

Deutscher Bundestag (1982b) Verhandlungen des Deutschen Bundestages, 130. Sitzung. *Stenographische Berichte* 9. Wahlperiode (25. November): 8005–8096.

Deutscher Bundestag (1983a) Verhandlungen des Deutschen Bundestages, 11. Sitzung. *Stenographische Berichte* 10. Wahlperiode (9. Juni): 525–627.

Deutscher Bundestag (1983b) Verhandlungen des Deutschen Bundestages, 13. Sitzung. *Stenographische Berichte* 10. Wahlperiode (15. Juni): 691–814.

Deutscher Bundestag (1985) Kleine anfrage der Abgeordneten Frau Kelly und der Fraktion Die Grünen. *Drucksachen des Deutschen Bundestages* 10 (2904).

Deutscher Bundestag (1986) Verhandlungen des Deutschen Bundestages, 243. Sitzung. *Stenographische Berichte* 10. Wahlperiode (6. November): 18737–18874.

Deutscher Bundestag (1987) Verhandlungen des Deutschen Bundestages, 4. Sitzung. *Stenographische Berichte* 11. Wahlperiode (18. März): 51–135.

Deutscher Bundestag (1988) Verhandlungen des Deutschen Bundestages, 133. Sitzung. *Stenographische Berichte* 11. Wahlperiode (1. Dezember): 8093–8244.

Deutscher Bundestag (1989) Verhandlungen des Deutschen Bundestages, 157. Sitzung. *Stenographische Berichte* 11. Wahlperiode (6. September): 11835–11972.

Deutscher Bundestag (1990a) Verhandlungen des Deutschen Bundestages, 221. Sitzung. *Stenographische Berichte* 11. Wahlperiode (23. August): 17437–17481.

Deutscher Bundestag (1990b) Verhandlungen des Deutschen Bundestages, 236. Sitzung. *Stenographische Berichte* 11. Wahlperiode (22. November): 18861–18935.

Deutscher Bundestag (1991) Verhandlungen des Deutschen Bundestages, 53. Sitzung. *Stenographische Berichte* 12. Wahlperiode (6. November): 4363–4442.

Deutscher Bundestag (1993) Verhandlungen des Deutschen Bundestages, 151. Sitzung. *Stenographische Berichte* 12. Wahlperiode (21. April): 12925–13002.

Deutscher Bundestag (1994a) Verhandlungen des Deutschen Bundestages, 202. Sitzung. *Stenographische Berichte* 12. Wahlperiode (13. Januar): 17411–17557.

Deutscher Bundestag (1994b) Verhandlungen des Deutschen Bundestages, 5. Sitzung. *Stenographische Berichte* 13. Wahlperiode (23 November): 37–156.

Deutscher Bundestag (1995) Verhandlungen des Deutschen Bundestages, 48. Sitzung. *Stenographische Berichte* 13. Wahlperiode (30. Juni): 3953–4044.

Deutscher Bundestag (1996) Unterrichtung durch die Bundesregierung: Bericht zum stand der bemühungen um rüstungskontrolle und abrüstung (Jahresabrüstungsbericht 1995). *Drucksachen des Deutschen Bundestages* 13 (4450).

Deutscher Bundestag (1999a) Verhandlungen des Deutschen Bundestages, 33. Sitzung. *Stenographische Berichte* 14. Wahlperiode (19. April): 2663–2696.

Deutscher Bundestag (1999b) Verhandlungen des Deutschen Bundestages, 35. Sitzung. *Stenographische Berichte* 14. Wahlperiode (22. April): 2761–2890.

Deutscher Bundestag (2001a) Verhandlungen des Deutschen Bundestages, 187. Sitzung. *Stenographische Berichte* 14. Wahlperiode (19. September): 18301–18343.

Deutscher Bundestag (2001b) Verhandlungen des Deutschen Bundestages, 192. Sitzung. *Stenographische Berichte* 14. Wahlperiode (11. Oktober): 18679–18853.

Deutscher Bundestag (2002a) Verhandlungen des Deutschen Bundestages, 10. Sitzung. *Stenographische Berichte* 15. Wahlperiode (14. November): 531–645.

Deutscher Bundestag (2002b) Verhandlungen des Deutschen Bundestages, 13. Sitzung. *Stenographische Berichte* 15. Wahlperiode (4. Dezember): 871–1009.

Deutscher Bundestag (2002c) Verhandlungen des Deutschen Bundestages, 8. Sitzung. *Stenographische Berichte* 15. Wahlperiode (7. November): 379–471.

Deutscher Bundestag (2003) Verhandlungen des Deutschen Bundestages, 35. Sitzung. *Stenographische Berichte* 15. Wahlperiode (20. März): 2857–2938.

Deutscher Bundestag (2004a) Verhandlungen des Deutschen Bundestages, 97. Sitzung. *Stenographische Berichte* 15. Wahlperiode (11. März): 8599–8726.

Deutscher Bundestag (2004b) Verhandlungen des Deutschen Bundestages, 139. Sitzung. *Stenographische Berichte* 15. Wahlperiode (12. November): 12783–12867.

Deutscher Bundestag (2006) Verhandlungen des Deutschen Bundestages, 60. Sitzung. *Stenographische Berichte* 16. Wahlperiode (26. Oktober): 5781–5966.

Devillers P (1970) L'évolution du conflit et les perspectives de solution (Vietnam). *Revue Française de Science Politique* 20(2): 330–348.

Devillers P (1974) La fin d'une guerre d'Indochine. *Revue Française de Science Politique* 24(2): 295–308.

Die Zeit (1952a) Die Ostpolitik des Kanzlers. *Die Zeit* 3. April, Nr. 14.

Die Zeit (1952b) Die Beweislast liegt bei der Opposition. *Die Zeit* 10. Juli, Nr. 28.

Die Zeit (1957a) Gemeinsame Außenpolitik. *Die Zeit* 13. Juni, Nr. 24.

Die Zeit (1957b) Die Ost-Mauer soll bröckeln. *Die Zeit* 3. Oktober, Nr. 40.

Die Zeit (1960) Die neue Weltkarte: Das Ost-West-Schema ist zu eng für die Realität von 1961. *Die Zeit* 30. Dezember, Nr. 53.

Die Zeit (1965a) Fenster zum Osten: Experimente der Bonner Ostpolitik in Rumänien. *Die Zeit* 21. Mai, Nr. 21.

Die Zeit (1965b) Politik mit dem Osten: Europa endet nicht mehr an der Elbe. *Die Zeit* 2. Juli, Nr. 27.

Die Zeit (1965c) Strategie für Deutschland: Anregungen für eine deutsche Wiedervereinigungspolitik. *Die Zeit* 10. Dezember, Nr. 50.

Die Zeit (1966a) Blick nach Osten: Realismus als Gebot deutscher Politik. *Die Zeit* 18. März, Nr. 12.

Die Zeit (1966b) Öffnung nach Osten? Die CDU rüttelt an außenpolitischen Dogmen. *Die Zeit* 25. März, Nr. 13.

Die Zeit (1967) Zwischenbilanz der Großen Koalition. *Die Zeit* 22. September, Nr. 38.

Die Zeit (1969a) Ist die deutsche Einheit noch ein Ziel? Der Bonner Deutschlandpolitik fehlt ein langfristiges Konzept. *Die Zeit* 23. Mai, Nr. 21.

Die Zeit (1969b) Das Ende der Doktrin: Längst hat die Hallstein-Formel ihre Wirkung verloren. *Die Zeit* 6. Juni, Nr. 23.

Die Zeit (1972) Weltpolitik 1972: Spiel auf mehreren Brettern. *Die Zeit.* 13. Oktober, Nr. 41.

Die Zeit (1974a) Vorrang für die Innenpolitik: Bundestag debattiert über Schmidts Regierungserklärung. *Die Zeit* 24. Mai, Nr. 22.

Die Zeit (1974b) Billigbombe für jedermann! Nach der indischen Atomexplosion. *Die Zeit* 5. Juli, Nr. 28.

Die Zeit (1976) Ein Westafrikanischer Bürgerkrieg als weltpolitisches Pulverfass. *Die Zeit* 9. Januar, Nr. 3.

Die Zeit (1982) Keine Angst vor den Grünen: Die SPD muss das Bündnis von Arbeitnehmern und kritischer Jugend erneuern. *Die Zeit* 24. September, Nr. 39.

Die Zeit (1983) Wohin treibt die SPD? Die Bundesrepublik braucht eine regierungsfähige Opposition. *Die Zeit* 11. November, Nr. 46.

Die Zeit (1993) Die Festung Europa und das neue Deutschland. *Die Zeit* 28. Mai, Nr. 22.

Die Zeit (1994) Russland will in Europa mitsprechen: Zu recht! *Die Zeit* 3. Juni, Nr. 23.

Die Zeit (1995) Die Gefahr liegt im Nichtstun. *Die Zeit* 24. März, Nr. 13.

Die Zeit (1996) Der Kalte Krieg ist noch lange nicht vorbei. *Die Zeit* 1. März, Nr. 10.

Die Zeit (2001) Einwanderung in der Nationalisierungsfalle: Nach dem Terror drohen neue Grenzen für Migranten in aller Welt. *Die Zeit* 14. Mai, Nr. 39.

Die Zeit (2005) Terror: Europas offene Wunde. *Die Zeit* 11. März, Nr. 11.

Die Zeit (2007) Die Klima-Kriege. *Die Zeit* 3. Mai, Nr. 19.

Die Zeit (2008) Vernetzte Sicherheit. *Die Zeit* 1. Mai, Nr. 19.

Die Zeit (2009) NATO: Wie ein Hammer auf der Suche nach Nägeln. *Die Zeit* 31. März, Nr. 11.

Diez E (1980) *Festschrift für Rudolf Bindschedler.* Bern: Stämpfli & Cie.

Doly G (1978) Sécurité de la France et Union Européenne. *Politique Étrangère* 43(3): 265–282.

Doty RL (1993) Foreign policy as social construction: A post-positivist analysis of US counterinsurgency policy in the Philippines. *International Studies Quarterly* 37(3): 297–320.

Doty RL (2003) *Anti-Immigrantism in Western Democracies: Statecraft, Desire, and the Politics of Exclusion.* London: Routledge.

Dunn LA (1995) Le nouvel agenda de la non-prolifération. *Politique Étrangère* 60(3): 681–694.

Eidgenössisches Departement für Auswärtige Angelegenheiten (1991) Quelques considérations sur l'adhésion à l'ONU: Neutralité, Notiz Roethlisberger an Pometta (9. Juni 1981). *BAR E* 2023 (A)1991/39-713.

Eidgenössisches Politisches Departement (1980) Protokoll der Besprechung über die Europäische Sicherheitskonferenz (16. Dezember 1969). *BAR E* 2001 (E)1980/83.

Elbe S (2009) *Virus Alert: Security, Governmentality, and the AIDS Pandemic.* New York, NY: Columbia University Press.

Ellsworth R (1978) New imperatives for the old alliance. *International Security* 2(4): 132–148.

Emirbayer M and Mische A (1998) What is agency? *American Journal of Sociology* 103(4): 962–1023.

Enders T and Siebenmorgen P (1988) Überlegungen zu einem sicherheitspolitischen Gesamtkonzept der Bundesrepublik Deutschland. *Europa-Archiv* 43(14): 385–392.

Erler F (1964) La République Fédérale, la Communauté Economique Européenne et la solidarité Atlantique. *Politique Étrangère* 29(5): 433–444.

European Security Strategy (2003) *A Secure Europe in a Better World*. Brussels: EU Council.

Eylau-Wagram P (1981) Propositions pour une stratégie française de 1980 à 1990. *Politique Étrangère* 46(1): 121–135.

Facon I (1999) L'armée russe, menace ou recours? *Politique Étrangère* 64(2): 291–306.

Fanzun J and Lehmann P (2000) Die Schweiz und die Welt: Aussen- und sicherheitspolitische Beiträge der Schweiz zu Frieden, Sicherheit und Stabilität 1945–2000. *Zürcher Beiträge* 57.

Farr R (1987) Social representations: A French tradition of research. *Journal for the Theory of Social Behaviour* 17(4): 343–369.

Fassbender B (1991) Zur staatlichen Ordnung Europas nach der deutschen Einigung. *Europa-Archiv* 46(13): 395–403.

Fearon J and Wendt A (2002) Rationalism vs. constructivism: A skeptical view. In: Carlsnaes W, Risse T and Simmons B (eds) *Handbook of International Relations*. London: Sage Publications, 52–72.

Feyerabend P (1975). How to defend society against science. *Radical Philosophy* 11(6): 3–8.

Fierke K (2002) Link across the abyss: Language and logic in international relations. *International Studies Quarterly* 46(3): 331–354.

Fischer T (2004) *Die Grenzen der Neutralität: Schweizerisches KSZE-Engagement und Gescheiterte UNO-Beitrittspolitik im Kalten Krieg 1969–1986*. Zürich: Chronos Verlag.

Floyd R (2010) *Security and the Environment: Securitization Theory and US Environmental Security Policy*. Cambridge: Cambridge University Press.

Foster J (2003) Representational projects and interacting forms of knowledge. *Journal for the Theory of Social Behaviour* 33(3): 231–244.

Foucault M (1982) The subject and power. *Critical Inquiry* 8(4): 777–795.

Foucault M (1991) Governmentality. In: Burchell G, Gordon C and Miller P (eds) *The Foucault Effect: Studies in Governmentality*. Hemel Hempstead: Harvester Wheatsheaf, 87–104.

François-Poncet J (1985) Quatre ans de politique étrangère socialiste. *Politique Étrangère* 50(2): 437–447.

Frank P (1970) Sicherheitsprobleme im Lichte des Moskauer Vertrags. *Europa-Archiv* 25(24): 867–876.

Frei O (1965) Die aussenpolitischen Bemühungen der DDR in der nichtkommunistischen Welt. *Europa-Archiv* 20(22): 843–852.

Freudenstein R (1998) Poland, Germany and the EU. *International Affairs* 74(1): 41–54.

Freymond JF (1990) Neutrality and security policy as components of the Swiss model. In: Milivojevic M and Maurer P (eds) *Swiss Neutrality and Security: Armed Forces, National Defence and Foreign Policy*. New York, NY: St. Martin's Press, 175–193.

Froment-Meurice H (2000) Une politique étrangère pour quoi faire? *Politique Étrangère* 65(2): 319–332.

Fuchs S (2001) Beyond agency. *Sociological Theory* 19(1): 24–40.

Furniss ES (1954) *France: Keystone of Western Defence*. Garden City, NY: Doubleday & Company.

Gabriel JM (1990) *Szenarien Schweizerischer Integrations- und Sicherheitspolitik.* St. Gallen: Hochschule St. Gallen, Institut für Politikwissenschaft.

Gabriel JM (1998) *Bericht Brunner: Stärken und Schwächen.* Zürich: ETH Zürich, Forschungsstelle für Internationale Beziehungen.

Gallois PM (1966) L'Alliance entre deux stratégies. *Politique Étrangère* 31(3): 217–236.

Gallois PM (1977) Sur une arme dont on ne sait que faire. *Politique Étrangère* 42(11): 35–62.

Galtung J (1984) Transarmament: From offensive to defensive defense. *Journal of Peace Research* 21(2): 127–139.

Gascuel J (1950) Vers une politique européenne. *Politique Étrangère* 15(4): 437–446.

Gasteyger C (1958) Der Atlantikpakt und das Problem der europäischen Sicherheit. *Europa-Archiv* 13(7): 1–12.

Gasteyger C (1995) Das internationale Umfeld: Eine aktuelle Beurteilung von Chancen und Risiken. In: Rhinow R (ed.) *Die Schweizerische Sicherheitspolitik im internationalen Umfeld.* Basel: Helbing & Lichtenhahn, 19–26.

Gasteyger C (1996) Neue Konturen europäischer Sicherheit. *Internationale Politik* 51(12): 21–31.

Gautier L (1999) L'Europe de la défense au portant. *Politique Étrangère* 64(2): 233–243.

Genscher HD (1980) Deutsche Aussenpolitik für die achtziger Jahre. *Europa-Archiv* 35(12): 371–386.

Géraud A (1937) L'assistance mutuelle franco-britannique. *Politique Étrangère* 2(2): 107–116.

Géraud A (1940) La France, la Grande-Bretagne et la paix future. *Politique Étrangère* 5(1): 13–23.

George S (1997) How to win the war of ideas: Lessons from the Gramscian right. *Dissent* 44 (Summer): 47–53.

Gerbet P (1956) La genèse du Plan Schuman. *Revue Française de Science Politique* 6(3): 525–553.

Gerring J (2005) Causation: A unified framework for the social sciences. *Journal of Theoretical Politics* 17(2): 163–198.

Giddens A (1976) *New Rules of Sociological Method: A Positive Critique of Interpretative Sociologies.* London: Hutchinson.

Giddens A (1979) *Central Problems in Social Theory.* Basingstoke: Palgrave Macmillan.

Giddens A (1984) *The Constitution of Society: Outline of Theory of Structuration.* Cambridge: Polity Press.

Giddens A (1995) *A Contemporary Critique of Historical Materialism.* Stanford, CA: Stanford University Press.

Giraud A (1990) Construction européenne et défense. *Politique Étrangère* 55(3): 513–524.

Glardet R (1960) Pouvoir civil et pouvoir militaire dans la France contemporaine. *Revue Française de Science Politique* 10(1): 5–38.

Gnesotto N (1990) Défense européenne pourquoi pas les douze. *Politique Étrangère* 55(4): 877–886.

Gnesotto N (1997) Elargissement de l'OTAN une responsabilité européenne. *Politique Étrangère* 62(1): 125–136.

Goetschel L, Barth M and Schwarz D (2005) *Swiss Foreign Policy: Foundations and Possibilities.* London: Routledge.

Gouldner A (1970) *The Coming Crisis of Western Sociology.* New York, NY: Basic Books.

Gouvernement Français (1972) *Livre Blanc sur la Défense Nationale*. Paris: Edocar Imprimerie.

Gouvernement Français (1994) *Livre Blanc sur la Défense*. Paris: Odile Jacob.

Gouvernement Français (2008a) *Défense et Sécurité Nationale: Le Livre Blanc*. Paris: Odile Jacob.

Gouvernement Français (2008b) *La France et l'Europe dans le Monde: Livre Blanc sur la Politique Étrangère et Européenne de la France*. Paris: Odile Jacob.

Gouvernement Français (2013) *Le Livre Blanc sur la Défense et la Sécurité Nationale*. Paris: Odile Jacob.

Gramsci A (1971) *The Modern Prince*. New York, NY: International Publishers.

Grant ML (1990) Renforcement de la CSCE: La réponse aux rêves européens? *Politique Étrangère* 55(3): 589–607.

Grappin P (1950) Le réarmement devant l'opinion allemande. *Politique Étrangère* 15(1): 71–86.

Grewe WG (1959) Ein Friedensvertrag mit Deutschland? *Europa-Archiv* 14(9/10): 301–321.

Gusterson H (1999). Missing the end of the Cold War. In: Weldes J, Laffey M, Gusterson H and Duvall R (eds) *Cultures of Insecurity: States, Communities and the Production of Danger*. Minneapolis, MN: University of Minnesota Press, 319–345.

Gutjahr L (1994) *German Foreign and Defence Policy after Unification*. London: Pinter Press.

Guzzini S (2000) A reconstruction of constructivism in International Relations. *European Journal of International Relations* 6(2): 147–182.

Guzzini S (2011) Securitization as a causal mechanism. *Security Dialogue* 42(4–5): 329–341.

Haftendorn H (1983) *Sicherheit und Entspannung: Zur Aussenpolitik der Bundesrepublik Deutschland 1955–1982*. Baden-Baden: Nomos.

Haftendorn H (1991) The security puzzle: Theory-building and discipline-building in international security. *International Studies Quarterly* 35(1): 3–17.

Hagmann J (2010) Beyond exceptionalism? New security conceptions in contemporary Switzerland. *Contemporary Security Policy* 31(2): 249–272.

Hagmann J (2013) Representations of terrorism and the making of counterterrorism policy. *Critical Studies on Terrorism* 6(3): 429–446.

Hagmann J and Dunn Cavelty M (2012) National risk registers: Security scientism and the propagation of permanent insecurity. *Security Dialogue* 43(1): 79–96.

Hagmann T and Korf B (2012) Agamben in the Ogaden: Violence and sovereignty in the Ethiopian-Somali frontier. *Political Geography* 31(4): 205–214.

Hall S (1992) *Modernity and its Feature*. Cambridge: Polity Press.

Hallsworth S and Lea J (2011) Reconstructing Leviathan: Emerging contours of the security state. *Theoretical Criminology* 15(2): 141–157.

Hanreider W (1989) *Germany, America, Europe: Forty Years of German Foreign Policy*. New Haven, CT: Yale University Press.

Hansen L (2006) *Security as Practice: Discourse Analysis and the Bosnian War*. London: Routledge.

Hardt M (1998) The global society of control. *Discourse* 20(3): 139–152.

Harmel P (1971) A la recherche de nouvelles formes de sécurité européenne. *Politique Étrangère* 36(2): 113–124.

Harré R (1993) *Social Being*. Oxford: Basil Blackwell.

Harré R and Madden EH (1975) *Causal Powers: A Theory of Natural Necessity*. Oxford: Basil Blackwell.

Hassner P (1976) L'avenir des alliances en Europe. *Revue Française de Science Politique* 26(6): 1029–1053.

Hay C (1995) Structure and agency. In: Marsh D and Stoker G (eds) *Theory and Methods in Political Science*. London: Macmillan, 189–206.

Heisbourg F (1988) Après le Traité. Aggiornamento pour une alliance. *Politique Étrangère* 53(1): 143–151.

Heisbourg F (1994) Sécurité l'Europe livrée à elle-même. *Politique Étrangère* 59(1): 247–260.

Heisbourg F (1995) La politique de défense française à l'aube d'un nouveau mandat presidential. *Politique Étrangère* 60(1): 73–83.

Hellmann G (2004) Sicherheitspolitik. In: Dittgen H and Schmidt S (eds) *Handbuch zur deutschen Aussenpolitik*. Wiesbaden: VS Verlag, 605–617.

Hermet G (1980) Entre l'utopie et la stratégie – la hiérarchie des nations dans le système mondial. *Revue Française de Science Politique* 30(2): 205–221.

Herzog R (1995) Die Grundkoordinaten deutscher Aussenpolitik. *Internationale Politik* 50(4): 3–11.

Hoffmann H (1995) Die Schweiz und die UNO. In: Rhinow R (ed.) *Die Schweizerische Sicherheitspolitik im internationalen Umfeld*. Basel: Helbing & Lichtenhahn, 57–72.

Hoffmann S (2000) La France dans le monde: 1979–2000. *Politique Étrangère* 65(2): 307–317.

Hollis M and Smith S (1990) *Explaining and Understanding International Relations*. Oxford: Clarendon Press.

Hoogensen G and Stuvoy K (2006) Gender, resistance and human security. *Security Dialogue* 37(2): 207–228.

Howorth J (2002) La France, l'OTAN et la sécurité européenne: *Statu quo* ingérable, renouveau introuvable. *Politique Étrangère* 67(4): 1001–1016.

Huysmans J (1998a) Revisiting Copenhagen: Or, on the creative development of a security studies agenda in Europe. *European Journal of International Relations* 4(4): 479–505.

Huysmans J (1998b) Security! What do you mean: From concept to thick signifier. *European Journal of International Relations* 4(2): 226–255.

Huysmans J (2006) *The Politics of Insecurity: Fear, Migration and Asylum in Europe*. London: Routledge.

Huysmans J (2008) The jargon of exception. On Schmitt, Agamben and the absence of political society. *International Political Sociology* 2(2): 165–183.

Hynek N and Chandler D (2013) No emancipatory alternative, no critical security studies. *Critical Security Studies* 1(1): 46–63.

Jacobs A and Masala C (1999) Germany's Mediterranean challenge. *Contemporary Security Policy* 20(2): 109–115.

Jahn E, Lemaitre P and Waever O (1987) European security – problems of research on non-military aspects. *Copenhagen Papers* 1.

Jameson F (1971) Introduction. In: Althusser L (ed.) *Lenin and Philosophy and Other Essays*. New York, NY: Monthly Review Press, vii–xiv.

Joffe J (1979) Die Aussenpolitik der Bundesrepublik Deutschland im Zeitalter der Entspannung. *Europa-Archiv* 34(23): 719–730.

Kaiser K (1969) Deutsche Aussenpolitik nach der tschechoslowakischen Krise von 1968. *Europa-Archiv* 24(10): 353–364.

Kaiser K (1986) SDI und deutsche Politik. *Europa-Archiv* 41(19): 569–578.

Kaiser K (1995) Deutsche Aussenpolitik in der Ära des Globalismus: Zwischen Interdependenz und Anarchie. *Internationale Politik* 50(1): 27–36.

Karst H (1959) La nouvelle Bundeswehr et la démocratie allemande. *Politique Étrangère* 24(1): 53–66.

Kawalkowski A (1964) Vers la fin d'une double hégémonie. *Politique Étrangère* 29(3): 260–282.

Kelstrup M (2004) Globalisation and societal insecurity: The securitization of terrorism and competing strategies for global governance. In: Guzzini S and Jung D (eds) *Contemporary Security Analysis and Copenhagen Peace Research*. London: Routledge, 106–116.

Keohane R (1988) International institutions: Two approaches. *International Studies Quarterly* 32(4): 379–396.

King G, Keohane R and Verba S (1994) *Designing Social Inquiry*. Princeton, NJ: Princeton University Press.

Kinkel K (1995) Die NATO-Erweiterung: Ein Beitrag zur gesamteuropäischen Sicherheit. *Internationale Politik* 50(4): 22–25.

Kissinger H (1966) Die deutsche Frage als Problem der europäischen und der internationalen Sicherheit. *Europa-Archiv* 21(23): 831–838.

Klein J (1978) La gauche française et les problèmes de défense. *Politique Étrangère* 43(5): 505–535.

Klein J (1983) Mythes et réalités de la défense de l'Europe. *Politique Étrangère* 48(2): 315–340.

Klotz A and Lynch C (2007) *Strategies for Research in Constructivist International Relations*. London: ME Sharpe.

Kolboom I (1989) Ostpolitik als deutsch-französische Herausforderung. *Europa-Archiv* 44(4): 115–124.

Krause K (1998) Critical theory and security studies: The research programme of 'critical security studies'. *Cooperation and Conflict* 33(3): 298–333.

Krause K (2011) Leashing the dogs of war: Arms control from sovereignty to governmentality. *Contemporary Security Policy* 32(1): 20–39.

Krause K and Williams MC (1996) Broadening the agenda of security studies: Politics and methods. *Mershon International Studies Review* 40(2): 229–254.

Kreis KM (1976) Der internationale Terrorismus: Ein unbewältigtes Problem der Staatengemeinschaft. *Europa-Archiv* 31(11): 367–376.

Kühner A (1991) Bewältigung von Katastrophen im 'Bericht des Bundesrates zur Schweizerischen Sicherheitspolitik im Wandel' vom 1. Dezember 1990. *Allgemeine Schweizerische Militärzeitschrift* 156(5): 252–253.

Kurki M (2006) Causes of a divided discipline: Rethinking the concept of cause in International Relations theory. *Review of International Studies* 32(2): 189–216.

Laclau E (1988) Metaphor and social antagonisms. In: Grossberg L and Nelson C (eds) *Marxism and the Interpretation of Culture*. Champaign, IL: University of Illinois Press, 249–257.

Laffey M and Weldes J (1997) Beyond belief: Ideas and symbolic technologies in the study of international relations. *European Journal of International Relations* 3(2): 193–237.

Landmann L (1980) Gedanken zur Konzeption der militärischen Landesverteidigung. *Allgemeine Schweizerische Militärzeitschrift* 146(5): 251–257.

Lange HJ (2003) *Die Polizei der Gesellschaft: Zur Soziologie der Inneren Sicherheit*. Opladen: Leske + Budrich.

Lasserre D (1967) *Etapes du Fédéralisme: Expérience Suisse*. Lausanne: Rencontres Suisses.

Laux J (1973) Prélude à la Conférence sur la Sécurité et la Coopération en Europe. *Politique Étrangère* 38(6): 675–696.

Layder D (1981) *Structure, Interaction and Social Theory*. London: Routledge.

Layder D (1997) *Modern Social Theory: Key Debates and New Directions*. London: UCL Press.

Le Monde (1948a) Le Président Truman donnerait mercredi un avertissement à l'URSS. *Le Monde* 13 mars: 1.

Le Monde (1948b) M. Attlee annonce que les communistes et les fascistes seraient écartés des postes intérressant la sécurité de l'Etat. *Le Monde* 12 mars: 4.

Le Monde (1948c) Le traité de Bruxelles. *Le Monde* 16 mars: 1.

Le Monde (1948d) Le pacte de Bruxelles a été signé hier au cours d'une cérémonie très simple. *Le Monde* 19 mars: 2.

Le Monde (1948e) Le Pacte de Bruxelles: Une révolution dans la politique extérieure britannique. *Le Monde* 19 mars: 2.

Le Monde (1948f) La formation de l'union Occidentale. *Le Monde* 20 mars: 1.

Le Monde (1949a) Après la signature du Pacte Atlantique: Les capitales s'interrogent sur les réactions possibles de Moscou. *Le Monde* 6 avril: 1–2.

Le Monde (1949b) Grande purge en Bulgarie. *Le Monde* 6 avril: 1.

Le Monde (1949c) La signature du Pacte Atlantique: Les discours officiels. *Le Monde* 6 avril: 2.

Le Monde (1950a) Washington n'envisage une réorganisation de la Communauté Occidentale que dans le cadre du Pacte Atlantique. *Le Monde* 9 mai: 1.

Le Monde (1950b) Débat entre l'Amérique et l'Europe. *Le Monde* 8 mai: 1.

Le Monde (1950c) Face aux soviets les allemands restent divisés. *Le Monde* 13 mai: 3.

Le Monde (1950d) Le gouvernement définit sa position: 'Pas de réarmement allemand sans unité européenne'. *Le Monde* 24 octobre: 1.

Le Monde (1950e) Les opinions de trois leaders. *Le Monde* 24 octobre: 2.

Le Monde (1950f) Le réarmement va-t-il renforcer les particularismes nationaux ou hâter l'unification de l'économie européenne? *Le Monde* 26 octobre: 3.

Le Monde (1954a) Le querelle de procédure est en réalité une bataille fondamentale sur la CED. *Le Monde* 31 août: 1.

Le Monde (1954b) Le débat sur l'armée européenne. *Le Monde* 31 août: 4.

Le Monde (1964) Paris confirme le retrait des officiers français des états-majors navals interalliés. *Le Monde* 29 avril: 1.

Le Monde (1966a) Tirez-nous de là, messieurs les Anglais. *Le Monde* 17 mars: 1.

Le Monde (1966b) Il s'agit de rendre la France à elle-même. *Le Monde* 14 avril: 2.

Le Monde (1966c) La France n'est pas un satellite des Etats-Unis. *Le Monde* 14 avril: 3.

Le Monde (1966d) Que les tenants du parti américain ne se fassent pas trop d'illusions! *Le Monde* 15 avril: 3.

Le Monde (1970) La débat de politique étrangère au Palais-Bourbon. *Le Monde* 29 avril: 5–6.

Le Monde (1973) M. Jobert: Le problème de la défense de l'Europe serait, cette année, à l'arrière-plan de toutes les discussions. *Le Monde* 21 juin: 8–9.

Le Monde (1976) L'augmentation du budget militaire: M. Giscard d'Estaing apporte peu de retouches à la politique de défense de la Ve République. *Le Monde* 7 mai: 1.

Le Monde (1978) L'Assemblée Nationale juge la politique étrangère. *Le Monde* 10 juin: 9–10.

Le Monde (1980) Le débat de politique étrangère à l'Assemblée Nationale. *Le Monde* 19 avril: 10.

Le Monde (1986) Le terrorisme en Europe et ses racines au Proche-Orient. *Le Monde* 8 octobre: 3.

Le Monde (1991) Paris et Washington réduisent leurs divergences sur la défense. *Le Monde* 8 juin: 1–2.

Le Monde (1995a) M. Chirac propose une politique étrangère à forte tonalité européenne. *Le Monde* 17 mars: Online.

Le Monde (1995b) L'alliance déstabilisée recherche un visionnaire. *Le Monde* 21 octobre: Online.

Le Monde (1998) Paris et Londres posent les bases d'une politique de défense commune. *Le Monde* 5 décembre: Online.

Le Monde (2002) Les clandestins. *Le Monde* 19 novembre: Online.

Le Monde (2004) L'OTAN a vocation à exporter la sécurité tous azimuts. *Le Monde* 17 janvier: Online.

Le Monde (2008) La place de la France. *Le Monde* 17 juin: Online.

Leveau R and Rifaï T (1974) L'arme du pétrole. *Revue Française de Science Politique* 24(4): 745–769.

Lewis P (2000) Realism, causality and the problem of social structure. *Journal for the Theory of Social Behaviour* 30(3): 249–268.

Lewis P (2002) Agency, structure and causality in political science: A comment on Sibeon. *Politics* 22(1): 17–23.

Liener A (1995) Die Sicherheitspolitik der Schweiz heute (Überblick). In: Rhinow R (ed.) *Die Schweizerische Sicherheitspolitik im internationalen Umfeld.* Basel: Helbing & Lichtenhahn, 37–46.

Lipschutz R (1992) Reconstructing world politics: The emergence of the global civil society. *Millennium: Journal of International Studies* 12(3): 389–420.

Lobo-Guerrero L (2012). *Insuring War: Sovereignty, Security and Risks.* London: Routledge.

Loescher G (1994) Les mouvements de réfugiés dans l'après-Guerre Froide. *Politique Étrangère* 59(3): 707–717.

Loretan W (1994) Warum dieser Kleinmut? Ja zu freiwilligen Schweizer Blauhelmen. *Allgemeine Schweizerische Militärzeitschrift* 159(5): 12–14.

Lund Petersen K (2012) Risk: A field within security studies. *European Journal of International Relations* 18(4): 693–717.

Lundborg T and Vaughan-Williams N (2011) Resilience, critical infrastructure, and molecular security: The excess of life in biopolitics. *International Political Sociology* 5(4): 367–383.

Mabillard R (1979) Die Armee und unsere Sicherheitspolitik. *Allgemeine Schweizerische Militärzeitschrift* 145(2): 53–58.

Mackintosh M (1968) Die Sowjetunion und die europäische Sicherheit. *Europa-Archiv* 23(6): 201–210.

Mahnke D (1971) Das Viermächte-Abkommen über Berlin: Bilanz und Aussichten. *Europa-Archiv* 26(20): 703–714.

Makki S (2004) Privatisation de la sécurité et transformation de la guerre. *Politique Étrangère* 69(4): 849–861.

Malvig H (2005) Security through intercultural dialogue? Implications of the securitization of Euro-Mediterranean dialogue between cultures. *Mediterranean Politics* 10(3): 349–364.

Mantovani M (1994) Sicherheitspolitische Öffnung im Dienste einer neuen nationalen Leitidee? *Bulletin zur Schweizerischen Sicherheitspolitik* 1994: 57–68.

Mantzke M (1990) Was bleibt von der DDR? Abschied von einem ungeliebten Staat. *Europa-Archiv* 45(24): 735–742.

Marcus G (1999). Foreword. In: Weldes J, Laffey M, Gusterson H and Duvall R (eds) *Cultures of Insecurity: States, Communities and the Production of Danger.* Minneapolis, MN: University of Minnesota Press, vii–xvi.

Maresca J (1995) L'après-Guerre Froide est terminée. *Politique Étrangère* 60(1): 57–72.

Mark W (1966) 'De quoi s'agit-il?' Unvollständige Konzeption der militärischen Landesverteidigung. *Allgemeine Schweizerische Militärzeitschrift* 132(8): 441–443.

Marsh D and Furlong P (2002) *Theory and Methods in Political Science.* Basingstoke: Palgrave Macmillan.

Martin L (1992) Nationale Sicherheit in einer neuen Weltordnung. *Europa-Archiv* 47(3): 59–70.

Mates L (1976) Europa nach der KSZE. *Europa-Archiv* 31(11): 357–366.

Mayer R (1954) Organisation européenne et coexistence pacifique. *Politique Étrangère* 19(3): 249–256.

McAnulla S (2002) Structure and agency. In: Marsh D and Stoker G (eds) *Theory and Methods in Political Science.* Basingstoke: Palgrave Macmillan, 271–291.

McDonald M (2008) Securitization and the construction of security. *European Journal of International Relations* 14(4): 531–587.

Menon A (2000) *France, NATO and the Limits of Independence, 1981–1997: The Politics of Ambivalence.* New York, NY: Palgrave Macmillan.

Mérand F (2007) Social representations in the European Security and Defence Policy. *Cooperation and Conflict* 41(2): 131–152.

Meynaud J (1962) Les groupes de pression sous la Ve République. *Revue Française de Science Politique* 12(3): 672–697.

Milliken J (1999). Intervention and identity: Reconstructing the West in Korea. In: Weldes J, Laffey M, Gusterson H and Duvall R (eds) *Cultures of Insecurity: States, Communities and the Production of Danger.* Minneapolis, MN: University of Minnesota Press, 91–117.

Mitzen J (2006) Ontological security in world politics: State identity and the security dilemma. *European Journal of International Relations* 12(3): 341–370.

Möckli D (2000a) Neutralität, Solidarität, Sonderfall. *Zürcher Beiträge* 55.

Möckli D (2000b) Vor einer neuen UNO-Abstimmung: Drei Erkenntnisse aus der Niederlage von 1986. *Bulletin zur Schweizerischen Sicherheitspolitik* 2000: 53–87.

Moïsi D (1985) L'épreuve de la réalité. *Politique Étrangère* 50(2): 317–319.

Moïsi D (1995) De Mitterrand à Chirac. *Politique Étrangère* 60(4): 849–855.

Moran TH (1996) Grand strategy: The pursuit of power and the pursuit of plenty. *International Organization* 50(1): 175–205.

Morgenthau HJ (1962) *Politics in the Twentieth Century.* Chicago, IL: Chicago University Press.

Morozov V (2004) Russia in the Baltic Sea region: Desecuritization or deregionalization? *Cooperation and Conflict* 39(3): 317–331.

Moscovici S (1973) Introduction. In: Herzlich C (ed.) *Health and Illness: A Social Psychological Analysis.* London: Academic Press, ix–xiv.

Musitelli J and Védrine H (1991) Les changements des années 1989–1990 et l'Europe de la prochaine décennie. *Politique Étrangère* 56(1): 165–177.

Mutimer D (1998) Reconstituting security? The practices of proliferation control. *European Journal of International Relations* 4(1): 99–129.

Mutimer D (2007) Critical security studies: A schismatic history. In: Collins A (ed.) *Contemporary Security Studies.* Oxford: Oxford University Press, 53–74.

Nerlich U (1993) Neue Sicherheitsfunktionen der NATO. *Europa-Archiv* 48(23): 663–673.

Neue Zürcher Zeitung (2000a) UNO – die Zeit ist reif: Joseph Deiss vor der Gesellschaft für Aussenpolitik. *Neue Zürcher Zeitung* 9. Juni: 13.

Neue Zürcher Zeitung (2000b) Ein Akt der aussenpolitischen Vernunft: Positive Haltung der Wirtschaft zu einem UNO-Beitritt. *Neue Zürcher Zeitung* 6. Oktober: 14.

Neue Zürcher Zeitung (2001a) Bewaffnung von Schweizer Friedenstruppen: Ein folgerichtiger sicherheitspolitischer Schritt. *Neue Zürcher Zeitung* 22. März: 15.

Neue Zürcher Zeitung (2001b) Dreistimmig für den UNO-Beitritt: Argumente des Bundesrats für die Vollmitgliedschaft. *Neue Zürcher Zeitung* 9. Januar: 13.

Neue Zürcher Zeitung (2002) 'Souverän sind nur die Vetomächte, die Schweiz und der Vatikan': Streitgespräch zwischen Ulrich Siegrist und Christoph Mörgeli zum UNO-Beitritt. *Neue Zürcher Zeitung* 25. Januar: 13.

Neue Zürcher Zeitung (2005a) Der Schweiz droht keine Kriminalitätswelle. *Neue Zürcher Zeitung* 20. Mai: 15.

Neue Zürcher Zeitung (2005b) Schengen aus der Sicht des Unternehmers. *Neue Zürcher Zeitung* 25. Mai: 15.

Neumann I (1999) *Uses of the Other: The East in European Identity Dormation*. Minneapolis, MN: University of Minnesota Press.

Nietzsche F (1887) *Zur Genealogie der Moral: Eine Streitschrift*. Leipzig: CG Naumann.

Noack P (1996) Zwischen Nationalismus und Globalismus: Ist die internationale Politik noch gestaltbar? *Internationale Politik* 51(1): 3–8.

Nunes J (2012) Reclaiming the political: Emancipation and critique in security studies. *Security Dialogue* 43(4): 345–361.

O'Tuathail G and Agnew J (1992) Geopolitics and discourse: Practical geopolitical reasoning in American foreign policy. *Political Geography* 11(2): 190–204.

Palewski JP (1964) Bilan d'une alliance. *Politique Étrangère* 29(2): 117–130.

Papademetriou DG (1994) Les effets des migrations internationales sur les pays d'accueil, les pays d'origine et les immigrants. *Politique Étrangère* 59(3): 671–688.

Parker I (1987) 'Social representations': Social psychology's (mis)use of sociology. *Journal for the Theory of Social Behaviour* 17(4): 447–469.

Peoples C (2011). Security after emancipation? Critical theory, violence and resistance. *Review of International Studies* 37(3): 1113–1135.

Petitpierre M (1980) Déclaration sur la position de la Suisse dans le monde et sa politique étrangere, 16–17 septembre 1947. In: Roulet L-E, Surdez M and Blättler R (eds) *Seize ans de Neutralité Active: Aspects de a Politique Étrangère de la Suisse (1945–1961)*. Neuchâtel: La Baconnière, 241–242.

Piiparinen T (2006) Reclaiming the human stratum, acknowledging the complexity of social behaviour: From the linguistic turn to the social cube in theory of decision-making. *Journal for the Theory of Social Behaviour* 36(4): 425–452.

Posner TR (1991) *Current French Security Policy: The Gaullist Legacy*. New York, NY: Greenwood Press.

Quermonne JL (1992) Trois lectures du traité de Maastricht. *Revue Française de Science Politique* 42(5): 802–818.

Rickenbacher I (1990) Sicherheitspolitik: Anspruchsvoll wie noch nie. *Allgemeine Schweizerische Militärzeitschrift* 156(6): 329–331.

Robin G (1995) A quoi sert l'OTAN? *Politique Étrangère* 60(1): 171–180.

Roe P (2008) The 'value' of positive security. *Review of International Studies* 34: 777–794.

Roe P (2012) Is securitization a 'negative' concept? Revisiting the normative debate over normal versus extraordinary politics. *Security Dialogue* 43(3): 249–266.

Roth M (1993) *Westliches Konzessionsverhalten in der Ost-West-Auseinandersetzung: Berlin-Frage, Deutschland-Frage, Europäische Sicherheit.* Frankfurt: Peter Lang.

Rovan J (1951) L'opinion allemande et la remilitarisation. *Politique Étrangère* 16(1): 59–74.

Rowe D (1999) World economic expansion and national security in pre-World War I Europe. *International Organization* 53(2): 195–232.

Rühe V (1988) Sécurité et maîtrise des armements. Uun point de vue allemand. *Politique Étrangère* 53(2): 453–458.

Rühe V (1995) Deutsche Sicherheitspolitik: Die Rolle der Bundeswehr. *Internationale Politik* 50(4): 26–29.

Rummel R (1983) Libertarianism and international violence. *Journal of Conflict Resolution* 27(1): 27–71.

Russett B (1993) *Grasping the Democratic Peace: Principle for a Post-Cold War World.* Princeton, NJ: Princeton University Press.

Ruth F (1982) Sicherheitspolitik der NATO: Abschreckung und Rüstungskontrolle. *Europa-Archiv* 37(5): 135–144.

Sager K (1996) Grüne Friedens- und Sicherheitspolitik: Was muss sich ändern? *Internationale Politik* 51(8): 43–49.

Salter M (2008) Securitization and desecuritization: A dramaturgical analysis of the Canadian Air Transport Security Authority. *Journal of International Relations and Development* 11(4): 321–349.

Sauder A (1996) Les changements de la politique de défense française et la coopération franco-allemande. *Politique Étrangère* 61(3): 583–597.

Scharping R (1994) La coopération franco-allemande face aux nouveaux défis. *Politique Étrangère* 59(2): 537–543.

Scheel W (1973) Aktuelle Probleme der Aussenpolitik der Bundesrepublik Deutschland. *Europa-Archiv* 28(13): 433–438.

Schelter K (1997) Bedrohung durch die russische Mafia. *Internationale Politik* 52(1): 31–36.

Schindler D (1984) *Dokumente zur Schweizerischen Neutralität seit 1945: Berichte und Stellungsnahmen der Schweizerischen Bundesbehörden zu Fragen der Neutralität 1945–1983.* Bern: Schriftenreihe der schweizerischen Gesellschaft für Aussenpolitik.

Schmidbauer B (1995) Illegaler Nuklearhandel und Nuklearterrorismus. *Internationale Politik* 50(2): 19–22.

Schmidt BC (2002) On the history and historiography of International Relations. In: Carlsnaes W, Risse T and Simmons B (eds) *Handbook of International Relations.* London: Sage Publications, 3–22.

Schmidt P (1996) Défis et perspectives de la politique de sécurité européenne de l'Allemagne. *Politique Étrangère* 61(3): 569–581.

Schöpflin G (1990) Das Ende des Kommunismus. *Europa-Archiv* 45(2): 51–60.

Schulz E (1971) Die DDR als Gegenspieler der Bonner Ostpolitik. *Europa-Archiv* 26(8): 283–292.

Schuster R (1963) Die Hallstein Doktrin: Ihre rechtliche und politische Bedeutung und die Grenzen ihrer Wirksamkeit. *Europa-Archiv* 18(18): 675–690.

Schutz A and Luckmann T (1973) *The Structures of the Life-World.* London: Heinemann.

Schweizerischer Bundesrat (1966) Bericht des Bundesrates an die Bundesversammlung über die Konzeption der militärischen Landesverteidigung. *Bundesblatt* I (853): 853–878.

Schweizerischer Bundesrat (1973) Bericht des Bundesrates an die Bundesversammlung über die Sicherheitspolitik der Schweiz. *Bundesblatt* II (11.740): 1–42.

Schweizerischer Bundesrat (1975) Bericht des Bundesrates an die Bundesversammlung über das Leitbild der militärischen Landesverteidigung in den achtziger Jahren (Armee Leitbild 80). *Bundesblatt* II (75.073): 1706–1728.

Schweizerischer Bundesrat (1979) Zwischenbericht zur Sicherheitspolitik. *Bundesblatt* I (79.085): 1-43.

Schweizerischer Bundesrat (1981) Botschaft über den Beitritt der Schweiz zur Organisation der Vereinten Nationen (UNO). *Bundesblatt* II (81.081): 497–696.

Schweizerischer Bundesrat (1990) Schweizerische Sicherheitspolitik im Wandel: Bericht 90 zur Schweizerischen Sicherheitspolitik. *Bundesblatt* III (90.061): 847–904.

Schweizerischer Bundesrat (1991) Botschaft über die Weiterführung der verstärkten Zusammenarbeit mit ost- und mitteleuropäischen Staaten. *Bundesblatt* IV (91.057): 553–634.

Schweizerischer Bundesrat (1993) Bericht über die Aussenpolitik der Schweiz in den 90er Jahren. *Bundesblatt* I (93.098): 153–242.

Schweizerischer Bundesrat (1999) *Sicherheit durch Kooperation: Bericht des Bundesrates an die Bundesversammlung über die Sicherheitspolitik der Schweiz (SIPOL B 2000)*. Bern: Schweizerische Eidgenossenschaft.

Schweizerischer Bundesrat (2000) *Aussenpolitischer Bericht 2000: Präsenz und Kooperation: Interessenwahrung in einer Zusammenwachsenden Welt*. Bern: Schweizerische Eidgenossenschaft.

Schweizerischer Nationalrat (1966) Militärische Landesverteidigung. *Amtliches Bulletin* I (9478): 474–496.

Schweizerischer Nationalrat (1974) Sicherheitspolitik: Bericht des Bundesrates. *Amtliches Bulletin* IV (11.740): 764–803.

Schweizerischer Nationalrat (1976) Armeeleitbild 1980. *Amtliches Bulletin* (75.073): 611–631, 820–822.

Schweizerischer Nationalrat (1980) Sicherheitspolitik: Zwischenbericht. *Amtliches Bulletin* I (79.085): 713–734.

Schweizerischer Nationalrat (1991) Sicherheitspolitik: Bericht 1990. *Amtliches Bulletin* III (90.061): 903–933.

Schweizerischer Nationalrat (1994) Aussenpolitik der Schweiz in den neunziger Jahren. *Amtliches Bulletin* I (94.3089): 174–227.

Schweizerischer Nationalrat (1999) Sicherheitspolitik der Schweiz. *Amtliches Bulletin*: Online.

Schweizerischer Nationalrat (2001) Für den Beitritt der Schweiz zur UNO: Volksinitiative. *Amtliches Bulletin*: Online.

Schweizerischer Ständerat (1966) Militärische Landesverteidigung: Konzeption. *Amtliches Bulletin* I (9478): 324–331.

Schweizerischer Ständerat (1973) Sicherheitspolitik: Bericht des Bundesrates. *Amtliches Bulletin* IV (11.740): 713–725.

Schweizerischer Ständerat (1976) Armeeleitbild 1980. *Amtliches Bulletin* II (75.073): 68–77.

Schweizerischer Ständerat (2000) Sicherheitspolitik der Schweiz 99.056. *Amtliches Bulletin* (21 March 2000): Online.

Searle JR (1995) *The Construction of Social Reality*. New York, NY: Free Press.

Senghaas D (1995) Deutschlands verflochtene Interessen. *Internationale Politik* 50(8): 31–37.

Sibeon R (1999) Agency, structure and social chance as cross-disciplinary concepts. *Politics* 19(3): 139–144.

Silvestri S (1988) La sécurité de l'Europe occidentale entre le nucléaire et le conventionnel. *Politique Étrangère* 53(1): 107–121.

Smith S (1999) The increasing insecurity of security studies: Conceptualizing security in the last twenty years. *Contemporary Security Policy* 20(3): 72–101.

Smith S (2005) The contested concept of security. In: Booth K (ed.) *Critical Security Studies and World Politics*. Boulder, CO: Lynne Rienner, 27–62.

Smouts MC (1974) Les suites institutionnelles de la Conférence sur la Sécurité et la Coopération en Europe. *Revue Française de Science Politique* 24(6): 1230–1236.

Snyder GH and Diesing P (1977) *Conflict Among Nations*. Princeton, NJ: Princeton University Press.

Spillmann K (1990) Schweizer Sicherheitspolitik heute und morgen. *Allgemeine Schweizerische Militärzeitschrift* 155(1): 14–19.

Spillmann K (1995) Von der bewaffneten Neutralität zur kooperativen Sicherheit. *Bulletin zur Schweizerischen Sicherheitspolitik* 1995: 1–16.

Spillmann K, Wenger A, Breitenmoser C and Gerber M (2001) *Schweizer Sicherheitspolitik seit 1945: Zwischen Autonomie und Kooperation*. Zürich: Verlag Neue Zürcher Zeitung.

Spillmann K, Wenger A, Fanzun J and Lehmann P (1999) Der Bericht Brunner: Impulse und Reaktionen. *Bulletin zur Schweizerischen Sicherheitspolitik* 1999: 9–34.

Stahel A (2006) *Niedergang des militärischen Operations Research und der Schweizer Armee: Eine Parallele?* Wädenswil: Institut für Strategische Studien.

Steinmetz G (1998) Critical realism and historical sociology. *Comparative Studies in Society and History* 40(1): 170–186.

Stones R (1996) *Sociological Reasoning: Towards a Post-Modern Sociology*. London: Macmillan.

Stones R (2001) Refusing the realism-structuration divide. *European Journal of Social Theory* 4(2): 177–197.

Strauss FJ (1960) La Bundeswehr et la défense de la République Fédérale. *Politique Étrangère* 25(1): 5–14.

Stritzel H (2007) Towards a theory of securitisation: Copenhagen and beyond. *European Journal of International Relations* 13(3): 357–383.

Stritzel H (2011) Security, the translation. *Security Dialogue* 42(4–5): 343–355.

Studienkommission für Strategische Fragen (1969) *Grundlagen einer strategischen Konzeption der Schweiz*. Bern: Schweizerische Eidgenossenschaft.

Studienkommission für Strategische Fragen (1998) *Bericht der Studienkommission für Strategische Fragen (Bericht Brunner)*. Bern: Schweizerische Eidgenossenschaft.

Stueber KR (2005) How to think about rules and rule-following. *Philosophy of the Social Sciences* 35(3): 307–323.

Stueber KR (2006) How to structure a social theory? *Philosophy of the Social Sciences* 36(1): 95–104.

Sylvester C (2010). Tensions in feminist security studies. *Security Dialogue* 41(6): 607–614.

Taylor M (1989) Structure, agency and action in the explanation of social change. *Politics and Society* 17(2): 115–162.

Tertrais B (2004) La guerre mondiale contre la terreur, 2001–2004. *Politique Étrangère* 69(3): 533–546.

Thompson JB (1989) The theory of structuration. In: Thompson J and Held D (eds) *Social Theory in Modern Societies: Anthony Giddens and his Critics*. Cambridge: Cambridge University Press, 56–76.

Thürer D (1995) Sicherheitspolitik und Neutralität. In: Rhinow R (ed.) *Die Schweizerische Sicherheitspolitik im internationalen Umfeld*. Basel: Helbing & Lichtenhahn, 121–136.

Torfing J (1999) *New Theories of Discourse: Laclau, Mouffe and Žižek*. Oxford: Blackwell.

Törrönen J (2001) The concept of subject position in empirical research. *Journal for the Theory of Social Behaviour* 31(3): 313–329.

Touraine M (1993) La représentation de l'adversaire dans la politique extérieure française depuis 1981. *Politique Étrangère* 43(5): 807–822.

Trachsler D (2001) Neutral zwischen Ost und West? Infragestellung der Konsolidierung der Schweizerischen Neutralitätspolitik durch den Beginn des Kalten Krieges 1947–1952. *Zürcher Beiträge* 63.

Tudyka KP (1966) Die DDR im Kräftefeld des Ost-West-Konflikts. *Europa-Archiv* 21(1): 17–28.

Umbach F (2004) Sichere Energieversorgung auch in Zukunft: Die Notwendigkeit einer europäischen Strategie. *Internationale Politik* 59(8): 17–28.

Unabhängige Expertenkommission Schweiz – Zweiter Weltkrieg (2001) *Die Schweiz, der Nationalsozialismus und der Zweite Weltkrieg*. Zürich: Pendo Verlag.

United Nations Development Programme (1994) *Human Development Report 1994: New Dimensions of Human Security*. New York, NY: UNDP.

Unser G (1994) Das Nein des Schweizervolkes zum Blauhelmgesetz. *Bulletin zur Schweizerischen Sicherheitspolitik* 1994: 1–12.

Valentin F (1990) Quelle défense pour quelle Europe? *Politique Étrangère* 55(3): 533–541.

Van Dongen L (1997) La mémoire de la Seconde Guerre mondiale en Suisse dans l'immédiat après-guerre (1945–1948). *Schweizerische Zeitschrift für Geschichte* 47(4): 709–729.

Verkuyten M (1995) Symbols and social representations. *Journal for the Theory of Social Behaviour* 25(3): 263–284.

Vernant J (1963) Fondements et objectifs de la politique extérieure française. *Politique Étrangère* 28(6): 459–466.

Vernant J (1970) Le Général de Gaulle et la politique extérieure. *Politique Étrangère* 35(6): 619–629.

Vernant J (1973) La conférence sur la sécurité et la coopération en Europe. *Politique Étrangère* 38(1): 13–25.

Villiger K (1995) Aktuelle Herausforderungen der Schweizerischen Sicherheitspolitik. In: Rhinow R (ed.) *Die Schweizerische Sicherheitspolitik im internationalen Umfeld*. Basel: Helbing & Lichtenhahn, 170–179.

Villumsen T (2011) Science and securitization: Objectivation, the authority of the speaker and mobilization of scientific facts. *Security Dialogue* 42(4–5): 385–397.

Von Baudissin W (1970) Grenzen und Möglichkeiten militärischer Bündnissysteme: Sicherheitspolitische Perspektiven im kommenden Jahrzehnt. *Europa-Archiv* 25(1): 1–10.

Von Braunmühl G (1983) Das Verhältnis zwischen West und Ost in Europa im Jahre 1983. *Europa-Archiv* 38(11): 325–334.

Von Schmoller G (1951) Die Revision des Besatzungstatues. *Europa-Archiv* 6(9): 3919–3927.

Von Tscharner B (1995) Die Schweiz und die OSZE. In: Rhinow R (ed.) *Die Schweizerische Sicherheitspolitik im internationalen Umfeld*. Basel: Helbing & Lichtenhahn, 73–86.

Waever O (1995) Securitization and de-securitization. In: Lipschutz R (ed.) *On Security*. New York, NY: Columbia University Press, 46–86.

Waever O (1999) Securitizing sectors? Reply to Eriksson. *Cooperation and Conflict* 34(3): 334–340.

Waever O (2004) Ole Waever's 10. The ten books that made academic me. *Tidsskriftet Politik* 7(4): 1–25.

Waever O (2011) Politics, security, theory. *Security Dialogue* 42(4–5): 465–480.

Waever O and Buzan B (2007) After the return to theory: The past, present and future of security studies. In: Collins A (ed.) *Contemporary Security Studies*. Oxford: Oxford University Press, 383–401.

Wagner W (1980) Das Ost-West Verhältnis nach der sowjetischen Intervention in Afghanistan: Die Eskalation der Enttäuschungen in der Periode der Détente. *Europa-Archiv* 35(5): 135–144.

Walker RBJ (1993) *Inside/Outside: International Relations as Political Theory*. Cambridge: Cambridge University Press.

Walker RBJ (2007) Security, critique, Europe. *Security Dialogue* 38(1): 95–103.

Wallace H (1947) Le monde d'après-guerre et la solidarité international. *Politique Étrangère* 12(3): 275–284.

Walt S (1991) The renaissance of security studies. *International Studies Quarterly* 35(2): 211–239.

Waltz K (1979) *Theory of International Politics*. Boston, MA: Addison-Wesley.

Weidenfeld W (1987) Neuorganisation der Sicherheit Westeuropas: Ein Beitrag zur aktuellen Diskussion. *Europa-Archiv* 42(9): 259–267.

Weidenfeld W (1995) Ernstfall Europa: Der Kontinent braucht konzeptionelle Klarheit. *Internationale Politik* 50(1): 11–19.

Weil P (1994) La politique de la France. *Politique Étrangère* 59(3): 719–729.

Weisenfeld E (1975) Les grandes lignes de la politique étrangère de la France. *Politique Étrangère* 40(1): 5–18.

Weisenfeld E (1986) François Mitterrand l'action extérieure. *Politique Étrangère* 51(1): 131–141.

Weldes J (1996) Constructing national interests. *European Journal of International Relations* 2(3): 275–318.

Weldes J and Saco D (1996) Making state action possible: The U.S. and the discursive construction of 'the Cuban problem', 1960–1994. *Millennium: Journal of International Studies* 25(2): 361–395.

Weldes J, Laffey M, Gusterson H and Duvall R (1999) *Cultures of Insecurity: States, Communities and the Production of Danger*. Minneapolis, MN: University of Minnesota Press.

Wendt A (1987) The agent-structure problem in international relations theory. *International Organization* 41(3): 335–370.

Wendt A (1992) Anarchy is what states make of it: The social construction of power politics. *International Organization* 46(2): 391–425.

Wendt A (1998) On constitution and causation in International Relations. *Review of International Studies* 24(5): 101–118.

Wendt A (1999) *Social Theory of International Politics*. Cambridge: Cambridge University Press.

Werthebach E (2004) Deutschland: Auf Terror schlecht vorbereitet. *Internationale Politik* 59(2): 29–33.

Westing AH (1989) The environmental component of comprehensive security. *Bulletin of Peace Proposals* 20(2): 129–134.

Wiegreffe WF (1976) *Grundgesetzänderungen zur 'Inneren Sicherheit' seit 1967*. Berlin: Freie Universität Berlin.

Wight C (2000) Interpretation all the way down? A reply to Roxanne Lynn Doty. *European Journal of International Relations* 6(3): 423–430.

Wight C (2002) Philosophy of social science and International Relations. In: Carlsnaes W, Risse T and Simmons B (eds) *Handbook of International Relations*. London: Sage Publications, 23–51.

Wilkinson C (2007) The Copenhagen School on tour in Kyrgyzstan: Is securitization theory useable outside Europe? *Security Dialogue* 38(5): 5–25.

Williams MC (2003) Words, images, enemies: Securitization of international politics. *International Studies Quarterly* 47(4): 511–533.

Winch P (1972) *The Idea of Social Science and its Relation to Philosophy*. London: Routledge.

Windsor P (1982) La puissance militaire, instrument de la politique soviétique. *Politique Étrangère* 47(1): 45–62.

Winkler TH (1995) Zur Geschichte der Schweizerischen Sicherheitspolitik seit 1945. In: Rhinow R (ed.) *Die Schweizerische Sicherheitspolitik im internationalen Umfeld*. Basel: Helbing & Lichtenhahn, 27–36.

Wolfers A (1952) 'National security' as an ambiguous symbol. *Political Science Quarterly* 67(4): 481–502.

XXX (1960) Coexistence, sécurité, désarmement. *Politique Étrangère* 25(3): 221–229.

Yost D (1990) La France dans la nouvelle Europe. *Politique Étrangère* 55(4): 887–901.

Zartmann IW (1964) Les relations entre la France et l'Algérie depuis les Accords d'Évian. *Revue Française de Science Politique* 14(6): 1087–1113.

Zinner PE (1988) Gorbatschows Politik gegenüber der Bundesrepublik Deutschland: Eine Zwischenbilanz. *Europa-Archiv* 43(8): 223–232.

Žižek S (1994) *Mapping Ideology*. London: Verso.

Zorgbibe C (1976) La France les initiatives d'une puissance moyenne. *Revue Française de Science Politique* 26(4): 724–734.

Index

Page numbers in *italics* denote tables, those in **bold** denote figures.

For Product Safety Concerns and Information please contact our EU
representative GPSR@taylorandfrancis.com
Taylor & Francis Verlag GmbH, Kaufingerstraße 24, 80331 München, Germany

www.ingramcontent.com/pod-product-compliance
Lightning Source LLC
Chambersburg PA
CBHW072123270326
41931CB00010B/1650

*9 7 8 1 1 3 8 2 3 6 6 1 5 *